Shakespeare and the 'Live' Theatre Broadcast Experience

RELATED TITLES FROM THE ARDEN SHAKESPEARE AND METHUEN DRAMA

Broadcast your Shakespeare: Continuity and Change Across Media
edited by Stephen O'Neill
ISBN 978-1-4742-9511-6

Shakespeare and YouTube, Stephen O'Neill
ISBN 978-1-4742-6317-7

Stage Directions and Shakespearean Theatre
edited by Sarah Dustagheer and Gillian Woods
ISBN 978-1-4742-5747-3

Shakespeare's Pictures: Visual Objects in the Drama, Keir Elam
ISBN 978-1-4081-7975-8

Shakespeare in the Theatre: Mark Rylance at the Globe, Stephen Purcell
ISBN 978-1-4725-8171-6

Shakespeare in the Theatre: Nicholas Hytner, Abigail Rokison-Woodall
ISBN 978-1-4725-8160-0

Queering the Shakespeare Film: Gender Trouble, Gay Spectatorship and Male Homoeroticism, Anthony Guy Patricia
ISBN 978-1-4742-3703-1

Ivo van Hove: From Shakespeare to David Bowie
edited by Susan Bennett and Sonia Massai
ISBN 978-1-350-03154-8

Shakespeare and the 'Live' Theatre Broadcast Experience

Edited by
Pascale Aebischer, Susanne Greenhalgh and Laurie E. Osborne

THE ARDEN SHAKESPEARE
LONDON • NEW YORK • OXFORD • NEW DELHI • SYDNEY

THE ARDEN SHAKESPEARE

Bloomsbury Publishing Plc, 50 Bedford Square, London, WC1B 3DP, UK
Bloomsbury Publishing Inc, 1359 Broadway, New York, NY 10018, USA
Bloomsbury Publishing Ireland, 29 Earlsfort Terrace, Dublin 2, D02 AY28, Ireland

BLOOMSBURY, THE ARDEN SHAKESPEARE and the Arden Shakespeare logo are
trademarks of Bloomsbury Publishing Plc

First published in Great Britain 2018
This paperback edition first published 2019

Copyright © Pascale Aebischer, Susanne Greenhalgh, Laurie E. Osborne and
contributors, 2018

Pascale Aebischer, Susanne Greenhalgh, Laurie E. Osborne and contributors
have asserted their right under the Copyright, Designs and Patents Act, 1988,
to be identified as the authors of this work.

For legal purposes the Acknowledgements on p. x constitute an extension of this
copyright page.

Cover image: *Hamlet*, directed by Lyndsey Turner at the Barbican.
© Sonia Friedman Productions, 2015. Photo by Ludovic des Cognets

All rights reserved. No part of this publication may be: i) reproduced or transmitted
in any form, electronic or mechanical, including photocopying, recording or by
means of any information storage or retrieval system without prior permission in
writing from the publishers; or ii) used or reproduced in any way for the training,
development or operation of artificial intelligence (AI) technologies, including
generative AI technologies. The rights holders expressly reserve this publication
from the text and data mining exception as per Article 4(3) of the Digital Single
Market Directive (EU) 2019/790.

Bloomsbury Publishing Plc does not have any control over, or responsibility for, any
third-party websites referred to or in this book. All internet addresses given in this
book were correct at the time of going to press. The author and publisher regret any
inconvenience caused if addresses have changed or sites have ceased to exist,
but can accept no responsibility for any such changes.

A catalogue record for this book is available from the British Library.

A catalog record for this book is available from the Library of Congress.

ISBN: HB: 978-1-350-03046-6
PB: 978-1-350-12581-0
ePDF: 978-1-350-03048-0
eBook: 978-1-350-03047-3

Typeset by RefineCatch Limited, Bungay, Suffolk

For product safety related questions contact productsafety@bloomsbury.com.

To find out more about our authors and books visit www.bloomsbury.com
and sign up for our newsletters.

CONTENTS

Illustrations viii
List of Contributors ix
Acknowledgements x
Note on the Text xi
List of Abbreviations xii

    Introduction: Shakespeare and the 'Live' Theatre Broadcast Experience   1
    Pascale Aebischer and Susanne Greenhalgh

Part One: Wide Angle

1. The Remains of the Stage: Revivifying Shakespearean Theatre on Screen, 1964–2016   19
   Susanne Greenhalgh

2. Shakespeare's New Marketplace: The Places of Event Cinema   41
   Susan Bennett

3. The Audience Is Present: Aliveness, Social Media, and the Theatre Broadcast Experience   59
   Erin Sullivan

4. Understanding 'New' Encounters with Shakespeare: Hybrid Media and Emerging Audience Behaviours   77
   Rachael Nicholas

Part Two: In the Theatre

5. A View from the Stage: Interviews with Performers   95
   Beth Sharrock

6   A View from the Stalls: The Audience's Experience in the Theatre During the RSC Live from Stratford-upon-Avon Broadcasts   103
    Julie Raby

Part Three: Close-ups

7   South Bank Shakespeare Goes Global: Broadcasting from Shakespeare's Globe and the National Theatre   113
    Pascale Aebischer

8   The Stratford Festival of Canada: Mental Tricks and Archival Documents in the Age of NTLive   133
    Margaret Jane Kidnie

9   Talawa and Black Theatre Live: 'Creating the Ira Aldridges That Are Remembered' – Live Theatre Broadcast and the Historical Record   147
    Jami Rogers

10 Cheek by Jowl: Reframing Complicity in Web-Streams of *Measure for Measure*   161
    Peter Kirwan

Part Four: Reaction Shots

11 The Curious Incident of Shakespeare Fans in NTLive: Public Screenings and Fan Culture in Japan   177
    Kitamura Sae

12 Shakespeare and the Theatre Broadcast Experience: A View from Hong Kong   185
    Michael Ingham

13 Very Like a Film: *Hamlet* Live in Bologna   193
    Keir Elam

14 Shakespeare at a Theatre Near You: Student Engagement in Northeast Ohio   199
Ann M. Martinez

15 Shakespeare from the House of Molière: The Comédie-Française/Pathé Live *Roméo et Juliette* (2016)   207
Pascale Aebischer

Epilogue: Revisiting Liveness   215
Laurie E. Osborne

Appendix: Digital Theatre Broadcasts of Shakespeare, 2003–17   227
   Rachael Nicholas
Index of Theatre Broadcasts of Shakespeare   243
Index of Names and Terms   245

ILLUSTRATIONS

Figures

- **3.1** Netlytic analysis of *A Midsummer Night's Dream* (Shakespeare's Globe, dir. Emma Rice, 2016) and *Romeo and Juliet* (KBTC, dir. Rob Ashford and Kenneth Branagh).   71
- **6.1** Track and crane cameras in the RST stalls.   107
- **13.1** Lumière Cinema programme note for the NTLive *Hamlet*, Bologna Cineteca.   195

Table

- **10.1** Camera positions, Cheek by Jowl's *Measure for Measure* broadcast (2015).   165

LIST OF CONTRIBUTORS

Pascale Aebischer
University of Exeter, UK

Susan Bennett
University of Calgary, Canada

Keir Elam
University of Bologna, Italy

Susanne Greenhalgh
University of Roehampton, UK

Michael Ingham
Lignan University, Hong Kong Special Administrative Region of the People's Republic of China

Margaret Jane Kidnie
University of Western Ontario, Canada

Peter Kirwan
University of Nottingham, UK

Kitamura Sae
Musashi University, Japan

Ann M. Martinez
Kent State University at Stark, USA

Rachael Nicholas
University of Roehampton, UK

Laurie E. Osborne
Colby College, USA

Julie Raby
York St John University, UK

Jami Rogers
University of Warwick, UK

Beth Sharrock
University of Birmingham, UK

Erin Sullivan
University of Birmingham, UK

ACKNOWLEDGEMENTS

The editors wish to acknowledge the kind assistance they have received from Gabriella Giannachi, Ollie Jones, Catherine Mallyon, Abigail Rokison and Florian Stadtler, all of whom helped out with information, ideas and advice. Judith Buchanan and John Wyver were influential members of the World Shakespeare Congress seminar in 2016 where we first shared ideas about theatre broadcasts; their forthcoming book, *Being There: Shakespeare and Live Broadcast Theatre*, will complement this volume and provide an additional focus on the RSC and some of the pre-histories of the medium. Thanks also to Anna Blackwell, Andrew Bretz, Lindsay Brandon Hunter, Joe Falocco, Gabriella Giannachi, Romano Mullin, Stephen O'Neill, Rosie Paice, Stephen Purcell, Erin Sullivan, Ayanna Thompson and Adrian Lester, and John Wyver for sharing their work ahead of publication.

We are grateful to Colby College and *Shakespeare Bulletin* for financial support and to Ludovic des Cognets, National Theatre Live and Sonia Friedman Productions for permission to reproduce the cover image of Lyndsey Turner's *Hamlet* at the Barbican Theatre, London, in 2015.

Flo Buckeridge (General Manager, NTLive), Chui-Yee Cheng (Film and Digital Distribution Manager, Shakespeare's Globe), Dominic Kennedy (Marketing and Education Manager, Cheek by Jowl) and John Wyver (Illuminations Media and Director, RSC Screen Productions) were all remarkably generous with their time, granting interviews, checking information and providing feedback on papers and drafts. This volume pays tribute to their labour and to that of all the often invisible members of the broadcast teams.

Finally, this book would not have happened without the assistance of Susan Furber, Lara Bateman and Mark Dudgeon and the enthusiasm and kind guiding hand of Margaret Bartley at Bloomsbury Publishing: many thanks to her for all she has done to support us and the field of Shakespeare Studies.

NOTE ON THE TEXT

All quotations from Shakespeare's plays refer to *The Arden Shakespeare Complete Works*, R. Proudfoot, A. Thompson, and D.S. Kastan (eds), London: Bloomsbury, 2011.

LIST OF ABBREVIATIONS

BME	Black and Minority Ethnic
KBTCLive	Kenneth Branagh Theatre Company Live
NESTA	National Endowment for Science, Technology and the Arts
NTLive	National Theatre Live
RSC	Royal Shakespeare Company
RSCLive	RSC Live from Stratford-upon-Avon
RST	Royal Shakespeare Theatre

Introduction:

Shakespeare and the 'Live' Theatre Broadcast Experience

*Pascale Aebischer and
Susanne Greenhalgh*

> *What ... new ways of experiencing theatre are there?*
> DAVID SABEL, Head of Digital (2009–16), National Theatre
> (cited in Groves 2012)

The theatre broadcast of Phyllida Lloyd's *Julius Caesar*, starring Harriet Walter as Brutus and set in a women's prison, premiered at the Edinburgh International Film Festival on 24 June 2017. On 12 July 2017, the day of its UK cinematic release, we watched it in our respective cinemas in Oxford and Exeter. Across separate locations and slightly staggered screening times, we participated in what, by virtue of limited distribution, was nevertheless a unique cultural experience, shaped by its inclusion in the cinemas' 'Screen Arts', 'Live Cinema' or 'Theatre Events' listings.[1] Reframed as a media event, the ephemerality of live performance translated into our awareness of being present for the one-off opportunity to access this landmark production in our local cinemas. Neither of us had been able to see the initial stage production at the Donmar Warehouse in 2012, nor had we seen its 2016 revival at the Donmar King's Cross. Restaged at the King's Cross venue, with an audience surrounding the square performance space, the production was live-captured by broadcast director Rhodri Huw, with John Wyver acting as producer on behalf of Illuminations Media. Phyllida Lloyd carried out a post-production edit of separately recorded material with the feeds live-captured by eight cameras across two performances to produce 'a dynamic and cinematic version for the screen' (Wyver 2017b). Our engagement with this production during and after the screening spoke to the important and ongoing shift in how audiences participate in an event, are present in the theatre and interact with one another and with stage performances of Shakespeare.[2]

Shakespeare and the 'Live' Theatre Broadcast Experience investigates some of the key issues raised by Lloyd's *Caesar*. The broadcast's involvement of audiences in a 'live'/'alive' experience despite the time lag between performance capture and reception contributes to ongoing debates regarding 'liveness' in performance and media culture.[3] Our ability to watch the production 'Together, Apart' (Way 2017) taps into the emerging modes of digital spectatorship and participation that concern us throughout this volume. As a lasting documentation of Lloyd's stage production that is nevertheless ephemeral in its limited theatrical release, it prompts questions regarding the status of the performance archive and puts pressure on the differentiation between an 'original' artwork and its mechanical reproduction. Additionally, Lloyd's *Caesar* exemplifies the importance of the broadcast team's prior experience, industry skills sets and creativity, as well as the medium's hybridity and evolution towards ever more cinematic forms.

Most significantly, perhaps, this broadcast is a telling example of how Shakespeare, thanks to his status as a secure and marketable global 'super-brand' (Bennett, Chapter 2) and through the staging challenges specific to early modern dramaturgy, functions within the broadcast industry: as a catalyst to 'launch or legitimate a new technology' (O'Neill 2017: 1). Shakespeare, Mark Burnett has shown, has long acted as a 'point of communal stability in the midst of competing art-forms' (2007: 8). By using Shakespeare as a critical lens through which to view theatre broadcasts, this book brings to the fore the extent to which 'Event Cinema' – which 'is forecast to achieve annual revenues of £60 million–80 million in the UK and $1 billion worldwide by 2019' (Reidy et al. 2016: 9) – is inextricably connected to Shakespeare as the main provider of content, a significant shaping influence regarding form and paratextual framing, and a focal point for global fan communities. And by using *experience* as an additional lens, we shift the discussion of theatre broadcasts from a historical concern with media genres and production methods, and from abstract debates regarding 'presence' and 'participation' in the theatre and its remediations, to a phenomenological concern with reception. Our emphasis on medium-specific modes of audience participation and the diverse ways in which Anglo-American and worldwide audiences engage with Shakespeare (and with one another) through digital media contributes to those debates, and in several chapters in this volume prompts a fundamental reassessment of what constitutes audience participation, interaction and immersion within this hybrid performance and media ecology.

As Susanne Greenhalgh shows in Chapter 1, live captures of performances of Shakespeare build on a long history of attempts to represent theatricality on television and cinema screens. The broadcasts we consider in this volume are part of the rapid proliferation of live digital captures of Shakespeare that began tentatively in 2003 with the BBC's broadcast of *Richard II* from Shakespeare's Globe and which exploded into life in 2009 with the launch of NTLive. Since then, the now considerable corpus of Shakespeare broadcasts listed in our filmography has developed its own conventions in response to the pressures and innovations created by originating companies, broadcast teams and receiving venues. In a rapidly evolving environment in which experimentation thrives and producers exchange both personnel and techniques, the Shakespearean origin of a significant proportion of theatre broadcasts acts as an important anchor. It roots the proliferation of new approaches to broadcasting and to involving remote audiences in interactions with each other and the performance in a tradition of televisual, cinematic and digital remediations of Shakespeare. This tradition, in turn, shapes audience expectations and the interpretative frameworks deployed by our authors.

Threaded through this volume, therefore, is a recognition that the medium of theatre broadcast is shaped not only by a 'confluence of economic necessity, industry trade practices, aesthetics and ... the expectations and constraints ... of theatrical institutions like the National Theatre or the RSC' (Wyver 2017a), but also by its predominantly Shakespearean content. In the broadcast repertoire of NTLive, Cheek by Jowl, and KBTCLive, a disproportionate amount of Shakespeare has hitherto been principally paired with 'classics' from European and North American traditions and a few new plays, effectively squeezing out much of British pre-twentieth-century non-Shakespearean drama from the repertoire.[4] In a theatrical landscape in which some of the most exciting work is site-specific and/or profoundly participatory in nature, with the audience involved in the co-creation of the performance and able to direct its trajectory (see, e.g., Lehmann 2006; Machon 2013), the corpus of text-based plays which has hitherto most consistently benefited from theatre broadcasts sits at the opposite end of the spectrum (see Weimann 2010).

Nevertheless, within the corpus of text-based drama that has been 'live' broadcast since 2003, Shakespeare's plays are among those that require the most direct interaction with theatre audiences. These interactive performance dynamics exert pressure on a medium which would otherwise lend itself most easily to forms of performance capture that, for the duration of the performance itself, deploy the fourth-wall convention and exclude the audience from the frame. As in many of the broadcasts discussed in this volume, what was at stake in Lloyd's *Caesar* was the reconfiguration, for a remote audience, of a specifically 'Shakespearean' form of theatrical presence: one which hinges on the fluid spatial dynamics and performer–spectator contact characteristic of the early modern thrust stage, where the performers' ability to move smoothly from theatrical illusion to moments of direct address asks that audience members contribute to the generation of character (see Aebischer, Chapter 7). Lloyd's *Caesar* built on conventions established in previous Shakespeare broadcasts from the Donmar Warehouse, the National Theatre and the RSC by deploying techniques that respond to Shakespeare's challenging mix of crowd scenes involving audience members as supplementary bodies, intimate moments of introspection which negate the presence of an audience and fight scenes that threaten to break the boundaries between stage and stalls. Broadcasts such as Lloyd's contribute to the creation of a stylistic genealogy of theatre broadcast techniques in which solutions to some of the challenges that are particular to Shakespearean performance today are gradually consolidated into shared medium-specific conventions that become part of the evolving 'grammar' of theatre broadcasting.

What unites all the digital recordings of Shakespeare we discuss in this book is the fact that they were captured in the theatre, in front of a 'live' audience. Where they differ is in their modes of production and distribution. These have an impact on the degrees of proximity, in terms of simultaneity of production and reception and in their mode of dissemination, between the recording and the theatrical experience of an ephemeral performance. With that in mind, the recordings we examine fall into three categories:

1 *'Live' theatre broadcasts* that are live-mixed during the capture and distributed simultaneously on television, in cinema or online; these might be accessed as a 'delayed live' or 'as live' screening to account for different time zones, or as an 'Encore' days, months or even years later.

2 *Theatre broadcasts* that are captured with multi-camera setup usually during two or more performances in the presence of a live audience, edited together in post-production, and then broadcast to cinemas/television/online stream.

3 *Recorded theatre* or 'edited theatrical film' (see Kirwan, Chapter 10) captured live, in more than one performance, mixed in post-production, and released later on DVD or as a Web-based stream or download rather than broadcast in cinema or on television.

As is already evident in these descriptions, the boundaries between these categories are permeable, since, once recorded, the theatrical material is available for 'stored content replay' so that it may reappear on any of a range of platforms, subject to any distribution and copyright restrictions which apply (Kidnie, Chapter 8).

Digital live captures of theatre also differ in the degree to which, in the course of preserving and disseminating a stage production, the creative potential of the technology is exploited. Its traces of studied theatricality notwithstanding, the premiere of Lloyd's *Caesar* at the Edinburgh International

Film Festival attests how this broadcast strains the generic limits of the medium by moving ever closer to film in its post-production edit. It thus situates itself at one end of the spectrum of broadcasts examined in this book, with the static single-camera livestream of Forced Entertainment's *Complete Works: Table Top Shakespeare* (2015) at the other end (see Nicholas, Chapter 4). These two broadcasts exemplify the two approaches to preservation of live performance André Gaudreault and Philippe Marion identify: *reproductive archiving* and *expressive archiving* (2015: 95). The first attempts to document the 'autonomous and "time-stamped reality" of the *pre-formed* artwork, which is sectioned off, filmed and recorded, in the moment of shooting'. Expressive archiving, by contrast, emerges from an external desire to negotiate with a medium's interpretive potentialities in a given time and place: 'What is added to the archive is the style of the creator ... what is being archived is no longer what happens *in front of* the camera, but, in a sense, what happens *behind* it' (96; original emphasis). Broadcast theatre offers a spectrum of 'expressive potentialities' arising from who is behind the camera; where, when and how the performance is filmed; how it is mixed together either 'live' or in post-production; and how it is framed by additional paratexts. These elements combine to make of theatre broadcasts something other than a transparent 'representation of one medium in another', in Jay David Bolter and Richard Grusin's basic and influential definition of 'remediation' (2000: 45). The more theatre broadcasts combine reproduction (or 'representation') with expression, the more urgently they challenge received definitions of what constitutes live performance and an original artwork.

In some cases, as Kirwan shows (Chapter 10), the capture of a single live performance may even exist in different versions aimed at different audiences (in this case, live-streamed general audiences and on-demand audiences in education settings). Even the apparent archival stability of the capture is unsettled here. Different mixes of the camera feeds capturing a single performance do not merely offer different viewpoints onto that performance: they constitute performances in their own right. If we take as seriously as we ought broadcast director Don Kent's description of his mixing of feeds as analogous to playing a musical instrument (see Aebischer, Chapter 15), it follows that each mix and re-mix constitutes an original performance that communicates a unique creative vision.

At the same time, each (re-)mix and individual feed is part of the physical corpus of documentary evidence of the ephemeral stage production, along with the 'scratch tapes', promptbooks, photographs, notes, props, costumes, etc. that form part of the conventional theatrical archive (see Kidnie, Chapter 8), and is part of the digital archive composed of audience responses and reviews on social media (see Sullivan, Chapter 3). These 'paradocumentary' arrays of material correlate with Jerome J. McGann's definition of the literary 'work' as 'comprehend[ing] the global set' of all the texts and specific processes of their production and consumption 'which have emerged in the literary production and reproduction processes' (McGann 1991: 32; see also Sant 2017). When, by analogy, a theatrical production like the Donmar *Caesar* is considered as a 'work', it can be seen to encompass all the distinct live performance events in the course of its run as well as their production and consumption through audio and theatre broadcasting. A theatre broadcast is therefore both an original performance in its own right *and* a component of the overarching work. Evidently, as Gabriella Giannachi points out, 'performance is not purely constituted by a live event and documentation does not solely lead to a process of retrospection' (2018: 218). Audiences may well experience a broadcast as their unique encounter with a production or choose to watch both the live production and screening, with each experience shaping their understanding of the production independently and together. The same broadcast, furthermore, can be experienced by some audience members as retrospective archival documentation of the production (see Kidnie, Chapter 8), or as a 'live' engagement with the work in one of its manifestations.

These multi-experiential possibilities are just one of the ways in which theatre broadcasts are characterized by an interplay of remediated theatrical, televisual and cinematic concepts and conventions which makes them an intrinsically hybrid art form.[5] Whereas the medium's most explicit theatricality consists in its capture of an entire and continuous performance on stage for a live audience, the use of multi-camera techniques and live editing derived from outside television broadcasts provides ways to offer 'an apparently direct and comparatively unmediated form of access to the staging' (Wyver 2014: 104) combined with a 'cinematic take on the theatre experience' that is mindful of the big-screen context of reception (Van Someren in Handley 2016).

This hybridity is evident in the current lack of an established terminology. As a cinematic genre, the term 'Event Cinema' has gained currency since the formation of an industry association of this name in 2012, replacing the previous label of 'alternative content', at least in the UK (see Bennett, Chapter 2). In her 2014 'Live Cinema Relays of Shakespearean Performance' guest-edited collection of reviews in *Shakespeare Bulletin,* Susanne Greenhalgh borrowed from Stuart Hall's 1971 analysis of television's relay function, typified by 'a straight relay from the Stratford stage' (12), when she used the term 'live relay' to describe this genre (see also Cochrane and Bonner 2014). The term, however, helps occlude the creative agency of the broadcast director and team. By using the term 'theatre broadcast' in this book, we acknowledge the creativity of the broadcast team along with the medium's televisual intersections and the move to transmission on multiple platforms, but shift the emphasis to the specifically theatrical features of the corpus considered in this book.[6] At the same time, we point to the ways the concept of 'broadcasting', which Stephen O'Neill reminds us stems from the scattering of seed and allows for an understanding of broadcast dissemination as part of a 'complex media ecology' (2017: 3–5), expands the critical focus into questions of mass dissemination, institutional imperatives, and audience impact.

Meanwhile the scare quotes for 'live' in our title and elsewhere recognize the spectrum of liveness and aliveness within which this medium operates especially when we move the focus from the medium's mode of production towards its reception at various degrees of temporal remove. If, in the early broadcasts by Shakespeare's Globe and NTLive, the simultaneity of performance, capture and reception dominated the paratextual framing of broadcasts and their marketing and contributed in significant ways to the audience's enjoyment of 'the "buzz" of a live experience' (NESTA 2010: 6), a more recent survey of audiences in England 'suggests that in fact "liveness" does not drive demand for Live-to-Digital, nor affect the quality of the audience experience' (Reidy et al. 2016: 13). Instead, in a globally connected world, broadcasts are, as Sarah Bay-Cheng explains, part of a wider 'mediated context' in which 'performance itself functions not as a discrete event but as a network of interrelated components, both on- and offline, both overtly mediated and immediate to various and dispersed recipients' (2012: 34, 35).

Lloyd's *Caesar* is once more a telling example. The marketing for the broadcast made no attempt to disguise the pre-recorded nature of the broadcast but presented it as part of such a network of interrelated components. Theatrical presence was reconfigured into our sense of *presentness*, the 'spatio-temporal perception and impression of [our]selves and others in the present moment' (Giannachi et al. 2012: 46). The audience's participation in the screening had no power to shape the broadcast – let alone the performance – and could be dismissed as mere 'passive optical spectatorship' (Reason 2015: 274). To do so, however, would be to deny the intensity of the sensation of 'being there' that was generated, on the one hand, by the broadcast's deployment of medium-specific effects of proximity, immediacy and point-of-view, and on the other hand by our experience of belonging to a physical and networked community of fans that spanned geographical locations and shared in the excitement of participating in a unique, ephemeral cultural event. Reflecting on the intermediality of twenty-first-century Shakespeare performances, Stephen Purcell observes that '[i]f "being there" remains, for now, the dominant criterion of liveness, then digital technologies are making it increasingly difficult to determine what, precisely, "being there" constitutes' (2014). Our experience of participation in Lloyd's *Caesar* validates Matthew Reason's call for 'a serious focus on reception processes, and an analysis of the manners in which actual audiences engage with different kinds of audience–performer relationships to produce different kinds of experiences' (2015: 275). The focus in this book on the reception of broadcasts in a range of settings addresses this need to examine how actual audiences engage with productions of Shakespeare through 'live' theatre broadcasting.

The viewing practices we examine in this book are, as Bay-Cheng explains, 'largely activated by and within mediated networks as part of an extended engagement with the play unbounded by the duration of the performance' as much as by expectations of simultaneity (33). As part of the media ecology, 'live' theatre broadcasts therefore force us to move our historical and critical investigations 'beyond the binary of the live and recorded, beyond the question of authenticity and presence (perhaps beyond the "liveness problem" itself)' (40). Accordingly, this mode of inquiry informs several of the essays as well as the epilogue in which Laurie Osborne uses her experience of recent Shakespeare theatre broadcasts to revisit her approach to 'liveness' in one of the first essays, within Shakespeare studies, to consider how the creation of a digital archive of performances deployed cinematic codes to generate effects of liveness (2006). Instead of concentrating on simultaneity of production and reception, we are concerned here with how audiences participate in the broadcast experience through a range of interactions, both in-person and digital, with broadcasts and fellow audience members across geographical and temporal divides. Conceived thus, engagement with a screened performance only partially maps onto the theatrical experience because it constitutes something else – the 'live' theatre broadcast experience that is the subject of this book.

As is evident in several discussions in this volume, even when an identical capture, framed by the same trailers and paratexts provided by the broadcasting company, is broadcast in different locations or via different platforms, the reception context and the extent to which spectators engage with supplementary materials as well as social media feeds can significantly alter how the broadcast – and, therefore, 'Shakespeare' – is experienced by an audience. Not only do different cultures respond to the same production in distinctive ways – with local codes governing affective responses such as laughter, which can either help or inhibit the experience of participation in a broadcast – but the politics of a production may play out in unexpected ways when distributed internationally. Far from being passive channels and consumers, international receiving venues shape the broadcasts in decisive ways. How audiences respond may even affect the shape of future broadcasts in their approach to subtitling (see, for example, Kitamura, Chapter 11). 'Access' to a production thus translates into participation in a shared cultural activity which is characterized by the priorities of distinctive local viewing communities as much as it is by global fan networks.

When viewed from a global perspective, the dominance of broadcasts produced by UK companies, many of which are supported by Arts Council funding, carries problematic overtones of cultural colonialism (Reidy et al. 2016: 22 and British Council 2016; see also Bennett, Chapter 2; Kidnie, Chapter 8; Ingham, Chapter 12). Despite the recent expansion of broadcasts to new companies which, like Shakespeare's Globe, Sonia Friedman Productions or KBTCLive adopt an unsubsidized entrepreneurial model, and the launch of Stratford Live on HD in Canada and the Comédie-Française's collaboration with Pathé Live in France, theatre broadcasts of Shakespeare still constitute a body of work dominated by a small number of key industry figures who move between high-profile London-based companies (NTLive, Almeida Live, The Donmar Warehouse, Shakespeare's

Globe) and Stratford-upon-Avon (RSCLive).[7] With Shakespeare officially recognized by the British Council as 'important for the UK' and as a potential 'soft power' contributor 'to the country's international priorities' (British Council 2016: 3), the international distribution of Shakespeare broadcasts from the UK is a politically charged activity seen as contributing to the country's 'ability to get what [it] wants through attraction rather than coercion or payment' (Nye cited in British Council 2016: 5).

Even Shakespeare's Globe ultimately did not manage to unsettle the English dominance of the genre when, through its Globe to Globe Festival in 2012 (live-streamed on The Space) the company reached out to thirty-six international companies who performed the plays in their own languages. Not only did the theatre's resident company itself perform the thirty-seventh play, the belligerently patriotic play *Henry V*, in English,[8] but the centrifugal impulse behind the Festival that propelled Shakespeare into so many different cultures resolved itself in a (reassuringly?) centripetal return to the centre, as one company after another performed for London audiences in Shakespeare's Globe, culminating in *Henry V*. Dominic Dromgoole, then artistic director of Shakespeare's Globe, succinctly articulated the trajectories behind the Festival: 'A Globe beside the Thames is where many of these plays began their extraordinary journey. Another Globe beside the Thames is delighted to be bringing these plays, dressed in the clothes of many peoples, back home . . .' ('Globe to Globe' 2012: 2).

The broadcasts of these Festival productions that are now available on Globe Player, just like the productions made available via the MIT Global Shakespeares platform, struggle to unsettle the imbalance of power that pitches English-language big-budget cinema broadcasts in English issuing from the UK against potential international competitors. Diana Henderson warns that the high production values of cinema broadcasts by NTLive, Shakespeare's Globe and RSCLive as well as Stratford Live on HD may, as their 'unintended consequence ... create a less patient, attentive online audience for the work of small companies without access to top-tier documentary filmmakers' (2017: 76). Digital technologies may have made it easier for companies to capture and disseminate their work, but differences in capital investment and state subsidy have so far led to an uneven playing field, both nationally within the UK and world-wide. This volume begins to redress the balance by considering the work of Stratford Live on HD and the Comédie-Française alongside a selection of global contexts of reception.

Shakespeare and the 'Live' Theatre Broadcast Experience: a road-map

We begin our examination of how Shakespeare broadcasts have affected the access to Shakespeare and the experiences of audiences worldwide with a

'Wide Angle' section which offers broad historical and conceptual perspectives on the history of theatre broadcast. Authors consider its marketing and emergent modes of audience interaction, together with the enculturation generated by the 'f(act) of recording and worldwide broadcasting', expanded digitally and globally via the 'proscenium arch' perspective of satellite technology (Tinnell 2011). Susanne Greenhalgh traces the emergent hybridity of medium and genre evident in the British media and theatrical ecologies of the mid-twentieth and early twenty-first centuries as the National Theatre, RSC and BBC competed to 'revivify' Shakespearean stage performances in different spatial configurations through film, television and live cinema broadcast. Susan Bennett approaches the phenomenon of 'Event Cinema' from the point of view of the worldwide neoliberal marketization of Shakespeare. She explains how star power, the widespread investment in digital HD projectors in cinemas, and the promotion of British culture come together to create a market for an experiential engagement with Shakespeare which draws on the playwright's cultural capital to generate returns on capital investments in digital equipment. Erin Sullivan and Rachael Nicholas explore the new forms of audience participation, including the distracted viewing practices characteristic of online audiences, enabled by the 'unparalleled changes in how audiences engage with live cultural experiences communally in cinemas and online' in the early twenty-first century (Live-to-Digital 2016: 9), whether through Twitter or the hybridization of a variety of new media narratives. Sullivan's theorization of experiential 'aliveness' in the digital sphere refines current understandings of 'liveness', while Nicholas demonstrates how spectatorial practices migrate from platforms such as Buzzfeed and Facebook Live to transform encounters with broadcast Shakespeare.

'In the Theatre' sharpens the focus onto the live broadcast experience at the RSC to pinpoint how, despite the rhetoric that captured performance will be 'just as on every other night', the paraphernalia of filming create a whole new set of cognitive prompts and para-experiences which transform the event for actors and audiences alike. Interviewing actors, Beth Sharrock finds that the hybrid character of the medium exerts pressure on them to balance film and theatre acting styles in order to stay faithful to the established trajectories of the production, while simultaneously responding flexibly 'in the moment' of the filmed performance. Julie Raby bears witness to how broadcast audiences are conscious of their presence at a unique event even as they are directed, through a range of instructions and cognitive prompts, to perform as lively and appreciative theatregoers. Between them, the essays in this section demonstrate the extent to which the presence of the cameras and broadcast teams has an impact on the live performance itself: documentation alters the shape of the object documented.

One of our aims in this book is to resist the tendency, in discussions of theatre broadcasts, to mix examples regardless of their origin in order to come to general conclusions regarding 'liveness' and media. Instead, by including chapters in the 'Close-ups' section that focus on individual companies and their approaches to broadcasting, we are promoting an understanding of how theatre broadcasts of Shakespeare's plays are profoundly affected, in form and mode of distribution, by different theatre companies and broadcast directors, as well as by the architecture of the originating theatres and the missions and performance styles of the companies. Pascale Aebischer and Peter Kirwan explain in their analyses of NTLive and broadcasts by Shakespeare's Globe and Cheek by Jowl how broadcast directors respond very individually to the idiosyncratic uses of theatrical space by specific companies and directors and, in the process, create distinctive house styles for their broadcasts (Chapters 7 and 10). While Kirwan demonstrates how Cheek by Jowl's aesthetic is affected by the livestream of its work, Aebischer explores how NTLive and Shakespeare's Globe use different techniques to generate, for their remote audiences, an experience of spatial and affective inclusion and immersion in the theatre or, conversely, to set up barriers to the experience of 'being there'. In turn, Margaret Jane Kidnie shows how Stratford Festival HD benefits from the environment of 'liveness' generated by screenings in Canada of NTLive productions even as the company's artistic director, Antoni Cimolino, is keen to distinguish his brand from those of his UK rivals, creating an archive of Shakespeare in Canadian accents (Chapter 8). Jami Rogers' interviews with creative team members involved in broadcasting Talawa and Black Theatre Live's Shakespeare productions reveal a similar desire to create a lasting record of the work of black and minority ethnic performers and to expand the types of 'Shakespeare' encountered by audiences in the online archive (Chapter 9). Such preservative broadcasts are examples of how, as Rebecca Schneider explains, the archive *performs*: that is, simultaneously enacts both the equation of performance with disappearance and the archive's own service of 'saving' (2011), as lasting records of significant Shakespeare productions that might otherwise be relegated to the margins of theatre history are created and curated for future generations.

In the final section, 'Reaction Shots', we expand the range of our enquiry to include points of view from selected locations around the globe. Once more, a 'one-size-fits-all' approach is exposed as unable to account for the very specific ways in which distinctive communities, and sometimes even cinemas within a single city, experience broadcast Shakespeare. For remote and international audiences, the introduction of Shakespeare theatre broadcasts has the capacity profoundly to affect their local theatrical ecology, introducing into it not simply more choice, but potentially also reinforcing the cultural dominance of the UK Shakespeare brand in a manner that leads to local acts of accommodation and resistance. Focusing her analysis on young female Cumberbatch and Shakespeare fans in Japan, Kitamura Sae describes a highly participatory media culture in which media convergence, as described by Henry Jenkins, is made more problematic by geographical distance and unsatisfactory Japanese-language subtitling (Chapter 11). This analysis, in turn, contrasts with the context of Hong Kong explored by Michael Ingham (Chapter 12). Here subtitling is available only in English, restricting access in a manner that is inherently political and speaks to the historical entanglement of China's newest territory with Britain's colonial past. Ingham's call for Chinese-language subtitling and his desire to see the broadcasts penetrate the wider Hong Kong community and cinemas in residential areas, as well as mainland China, finds an echo in Keir Elam's description of how the 2015 NTLive broadcast of Lyndsey Turner's 2015 *Hamlet* was framed by the arthouse Cinemateca and the more commercial multiplexes in Bologna (Chapter 13). The paratexts produced by the receiving venues themselves have the power to shape reception, orienting viewers towards experiencing Shakespeare as either part of 'high' cinematic culture and a tradition of Shakespeare on film, or, conversely, as part of a star-oriented popular film culture. In some places, as evident from Ann Martinez' account of watching the same broadcast with her students in rural Ohio (Chapter 14), receiving venues go out of their way in order to physically mirror the experience of theatregoing for their cinema audiences. Thus prompted into thinking of themselves as theatre audiences, Martinez' students responded with a mixture of frustration at not seeing every part of the stage as they would have in the theatre with excitement at being able to access the show and discuss it in class. And whereas all these 'Reaction Shots' confirm the dominance of NTLive in the international cinema circuit, Aebischer's account of the Comédie-Française's first broadcast of a Shakespeare play to Francophone regions acts as a reminder of how Shakespeare may give authority to non-Anglophone broadcasting ventures in regions that have resisted NTLive's penetration and that rely on alternative traditions of theatre broadcasting and Shakespearean performance (Chapter 15).

Collectively, the essays in this volume thus speak to current debates regarding modes of spectatorship in a media-saturated environment. They confront the arguments about the ontology of performance and its dependence on presence and liveness that have dominated the critical discussion of theatre broadcasting to date with viewing practices that unsettle received definitions and require that we rethink essential concepts. Our essays span the whole range of modes of presence from the physical co-presence of performers and spectators in the theatre at the time of the broadcast, via the 'distributed presence' remote viewers experience when watching a broadcast in a cinema, through to the distracted viewing practices typical of online audiences and the experiences of audiences in non-Anglophone countries, for whom the broadcasts may undergo an additional time-delay and layer of remediation through subtitling. We thus shift the focus from the ontology of performance as residing in the co-presence in a single time and space of performer and spectator towards the broadcast spectators' *experience* and *practices of presence and participation*. In doing so, we are redirecting attention towards the devices of inclusion, immersion and interaction deployed within the performance captures, the framing of the broadcasts by companies and receiving venues, and the critical and creative involvement of audiences. Our authors argue that spectators of theatre broadcasts, far from being passive consumers of a pre-fabricated product that restricts their spectatorial agency (Cochrane and Bonner 2014: 127), are active constituents of a networked community of fans. They contribute to the 'live' broadcast experience through their individual and collective performances as audience members within the receiving venue, as well as through their engagement with one another and with companies and individual performers via social media.

As theatres reinvent themselves as multi-media companies who distribute their work on multiple platforms, and as receiving venues add their own cognitive prompts to simulate (for their audiences) either the experience of being in the theatre or, conversely, frame broadcasts as part of film culture, what constitutes watching a stage production of Shakespeare undergoes a fundamental shift. It is not simply the medium itself that is a hybrid combination of stage production, televisual conventions derived from decades of outside broadcasting practices, and cinematic or online distribution and the codes that govern these platforms. Rather, practices of spectatorship themselves respond to the hybridity of the contexts of reception by transmediating Shakespearean modes of participation in the theatre into their digital counterparts. At the same time, they importantly constitute new forms of engagement with Shakespearean stage performance that are not co-extensive with spectatorship in the theatre. These are the 'significant and distinct' experiences generated by theatre broadcasts which audiences overwhelmingly reported in the 2016 'From Live-to-Digital' survey (Reidy et al. 2016: 12), and these diverse spectatorial practices and experiences demand to be explored and theorized in their own right. Our volume begins to do so, challenging our readers to re-think, quite fundamentally, the ideological and political implications of consuming Shakespeare through theatre broadcasts, the role of Shakespeare in a globally-connected media environment, and what constitutes spectatorship of Shakespearean stage performance in the age of global digital theatre broadcasting.

Notes

1 Categories used by Picturehouse Cinemas, QFT Belfast and Trinity Theatre, respectively.

2 *Julius Caesar* was broadcast on BBC4 on 17 June 2018, with the other two plays in Lloyd's trilogy, *Henry IV* and *The Tempest*, streamed on BBC iPlayer.

3 These debates, as part of a broader context of mechanical reproduction and remediation, have shaped much of the work on theatre broadcasting to date. See, in particular, work by Phelan ([1993] 2005), Auslander ([1999] 2008), Fischer-Lichte (2008), Barker (2013), Wardle (2014).

4 The exceptions in the NTLive repertoire are the broadcasts of Boucicault's 1841 *The London Assurance* (2010), Goldsmith's 1773 *She Stoops to Conquer* (2012), Pinero's 1885 *The Magistrate* (2013), the late fifteenth-century morality play *Everyman* (2015), and Farquhar's 1707 *The Beaux' Stratagem* (2014). Shakespeare's Globe is, to date, the only company to have produced two theatre broadcasts of plays by contemporaries of Shakespeare's in Marlowe's *Doctor Faustus* (2012; captured 2011) and Webster's *The Duchess of Malfi* (2014; see Kesson 2015 and Aebischer forthcoming for analyses of this broadcast). The RSC's 2015 production of Jonson's *Volpone*, which was live-captured, has not yet been released.

5 For an in-depth discussion of the history, production methods and possible futures of screen remediations of Shakespeare (with a particular, though not exclusive, focus on the work of the RSC), see Buchanan and Wyver's forthcoming *Being There: Shakespeare and Live Broadcast Theatre*.

6 Wyver's proposal that we adopt the term 'multims' to recognize the ways broadcasts are shaped by multi-camera capture puts the emphasis on the mode of production and consequently shapes the corpus differently, excluding single static camera broadcasts like *Complete Works: Table Top Shakespeare* and including productions like Toneelgroep Amsterdam's *Roman Tragedies*, which incorporate multi-camera capture as part of the stage performance (2017a). Friedman's term 'cinemacast' (2016: 458), in turn, confines the corpus to cinematic distribution and excludes the burgeoning expansion of online streams and television broadcasts we also consider in this volume (see Sullivan, Chapter 3; Nicholas, Chapter 4; Aebischer, Chapter 7; Rogers, Chapter 9; Kirwan, Chapter 10).

7 Rachael Nicholas' filmography at the end of this book reveals the extent to which, in particular, broadcast director Robin Lough and broadcast producer John Wyver move between companies and between them have creative input into the majority of broadcast ventures in the UK today.

8 Tellingly, Shakespeare's Globe approached the broadcast dissemination of this production separately, treating it as a Shakespeare's Globe recorded theatre DVD which was only released in 2013 (see Aebischer, Chapter 7, for the distribution strategies of Shakespeare's Globe).

References

Aebischer, P. (forthcoming), *Shakespeare, Spectatorship and Technologies of Performance*, Cambridge: Cambridge University Press.

Auslander, P. ([1999] 2008), *Liveness: Performance in a Mediatized Culture*, London: Routledge.

Barker, M. (2013), *Live to Your Local Cinema: The Remarkable Rise of Livecasting*, Kindle Book, Basingstoke: Palgrave Macmillan.

Bay-Cheng, S. (2012), 'Theater is Media: Some Principles for a Digital Historiography of Performance', *Theater*, 42 (2): 27–41.

Bolter, J.D. and R. Grusin (2000), *Remediation: Understanding New Media*, Cambridge, MA: The MIT Press.

British Council (2016), 'All the World's'. Available online: https://www.britishcouncil.org/sites/default/files/all_the_worlds.pdf (accessed 27 September 2017).

Buchanan, J. (2016), 'Being There: Shakespearean Event Cinema, 1964', 'Recreating Shakespearean Performance Cultures Worldwide: Live digital relay as creative practice?' (seminar), World Shakespeare Congress, Stratford-upon-Avon and London.

Burnett, M.T. (2007), *Filming Shakespeare in the Global Marketplace*, Houndmills: Palgrave Macmillan.

Cochrane, B. and F. Bonner (2014), 'Screening from the Met, the NT or the House: What Changes with the Live Relay', *Adaptation*, 7 (2): 121–33.

Fischer-Lichte, E. ([2004] 2008) *The Transformative Power of Performance: A New Aesthetics*, trans. S.I. Jain, London: Routledge.

Friedman, M.D. (2016), 'The Shakespeare Cinemacast: Coriolanus', *Shakespeare Quarterly*, 64 (4): 457–80.

Gaudreault, A. and P. Marion (2015), *The End of Cinema? A Medium in Crisis in the Digital Age*, trans. T. Barnard. New York: Columbia University Press.

Giannachi, G., N. Kaye and M. Shanks (2012), *Archaeologies of Presence: Art, Performance and the Persistence of Being*, London: Routledge.

Giannachi, G. (2018), 'The Intention of the Artist and the Point of View of the Audience: Performance Documentation Revisited', in G. Giannachi and J. Westerman (eds), *Histories of Performance Documentation: Museum, Artistic, and Scholarly Practices*, London: Routledge, 182–97.

Greenhalgh, S. (2014), 'Guest Editor's Introduction', in S. Greenhalgh (ed.), 'Special Reviews Section: Live Cinema Relays of Shakespearean Performance', *Shakespeare Bulletin* 32 (2): 255–61.

Groves, N. (2012), 'Arts Head: David Sabel, Head of Digital, National Theatre', *The Guardian*, 10 April. Available online: https://www.theguardian.com/culture-professionals-network/culture-professionals-blog/2012/apr/10/david-sabel-digital-national-theatre (accessed 29 September 2017).

Hall, S. (1971), 'Television and its Relation to Culture', Part IV, *Innovation and Decline in Cultural Programming on British Television*, UNESCO Report, Birmingham: Centre for Contemporary Cultural Studies, University of Birmingham. Available online: http://www.birmingham.ac.uk/Documents/college-artslaw/history/cccs/stencilled-occasional-papers/9and25to37/SOP34.pdf (accessed 28 September 2017).

Handley, L. (2016), 'Filming National Theatre Live with Tim van Someren', *The Telegraph*, 25 November. Available online: http://www.telegraph.co.uk/theatre/national-theatre-live/filming-with-tim-van-someren/ (accessed 8 September 2017).

Henderson, D. (2017), 'This Distracted Globe, This Brave New World: Learning from the MIT Global Shakespeares' Twenty-First Century', in Stephen O'Neill (ed.), *Broadcast Your Shakespeare*, London: Bloomsbury Arden Shakespeare, 67–86.

Kesson, A. (2015), '"Trying Television by Candlelight": Shakespeare's Globe's *The Duchess of Malfi* on BBC4,' in J. Wyver (ed.), 'Not Shakespeare on Television and Beyond', *Shakespeare Bulletin*, 33 (4): 609–21.

Lehmann, H.-T. (2006), *Postdramatic Theatre*, trans. Karen Jürs-Munby, London and New York: Routledge.

Machon, J. (2013), *Immersive Theatres: Intimacy and Immediacy in Contemporary Performance*, Basingstoke: Palgrave Macmillan.

McGann, J.J. (1991), *The Textual Condition*, Princeton, New Jersey: Princeton University Press.

MIT (2010–), 'Global Shakespeares: Video & Performance Archive.' Available online: http://globalshakespeares.mit.edu/# (accessed 12 September 2017).

NESTA (2010), 'Beyond Live: Digital Innovation in the Performing Arts,' Research Briefing, February 2010. Available online: https://www.nesta.org.uk/sites/default/files/beyond_live.pdf (accessed 12 September 2017).

O'Neill, S. (2017), 'Introduction: "Sowed and Scattered" – Shakespeare's Media Ecologies', in S. O'Neill (ed.), *Broadcast Your Shakespeare*, London: Bloomsbury Arden Shakespeare, 1–23.

Osborne, L.E. (2006), 'Speculations on Shakespearean Cinematic Liveness', *Shakespeare Bulletin*, 24 (3): 49–65.

Phelan, P. ([1993] 2005), *Unmarked: The Politics of Performance*, London: Routledge.

Purcell, S. (2014), 'The Impact of New Forms of Public Performance', in C. Carson and P. Kirwan (eds), *Shakespeare and the Digital World: Redefining Scholarship and Practice*, Cambridge: Cambridge University Press, Chapter 16, Kindle Book.

Reason, M. (2015), '*Participations* on Participation: Researching the "Active" Theatre Audience', *Participations*, 12 (1): 271–80.

Reidy, B.K., B. Schutt, D. Abramson and A. Durski (2016), 'From Live-to-Digital: Understanding the Impact of Digital Developments in Theatre on Audiences, Production and Distribution,' Arts Council England, October 2016. Available online: http://www.artscouncil.org.uk/publication/live-digital (accessed 8 September 2017).

Sant, T., ed. (2017), *Documenting Performance: The Contexts and Processes of Digital Curation and Archiving*, London: Bloomsbury.

Schneider, R. (2011), *Performing Remains: Art and War in Times of Theatrical Reenactment*, London: Routledge.

Tinnell, J. (2011), 'All the World's a Link: the Global Theater of Mobile World Browsers', *enculturation: a journal of rhetoric, writing and culture*, 12. Available online: http://www.enculturation.net/all-the-worlds-a-link (accessed 27 September 2017).

Wardle, J. (2014), '"Outside Broadcast": Looking Backwards and Forwards, Live Theatre in the Cinema – NT Live and RSC Live', *Adaptation*, 2 (1), 134–52. Available online: https://doi.org/10.1093/adaptation/apu017 (accessed 27 September 2017).

Way, G. (2017), 'Together, Apart: Liveness, Eventness and Streaming Shakespearean Performance', *Shakespeare Bulletin*, 35 (3): 389–406.

Weimann, R. (2010), 'Performance in Shakespeare's Theatre: Ministerial and/or Magisterial?', in D. Schalkwyk (ed.), *The Shakespearean International Yearbook* 10, Abingdon: Routledge, 3–29.

Wyver, J. (2014), '"All the Trimmings?": The Transfer of Theatre to Television in Adaptations of Shakespeare Stagings', *Adaptation*, 7 (2), 104–20.

Wyver, J. (2017a), '"Make Choice; and, See": Towards a Poetics of Multims', Shakespeare, Media, Technology and Performance (conference), University of Exeter, 24 June.

Wyver, J. (2017b), 'First Julius Caesar Thoughts', *Illuminations*, 24 July. Available online: http://www.illuminationsmedia.co.uk/29026-2/ (accessed 7 September 2017).

PART ONE

Wide Angle

1

The Remains of the Stage:

Revivifying Shakespearean Theatre on Screen, 1964–2016

Susanne Greenhalgh

'Is cinema the successor, the rival, or the revivifier of the theatre?' Susan Sontag's question continues to resonate fifty years after she posed it (1966: 33), especially when augmented by Philip Auslander's observation that 'at the level of cultural economy, theatre (and live performance generally) and the mass media are rivals, not partners' (2008: 1). In Britain, the BBC has broadcast Shakespearean performance since it began its television service (Wyver 2016). To date, there have been three periods in which stage-derived Shakespeare films for cinema have been produced with particular frequency: the first decades of silent filming, the 1960s and the period since 2009, during which theatre performances have been filmed live for digital streaming to cinema audiences around the world. As Adele Anderson observes about 'cinecast' opera, such practices 'are the product of multiple artistic developments interacting, as they always have done, with business pressures and critical reception, and they are not without historical precedent' (2012: 186).

Live theatre broadcast of Shakespeare has its origins in the intertwined histories of the major theatrical and media institutions in the UK: the National Theatre, the Royal Shakespeare Company (RSC) and the BBC. The last half century has seen a transition from the dependency of theatre companies on cinema and television as the means of preserving and enabling access to their work, to the present situation when stage content can be designed from the start with broadcasting in mind, and produced and filmed independently by the institutions themselves. The interrelated institutional and theatrical imperatives in the 1960s and 2010s include the shifting priorities of broadcasters, film producers and theatres regarding screened performance, the choice of studio-set or outside broadcast filming on location, and the impact of the national and international celebrations of Shakespeare, in 1964, 2012 and 2016.

This broad historical survey is focused in terms of the relation between 'the locale of performance and the kind of cultural space [the] company was trying to fashion for itself' (Shaughnessy 2005: 92). While, as Laurie Osborne has noted, 'early filmed stage productions often invoke the spatially limited structure of the proscenium stage in ways that register the liveness in filmed theatre' (2006: 54–5), the 1960s was the period in which the open stage developed in reaction against what was perceived as the two-dimensional, cinema screen-like effects of the proscenium stage. Richard Hornby has argued for the inter-connection of such developments in stage space and the capacity of film to capture performance effectively: 'Half a century of theatre architecture, moving us from proscenium to open-stage configurations, has itself been an important factor in enabling effective televising of stage productions' (Hornby 2011: 198). I argue that the reconfiguration of theatre space in the twenty-first century continues to play a significant part in the development of live theatre broadcast.

Two 1960s films encapsulate the issues involved in translating theatre space for the screen. The National Theatre's *Othello,* directed for the stage by John Dexter and on film by Stuart Burge in 1965, offered a televisually influenced studio remediation of the Old Vic's proscenium arch stage. By contrast, Tony Richardson's in-the-round *Hamlet,* filmed at the Roundhouse in 1969, was an explicit attempt to 'free' theatre from the artistic restraints represented by traditional theatrical architecture. Both Burge and Richardson were experienced theatre and television directors, and in different ways these two films can be viewed as laying the foundations for the hybridity of theatrical, televisual and cinematic conventions which has become accepted as a marker of the live theatre broadcast.

These conventions are spatial as well as intermedial, since the first decision to be made in translating any performance to screen is where it will be filmed. The history of filming stage productions documents the interplay of 'constructed' and 'abstracted' space: the architectural qualities of the original venue(s) and stages, the ways in which that spatial ordering is present or absent on screen, and how cultural meaning is affected by different forms of spatial remediation (see Tompkins 2014). Full understanding of the transformation of the National Theatre and RSC into media production companies in the second decade of the twenty-first century requires awareness of the significance of the theatres' thrust or open stages for this process, and the impact these developments have in turn had on the reinvigoration of theatre broadcasts on television and online in a period of rapid expansion of digital technologies and inter-connectivity. Shakespearean commemoration and celebration formed a productive context in which experimenting with new media developments and technologies for performance capture could be authorized. These memorializing and innovating impulses coalesced within the live broadcast medium when the National Theatre and RSC appropriated 'event' cinema and television to celebrate their own past histories and present spatial and cultural identities in *50 Years on Stage* (2013) and *Shakespeare Live!* (2016).

'Actual performance' on screen in the 1960s

The 1960s was a vibrant decade for the interaction of theatre and the 'recording arts' in Britain. Theatre, film and television were all expanding and experimenting, and actors and directors were increasingly moving freely between the different media. In pragmatic terms, then and now, 'films offered stage talent tempting opportunities for wider audiences and greater income', while the stage, in turn, 'offered the cinema pre-sold publicity, cultural prestige, and a magic gateway to ecstatic, patriotic reviews' (Brown 1986: 144–5). In broadcasting, the BBC's long tradition of transmitting theatre extracts and plays was imitated by the commercial channels in their early years, as made-for-television adaptations for anthology series, and as occasional outside broadcasts, a televisual mode which relocates filming from the studio to other spaces, not necessarily outdoors, and may be transmitted live or recorded (see Wyver 2014, 2015c; Wrigley and Wyver 2018).

However, the arrival of commercial television in 1955 had created a competitive environment for both broadcasting and the British film industry. By the end of the 1950s, the circuit-owning big producers and distributors, such as Rank and Associated British Picture Corporation, were growing cautious in the face of falling box-office receipts and declining government support (Drazin 2014: 15–20). Increasingly 'independent' production relied on the willingness of American studios and distributors to co-fund projects in a British creative culture beginning to be perceived as excitingly innovative and 'swinging'. Woodfall Films, founded in 1959 by stage and film director Tony Richardson, the playwright John Osborne and the Canadian producer Harry Salzman, began its cinematic 'New Wave' with adaptations of successful Royal Court stage productions such as Osborne's *Look Back in Anger* (1959) and *The Entertainer* (1960), and Theatre Workshop's *A Taste of Honey* (1961). These productions took their subjects out of the theatre or the studio into realistic location settings, still filmed in black and white but exploiting the new technical potential for complex soundtracks. Other theatre directors, like Lindsay Anderson, Peter Hall and Peter Brook, also became film directors, not only of original cinematic creations but, in the latter two cases, shooting versions of their own Shakespeare productions. In a post-war era that saw the emergence of the Arts Council in 1946 and the subsequent growth of subsidized theatres, access was becoming an important measure of institutional 'public value', understood as a composite of democratic, cultural, educational, social and global values. Filmed or televised stage productions offered the opportunity simultaneously to memorialize celebrated performances, and to enable audiences beyond the time and place of the original theatrical staging some kind of access to the experience.

However much cinema might attract audiences, television remained the mainstay for filmed theatre. The BBC seized the opportunity to schedule Shakespeare-based programming throughout 1964. Landmark productions were commissioned, notably *Hamlet at Elsinore*, directed by Philip Saville, which was the first television play to be filmed entirely as an outside broadcast. The celebrations of Shakespeare's birthday were also broadcast live from Stratford-upon-Avon, while related features, documentaries and recordings of theatre productions continued for the rest of the year, and the corporation even chose Shakespeare's birthday week and a production of the musical *Kiss Me Kate* for the launch of its second channel (see Greenhalgh 2007: 656, 691).

A number of stage-derived broadcasts of Shakespeare reflect the two approaches to televising theatre current at the time: live or recorded continuous performance in the studio, and outside broadcast from a theatre. Although studio production was increasingly condemned for its 'theatricality' when employed in general television drama, it remained a staple, alongside a discernible increase in stage-derived outside broadcasts. The quatercentenary year was inaugurated by a recording of the RSC's *commedia dell'arte* production of *The Comedy of Errors*, captured live in front of an audience at the company's new London base at the Aldwych Theatre. Both the Bristol Old Vic's *Love's Labour's Lost* at the Theatre Royal (1964) and *Coriolanus* (1965), a National Youth Theatre production filmed at Chichester Festival Theatre, highlight their theatrical location by opening with panning shots of the auditorium and audience, with laughter and applause recorded as effectively as the actors' dialogue. In other broadcasts the theatre setting is downplayed and only the action on stage is shown, or the theatre serves solely as a replacement studio set, as in the National Youth Theatre's *Julius Caesar* (1964), or its *Troilus and Cressida* (1966).[1]

It was the output of the two major subsidized theatre companies, the RSC, launched in 1961 under the artistic directorship of Peter Hall, and the National Theatre, led by Laurence Olivier from 1962, which was the focus of most media attention, however. Surveying the theatre scene in 1966, Irving Wardle described the two companies in these terms:

> Given the presence of Olivier as a figurehead, the popular character of much of the repertoire, and the very name of the organization, the National Theatre has acquired the reputation of being a permanently sold-out middle-class Mecca – the new home of the audiences who abandoned the West End. The Royal Shakespeare, on the other hand, through its shortage of money, its crusade to attract young audiences, and

its much publicized espousal of new playwrights and cult movements (such as the Theatre of Cruelty), has come to be regarded as an avant-garde stronghold.

(111)

Wardle also noted the significance of recordings for these institutions' finances. The RSC's Arts Council grant provided only half its running costs. Performance recordings could not only disseminate its productions more widely, fulfilling a public service remit that justified government subsidy, but could potentially open up new income streams which would enable Hall to realize his goal of making this provincial theatre in Stratford-upon-Avon a major national and international player. That other leading British public service provider, the BBC, was an obvious partner and from 1962–3 the corporation studio-recorded and distributed seven of the company's plays (see Wyver 2015a, 2015b). All these productions were directed for television by BBC staff producers, but the RSC also looked beyond British broadcasting to the international potential of cinema. In 1966 the American company Filmways agreed to make three major films of past RSC productions. Of these only Peter Brook's *King Lear* (1969) and Peter Hall's *A Midsummer Night's Dream* (1969) were completed, both filmed on location.

In 1964, the RSC's Stratford-upon-Avon auditorium was turned into a multi-camera, outside broadcast-cum-television studio for eight weeks to film Peter Hall and John Barton's three-part *The Wars of the Roses*, broadcast the following year (see Wyver 2015a). Performance of the history plays as cycles constitutes a type of '"event theatre", ideal projects for celebratory, commemorative occasions' which can also enable 'theatre companies to use these monumental plays as a proving ground for their own reputations' (Hagerman 2010: 116). The RSC/BBC collaboration did not simply preserve a historic piece of theatre while simultaneously announcing the arrival of a radical, politicized approach to staging Shakespeare. Through its use of the Royal Shakespeare Theatre (RST) as its location, the BBC marked the significance of the Royal Shakespeare Company's arrival on the cultural landscape, preceding the broadcasts with a 'behind-the-scenes' documentary about the production. On film the theatre became 'a hybrid physical space' created by 'a visual language weaving together strands of theatre, television technique and film style' (Wyver 2015a: 28). That the BBC archived a stage production mounted to mark the 1964 Shakespeare anniversary was significant even though the recordings were not transmitted until a year later, in the weeks leading up to Shakespeare's birthday. Such memorializing Shakespeare offers 'an insight into the past at the same time as it invites us to contemplate alternative bonds of association and as yet untested commemorative possibilities' (Burnett 2011: 461). The broadcast of *The Wars of the Roses* belongs alongside a whole range of images and symbols, events and ceremonies, relayed to audiences direct and live, whereby the BBC synthesizes components of social life into a 'national culture' in which

Shakespeare plays a key role (Scannell and Cardiff 1991: 277–8). As Shakespearean commemoration, even when delayed, the BBC's broadcasts of the RSC's histories articulated both desire for affirmation of national identity and a theatrical discourse that challenged such notions, thus serving the cultural purposes of both company and broadcaster.

While the nascent National Theatre was to some extent better funded than the RSC, it also ran at a deficit (Rosenthal 2013: 114). The new company needed to be able to offer the actors it had attracted from the West End or the Royal Court salaries sufficient to keep them in the theatre rather than defecting to better paid film or television roles. One solution was to ensure that their own theatre work was filmed or televised, and, like CBS in the United States, the BBC was keen to come to a contractual arrangement to regularly broadcast selected National Theatre productions. However, there was another option in the form of British Home Entertainment, a Pay TV consortium founded by the film producer Lord Brabourne and Anthony Havelock-Allan. This company aimed at delivering 'quality productions to discerning audiences' shot on film but intended for television reception, and Olivier also happened to be one of its non-executive directors (Rosenthal 2013: 110–14). During a pilot from 1963 to 1968, the company wired a programme of sport and cultural offerings to meter-fed television sets in 150,000 households in London and Sheffield, as well as screening some of them in cinemas (Rosenthal 2013: 110–14). Between 1962 and 1965, Olivier was artistic director of the Chichester Festival Theatre and British Home Entertainment filmed *Uncle Vanya* (1963) there. The screen director was Stuart Burge, also a theatre director at Chichester, who had previously directed a BBC studio version of *Julius Caesar* in 1959 (see Wyver 2012). *Uncle Vanya* acknowledged its theatrical origins by beginning with a silent camera journey through the new theatre into a full auditorium, briefly setting the theatrical scene in a way that has become an established convention of the NTLive, RSCLive, and KBTCLive films. However, the sense of theatre location and audience presence was removed for the rest of the production, which was filmed in a dominantly televisual style, with the stage treated as a studio set. *Uncle Vanya*'s hybridity was also evident in its transmission history: as television broadcasts by British Home Entertainment and National Educational Television in America, and later as US cinema screenings. The next National Theatre screen project would look first to cinema, rather than television, in order to make its mark internationally as well as nationally.

'Not film sets, not stage sets': the National Theatre's studio *Othello*

The Old Vic was the National Theatre's home for its first eight years while the South Bank complex was planned, designed and built. After a less than successful opening production of *Hamlet* in 1963, the company needed a hit, as well as a landmark production in honour of the 400th anniversary of Shakespeare's birth. In 1964 Olivier took on one of the few major Shakespearean roles he had not yet played, in a stage production of *Othello*, designed by Jocelyn Herbert. *Othello* was conceived for and mostly played in proscenium arch theatres. But influenced by his experiences of its open stage performances at Chichester, Olivier had tinkered with the Old Vic stage by extending the forestage, leaving very little space in the wings. Herbert created a minimalist design which, with the aid of a traverse curtain used almost cinematically as a 'wipe', enabled continuous stage action. The first scene was played at night with Brabantio's balcony in the side of the proscenium, while after the Venetian scenes the cut-out metallic façade was flown out to be replaced by a huge stone archway for Cyprus. Curtains, seating and a huge doorway were added for the interiors. For the last scene the bed, screened by a translucent curtain, was lit by a single Moorish hanging lamp.

It was inevitable that the critical and popular success of this quatercentenary year production would attract the interest of the BBC and others in recording the production for posterity. Film studios interested initially included Warner Brothers, which proposed an electronovision version on the model of the Gielgud/Burton *Hamlet,* broadcast the previous year (see Buchanan 2016), but it was British Home Entertainment which would go on to film the production in 1965, with Burge again directing (see Rosenthal 2013: 110–14). The National Theatre saw the value of providing access to a sold-out production as well as replacing the expense and time-commitment of an international tour with 'event cinema': in the US, Columbia would distribute the film for two days only to each venue to enhance its status as a 'once in a lifetime' experience. While *Othello* has become an embarrassment, both for its perceived racism and for its disappointing quality as a film, 'chopped up into dozens of takes in a sterile studio' (Rosenthal 2013: 794), it is significant as the most explicit attempt by the emergent National Theatre to control transmission of its work to a wider audience. The film's translation of theatrical space, and its hybrid cinematic and televisual aesthetic, make it readable as an example of 'expressive' rather than 'reproductive' archiving (Gaudreault and Marion 2015: 95; see also Introduction). In the trailer for the American screenings, Olivier announced that the film's aim was to 'preserve and enhance this *Othello* and more or less present it as one might have seen it at the National Theatre', recreating completely 'the atmosphere, effect and immediacy of the theatre performance'. Such a statement would not be out of place in the marketing of a show broadcast by NTLive or RSCLive.

William Kellner's translation of Herbert's set design into studio scenery fulfilled the remit that Olivier described in the trailer for the American release – 'a film of a performance shot against not film sets, not stage sets, but backgrounds to the situation' – by both expanding and compressing the performance space. The second story of the Venetian façade is never seen in the film, and the monumental Cypriot arches are very rarely shown in their full height. The film's opening scene, played at the Old Vic in semi-darkness by the proscenium arch, places the well-lit balcony centre-screen, producing a crucially different spatial, as well as performance, dynamic from that seen in the theatre. On film, the arrival of the Venetians and Othello's abuse of Desdemona are located in the exterior setting rather than the interior used on stage. Kellner's added flats closed off the sightlines, creating a labyrinthine feel that also produces a dislocating, abstract effect, often highlighted by Burge's overtly angled use of his three cameras. Archived on film, *Othello* embodied the National Theatre's artistic achievement to date, but the failure fully to capture the Old Vic stage also expressed ambivalence towards its temporary home, destabilizing its intended evocation of the new company's place in the national culture. On film *Othello* occupies a kind of no-man's-land, neither a recreation of its originating stage nor a cinematic *mise en scène* opening out into a realist Cyprus. When the film was made, the modernist design of the new National Theatre complex was still being formulated, following the appointment of Denys Lasdun as architect in 1963. The film's tendencies towards abstracted space gesture towards an overall modernist feel, underwritten by the font of the film's opening titles, which did not yet exist as constructed space in the form of a physical building and stage. The spatial uncertainties encoded in the filmed *Othello* dramatize the National Theatre as a company still tied to a theatrical past as it awaited its future home on the South Bank.

Burge's direction, with its frequent close-ups and mid-shots, has often been dismissed as too televisual although its 'respectable cinematic design' was acknowledged, even if the film still felt 'theatrically confined' (Crowther 1966). As Stephen Buhler observes, Burge's three cameras frequently take the viewpoint of an audience member sitting 'in front' in a proscenium arch theatre, most notably through repeated low angle shots of Frank Finlay's Iago, which ensured that he mostly appears to look down at the audience (2012: 40). Burge's wide angle shots can be viewed as both cinematic and theatrical in their exploitation of the widescreen ratio, allowing spectators to choose their own focus and gaze as though in a theatre, as when Olivier and Finlay stand at opposite ends of the stage. Including as well the breathing of supposedly dead characters shown in close-up and the possibly intentional retention of shots of Olivier's smudged black make-up on Maggie Smith's face, in a murder scene apparently shot as much as possible in one take to capture the immediacy of the stage production, the film retains reminders of the artifice, errors and risks of theatre which privilege moments that 'provenance-stamp' the performance as theatrical. However, although the cinema advertising promised an 'actual performance of the National Theatre', Burge's hybrid theatrical, televisual and cinematic styles could not compensate for the absence of both stage and audience.

In-house at the Roundhouse: Richardson's *Hamlet*

By the end of the decade, the National Theatre and RSC had established themselves as the key British theatre institutions. This status was reinforced by media coverage and filmed restagings of their work, which even in the years after the quatercentenary continued to centre on Shakespeare. Whether their theatres should employ proscenium or open staging also became a focus for debate. At the RSC, Hall had failed in his bid for Arts Council funding to reconstruct the RST to include 'a new false proscenium arch' alongside 'an apron stage that jutted fourteen feet into the auditorium' (Beauman 1982: 239), while debate about the desirability of flexible theatre spaces for the National Theatre's South Bank complex was resolved in favour of including both in the form of the proscenium Lyttelton and the Olivier's open stage.

If the National Theatre's *Othello* had been 'trammelled by its aim of reproducing the theatre production's action on an expanded version of the stage set' in the Pinewood studio (Jackson 2014: 103–4), a venture in 1969, independent of either the National Theatre or the RSC, responded to their respective attempts to bring the stage to the screen by using filmed theatre as an act of resistance against the 'controlled relationship between stage and auditorium of the traditional theatre building' (McAuley 2006: 17). Tony Richardson intended both his theatre production and his film of *Hamlet* at the Roundhouse as full-scale assaults on the proscenium stage, embodied by the National Theatre's 'formalized shape ... at the Old Vic' (Richardson in Morley 1969: 7). The goal expressed in the accompanying manifesto was to 'free' theatre socially as well as spatially, and restore a sense of the 'presence that the proscenium theatre has weakened and debilitated' (qtd. in Hunt 1969: 602). To this end, he set up an in-house production, creating a whole new theatre within the industrial architecture of an unused train shed in Camden, part-funded by his film-making in Hollywood:

> We decided to confine ourselves to the inner circle. We hung thick black drapes from the gallery down between the columns. We built a low semi-circular stage, and curving seats on three sides, so that it was like a half circus ring within a circle, and we suspended baffle-boards above the stage and audience to confine the sound. ... It was an exciting space that needed no scenery as such. With entrances possible from all sides, and a few raised blocks if we needed sitting areas, action could be swift, and angles and acting-areas could change constantly.
>
> (RICHARDSON 1993: 37)

Hilary Spurling waxed lyrical about the result:

it would be hard to imagine a more magical background for the play than the winding passages, the dim, interlocking ante-rooms, the impression of brilliant light, and warmth against the black hangings and thick stone walls of this strange and beautiful building. A ring of slender pillars surrounds both stage and auditorium, so that the audience is enclosed in the same space as the play, under the vast, shadowy, domed roof.

(1969: 19)

Richardson's television background had left him with a dislike of studio shooting, and he had employed a mix of live broadcast and film in his BBC production of *Othello* in 1955. He shared the preference for location articulated by Troy Kennedy Martin in his notorious 1964 denunciation of studio-shot television drama. Robert Shaughnessy notes the film's deployment of 'a cinematic discourse . . . analogous to its particular theatrical aesthetic of the "empty space"' (2006: 72). The film empties the space still further, turning the stage and the Roundhouse architecture into a *mise en scène* in which darkness becomes a background for angled, expressive mid-shots and close-ups which abstract actors from their surroundings to highlight moments of individual performance 'presence' in ways which have become part of the grammar of current live theatre broadcasts, as in Phyllida Lloyd's *Julius Caesar*. Such televisual close-ups throughout are combined with overtly filmic elements so that camera views are often framed and filmed through objects such as the spectacles worn by Horatio and borrowed briefly by Hamlet.

However much the location shooting means that the 'brick, the dust, and the darkness form part of this world in the film as they did for audiences in the stage performances at the Round House [sic]' (Mullin 1976: 124), the wide semi-circular stage is literally never seen in the film, even in the play scene. As with the BBC's *The Wars of the Roses*, Richardson's *Hamlet* endeavours to enhance capture of the theatre experience by filming on location in the theatre, but in the absence of an audience the combination of televisual and cinematic conventions means that despite the film's blend of 'overt theatricality and the quasi-documentary real' the stage ultimately remains the equivalent of a film studio (Shaughnessy 2006: 73). Intended as a radical assertion of the power of the open stage, Richardson's restaging of his production instead creates a sequence of 'sceneless stages' in which the originating theatre disappears (Mullin 1976: 130), much as it does in the National Theatre's filmed *Othello*. *Hamlet* points forward to the potential of 'in-house' production as a means to independent control of institutional self-representation, a prospect which reappears with the emergence of live broadcasts to cinema. But without an audience, its representation of the stage lacks the sense of theatrical 'presence' it aimed to restore.

Live theatre broadcast as commemoration and celebration

In the next five decades, film of National Theatre and RSC Shakespeare productions migrated mostly either to restagings in television studios or to observational documentaries capturing rehearsals or brief scenes on stage (see Greenhalgh 2007: 667–70). Beginning with a studio version of Zeffirelli's *Much Ado About Nothing* (BBC1, 1967) which exploited multi-camera shooting to open up the Old Vic's 'very two-dimensional production' (Adams 1967: 11) and take the viewer into the heart of the action (Rosenthal 2013: 113–14), all subsequent filmed National Theatre Shakespeare was studio-shot (*The Merchant of Venice* [Thames, 1974]; *Richard II* [BBC2, 1997]; *King Lear* [BBC2, 1998]; *The Merchant of Venice* [BBC2, 2001]). The same was true at the RSC, where, except for *The Comedy of Errors* (ATV, 1978), filmed on the main stage, Trevor Nunn's productions of *Antony and Cleopatra* (ATV, 1974) and *Macbeth* (Thames, 1979) were all multi-camera studio restagings without audiences, whether originating on the proscenium arch main stage or in The Other Place black box studio theatre, as were his *Othello* (1990, BBC2) and 2008 *King Lear* (More4).

Other than two live Shakespeare broadcasts, *The Comedy of Errors* and *Twelfth Night* from New York's Lincoln Center in 1987 and 1997, as part of the PBS 'Great Performances' series, and two BBC4 broadcasts from Shakespeare's Globe in 2003–4, television broadcasts of Shakespeare on stage seemed relegated to the past. The year 2009 was a pivotal one for the emergence of new digital outlets for filmed theatre (see Wade 2011: 55). The National Theatre's decision in that year to live broadcast selected performances from its two main theatres to cinemas restored both stage and audience to the screen. Pioneered from 2006 by 'Met Live in HD' from New York's Metropolitan Opera, with two Shakespeare operas part of its second season in 2007, live performance broadcasts were enabled by the conjunction of technological advances in High Definition digital filming and satellite distribution to cinemas (see Bennett, Chapter 2). As with previous forms of recorded theatre the intent was to expand audiences, 'democratize' access to high culture and prolong production life and profits by leading arts institutions. Encouraged by how well the broadcast of his Lincoln Center *Twelfth Night* ten years before had generated a sense of live, simultaneous experience, artistic director Nicholas Hytner envisaged theatre broadcasts as providing a contemporary equivalent of 'Laurence Olivier at the Old Vic in my local cinema' (Hytner 2017: 270).[2] Shakespeare was central to Hytner's policy that the National Theatre's repertoire should 'explore both the state of the nation and the boundaries of the theatre ... to be the big, public alternative to the studio theatres' (2017: 38–39). 'National Shakespeare' should therefore be 'public Shakespeare' (2017: 207), broadcast from the open Olivier stage to both a UK and international audience (see

Chapter 7 for the ubiquity of the Olivier for Shakespeare broadcasts to date). NTLive, which launched in 2009 with *Phèdre,* included *All's Well that Ends Well* in its first season and to date has broadcast eleven further Shakespeare productions.

Digital Theatre was also launched by Robert Delamere and Tom Shaw in 2009 to 'capture' live theatre productions for pay-to-view streaming, download and cinema broadcast from 2013. To date it has recorded *The Comedy of Errors* (RSC/Told by an Idiot, 2009), *As You Like It* (RSC, 2010), *Much Ado About Nothing* (Sonia Friedman Productions, 2011), *Macbeth* (Liverpool Everyman and Playhouse, 2011) and *King Lear* (Almeida, 2012). It also hosts RSCLive and Shakespeare's Globe recordings. Accessible in many locations, digital media for the broadcast of high quality content across a range of platforms became available at a time when productions of theatre plays had largely vanished from television schedules (Marshall 2012; Purves 2013; Wyver 2013; Trueman 2015). According to Dominic Cavendish, the size of audiences now watching broadcasts from the Olivier means 'the National's output has acquired the trappings of a mass medium' (2013). The turn to theatre broadcast at the National Theatre and the RSC was largely shaped by theatre directors who, like those of the 1960s, were experienced in filming stage plays. Benefiting from the availability of freelance screen directors with television backgrounds, the theatres could become media production companies in their own right: able 'to influence their own destinies – and avoid having their productions filtered through the fickle editorial views of a local broadcaster' (Marshall 2012). No longer dependent on the BBC or other producers to remediate their products, theatre institutions could control the direct access to high quality experience which confirmed their public value.

Ten years before NTLive's first Shakespeare broadcast, the RSC had experimented with filming in front of an audience to create an example of 'recorded theatre' (see Introduction). Gregory Doran's main house *The Winter's Tale* was filmed live by Robin Lough at the Barbican on 22 and 23 April 1999 as a co-production with Heritage Theatre for straight-to-video release. The film starts with shots of the audience, whose response is heard throughout. Lough begins each scene with an establishing wide shot, framed by the theatre's proscenium arch. The filming mostly remains within that frame, except during Antony Sher's direct address as Leontes, when Lough chooses side shots which include the audience (see Chapter 7 for more on Lough's handling of direct address). As Susannah Clapp noted, Doran's staging registered the need for 'a redesign of the [Stratford] stage . . . aimed at bringing audience and actors closer together' (1999). The recording of *The Winter's Tale* looks forward to the possibilities that would open up for live broadcast theatre once the RST was redesigned in 2012. Doran's *Macbeth* (BBC4, 2001), however, was transplanted from the Swan to the Roundhouse by John Wyver's company, Illuminations, in a production which was filmed cinematically in one-camera takes to exploit its atmospheric location as Richardson had done three decades earlier (see Greenhalgh 2003; Wyver 2015b). While Illuminations filmed both Doran's *Hamlet* (BBC2, 2009) and his African *Julius Caesar* (BBC2, 2012) on location, the crowd scenes from *Julius Caesar* which were captured in the newly reconfigured Royal Shakespeare Theatre (RST) were precursors of a shift to a stage where live theatre broadcast could flourish.

Meanwhile, other institutions were producing their stage Shakespeare on screen. Shakespeare's Globe started screening its Shakespeare productions as delayed broadcasts in the UK, Australia, New Zealand and the US from 2011 (see Aebischer, Chapter 7). In 2012 the Cultural Olympiad which accompanied Britain's hosting of the Olympic Games inevitably put Shakespeare at its heart, in the form of the 'World Shakespeare Festival' (RSC), 'Globe to Globe' (Shakespeare's Globe), and the 'Shakespeare Unlocked' season (BBC). In partnership with Arts Council England (ACE), the BBC piloted the digital platform 'The Space', which livestreamed a number of the Cultural Olympiad performances, while the *Guardian* newspaper website streamed Polish theatre company TR Warszawa's 'cinematic' *2008: Macbeth* from the Edinburgh International Festival (Dickson 2012), a development initiated by *The Times*, which offered downloads of Digital Theatre's *The Comedy of Errors* in 2010, and subsequently imitated by *The Telegraph* in partnership with Cheek by Jowl (see Kirwan, Chapter 10). In America BroadwayHD followed the same Web-based model as Digital Theatre from 2014, but initiated its repertoire with cinema showings of *Romeo and Juliet*, the first production on Broadway since 1977, starring Orlando Bloom and Condola Rashād.

The RSC's move into live broadcast in 2013 was initiated by Doran in his first year as artistic director, and benefited from his established collaborations with Wyver and Lough as well as the experience of NTLive, especially regarding contractual and distribution arrangements (see Wyver 2015b). The transformation of the RST into an all-enveloping auditorium with a deep thrust stage not only brought actors and audience together but allowed flexible and creative mobilization of the usual half-dozen or so cameras employed for broadcasts, positioned along the back of the side stalls and on tracks in the centre. RSCLive's distinctive use of the crane camera enabled 'expansive and spectacular shots', taking in audience and the whole of the stage in order to convey the 'full playing area' (Wyver 2015b: 293), while homing in subtly on details of performance from a variety of theatre perspectives, from stage-floor to gallery level.

The vast majority of Shakespeare productions broadcast have been screened from open stage venues, from the intimate studio-style Donmar Warehouse (*King Lear*, 2011; *Coriolanus*, 2014) to Stratford Festival's vast thrust stage theatre in Ontario, Canada which provides access to previously recorded performances via CBC television, North American cinemas, and online (see Kidnie, Chapter 8). In 2015 the Royal Exchange, Manchester, with support from the British Council, edited its in-the-round *Hamlet*, starring Maxine Peake as the prince, from three recorded performances for broadcast to cinemas and available to purchase on DVD. Kenneth Branagh Theatre Company Live (KBTCLive) filmed its West End season at the Garrick (2015–16), comprising *The Winter's Tale*, *Romeo and Juliet*, and *The Entertainer*, and apart from Lyndsey Turner's *Hamlet*, mounted at the Barbican by Sonia Friedman Productions in 2015, KBTCLive is the only British venture to date to have live broadcast Shakespeare from a proscenium arch theatre.[3]

The additional funds and effort invested in the 2016 commemoration of Shakespeare's death led to a peak in broadcasts. In addition to content on the BBC's and British Council's 'Shakespeare Lives' worldwide online platform, Almeida Live was inaugurated by Rupert Goold's *Richard III*, while the Comédie-Française mounted *Roméo et Juliette* in association with Pathé Live (see Aebischer, Chapter 15). The year 2016 also saw Shakespeare broadcasts across a range of platforms by smaller, more diverse or experimental companies. Forced Entertainment's *Table Top Shakespeare*, Cheek by Jowl's *The Winter's Tale* and Tara Arts' *Macbeth* were live-streamed (see Nicholas, Chapter 4, and Kirwan, Chapter 10). Meanwhile Talawa's *King Lear* was recorded at the Royal Exchange Manchester, made available on the 'Shakespeare Lives' website or BBC iPlayer, in selected cinemas, and as a BBC4 broadcast on Christmas Day (see Rogers, Chapter 9). Whereas for decades the BBC had largely ignored live theatre as a source of programming (Plunkett 2013; Wyver 2013; Trueman 2015), under the leadership of Tony Hall, previously chair of the Cultural Olympiad committee, its new openness to the genre was cemented by the hosting, again on the 'Shakespeare Lives' website and BBC iPlayer, of Shakespeare's Globe's first online broadcast, Emma Rice's controversial *A Midsummer Night's Dream* (see Sullivan, Chapter 3, and Aebischer, Chapter 7). The BBC's renewed embrace of Shakespeare on stage continued in 2018 with broadcasts of Illuminations's films of the Almeida's *Hamlet* on BBC2 and the Donmar Warehouse *Julius Caesar* on BBC4 (see Aebischer and Greenhalgh, Introduction), together with the streaming of the other two parts of Phyllida Lloyd's all-female trilogy, *Henry IV* and *The Tempest*, on BBC iPlayer.

Shakespearean commemoration is a 'paradoxical operation that remembers him best when it makes him new' (Calvo and Kahn 2015: 14). In the 1960s, at an earlier phase of the interwoven history of staging Shakespeare and filming performances, theatre and media institutions responded to moments of Shakespearean celebration with limited but important technological and artistic innovations that in turn spurred shifts in staging and forms of archiving, through the choice of studio or outside broadcast for the filming of Shakespearean performance. Between 2012 and 2016, analogous commemorative energies were at work in a period of even more rapidly accelerating technologies of representation. These inspired not only further innovations in theatre broadcasting but also revisions of staging, and extensions of performance beyond the framing of those theatre and media institutions that were previously so influential. These shifts in relationships between theatre and media practices are evident in two live broadcasts in which institutional self-fashioning through Shakespearean performance takes the form of celebratory commemoration: *50 Years on Stage* (NTLive) and *Shakespeare Live!* (RSCLive).

50 Years on Stage and *Shakespeare Live!*

Unlike the RSC, the National Theatre was not greatly involved in the 2012 appropriation of Shakespeare for 'Britain's soft power message of multicultural acceptance and celebration' (Sullivan 2015: 307). Instead, in November 2013, the company celebrated its fiftieth anniversary with a live broadcast to cinemas of a gala performance, *50 Years on Stage*, which was also transmitted on BBC2 to a British television audience of 947,000. The BBC trailed the programme as 'live and for one night only', while the National Theatre billed it as an 'once-in-a-lifetime performance', both institutions highlighting the promise of immediacy and unrepeatability that have become unique selling propositions for this kind of 'alternative content' cinema event. David Sabel, the evening's executive producer, claimed the event was 'the National's equivalent of the Olympics opening ceremony'. It wasn't simply 'logistical daring' that marked its significance, but the way in which it made the National Theatre 'the South Bank's answer to Broadcasting House', since the 'broadcast element ... [was] being created by us at the same time as the event itself' (Sabel in Cavendish 2013).

Compiled by Hytner and directed by Tim van Someren, the event employed the hybrid format of a televised awards show, mixing archival film, made-for-television documentary inserts and a succession of live performances to recreate selected theatrical highlights from the last half century. Reflecting the show's title, the core image was that of the Olivier stage itself, a bare wooden circle covering the theatre's drum revolve, by means of which streamlined replicas of the original sets appeared, while films were screened on monitors on either side. Theatricality was further emphasized by van Someren's frequent sweeping shots of the whole auditorium and applauding audience.

The live re-enactments inevitably began with the first scene of *Hamlet*, as had the first night of the National Theatre in 1963; the casting of Adrian Lester as Marcellus and Anna Maxwell Martin as Horatio marking the differences in theatrical attitudes to race and gender between that time and now. Judi Dench reprised her performance as Cleopatra in Peter Hall's 1987 *Antony and Cleopatra* and Simon Russell Beale his millennial Hamlet. However, despite Hytner's stress on the night's status as live theatre, and the claim that only a few minutes came from the video archive, the subsequent snatches of Shakespeare were all from television broadcasts in the form of awards footage of Richard Eyre's *Richard III* and the Illuminations restaging of *Richard II* and BBC2's *King Lear*. Live and recorded performances were brought together in the penultimate sequence. When Lester and Rory Kinnear replayed their roles as Othello and Iago in Hytner's 2013 production, at the moment that they embraced after Iago's vow to dedicate himself to Othello's service (3.3), they were briefly replaced by an audio recording of Olivier and Frank Finlay speaking the next few lines on the stage of the Old Vic in 1965. In a show designed to embody 'the way we've always sought to play the past and the present against each other . . . to reflect the nation on our stages' the interplay of theatrical and mediated performance disclosed the National Theatre's ambivalence concerning its own history of remediation (Hytner in Haill 2013: 18), even as it celebrated the live broadcast medium as a means to archive its history and influence its own destiny.

By contrast, the *Shakespeare Live!* outside broadcast from the RST, devised by Gregory Doran, was not directly a commemoration of the RSC's stage history but in its representation of a diverse and popular Shakespeare whose influence was international and intermedial, it reflected the company's current agenda as well as its media history. Unlike the NTLive broadcast, it was a co-production with the BBC and the Open University, directed by Bridget Caldwell, who had previously filmed the outside broadcast of the Richard III reburial in Leicester and the Talawa *King Lear*. Its format borrowed from the type of variety show, derived from music hall, which used to be a staple of Saturday night television fifty years ago, 'with favourite scenes from the greatest plays performed by a cast of household names' (McCrum 2016). It was also televisual in its reliance on the pairing of David Tennant with Catherine Tate as presenters. The broadcast evoked both their long-running partnership as Doctor and companion in the BBC's globally successful *Doctor Who*, as well as their later roles on stage as Beatrice and Benedick recorded by Digital Theatre.

According to Erin Sullivan, filming in the RST 'stage-scape' offers potential for a 'more open, contingent, unpredictable – in a word, theatrical– point of view' compared with the 'stable *mise-en-scène*' of conventional filming (2014: 274). Unlike *50 Years on Stage*, *Shakespeare Live!* blended theatre, film and television seamlessly. Robert Jones's design recycled the shiny black flooring he had used in the 2008 *Hamlet* and was dominated by a neon-lit proscenium arch, onto the frame of which different visual images could be projected, and behind which a monitor screen was lowered to show film clips. In a show constructed around Shakespeare's afterlives in media and the arts, this evocation of a proscenium arch on the RST thrust stage signified cinema, but also recalled Elizabeth Scott's 1932 design and Peter Hall's early plans for a reinvented, multi-purpose stage. As well as ballet, jazz, opera and hip-hop, throughout the evening cinema based on theatre was evoked through performance of song and dance from filmed musicals. Arts documentary-style sequences on Shakespeare's life were presented by Joseph Fiennes, the lead in *Shakespeare in Love* (1998) while film of *uMabatha*, a Zulu version of *Macbeth* (1972) and Ninegawa's 'cherry blossom' version of the play (1985) represented Shakespeare's global influence. Overt echoes of actors' stage performances were continually juxtaposed with reminders of their media appearances. Both RSCLive clips were from the histories, but the choice of the play-within-a-play scene from *Henry IV, Part 1* and the wooing scene from *Henry V* underplayed any nationalist subtexts. The RSC's *Shakespeare Live!* displayed none of the National Theatre's ambivalence about its televisual history but instead celebrated a long-term partnership with the BBC in the service of a Shakespeare embodying the public and increasingly international value both institutions seek to represent and disseminate.

Conclusion

Kate McLuskie and Kate Rumbold suggest that in the twenty-first century, theatre institutions such as the National Theatre, RSC and Globe have exploited the geo-historical significance and materiality of their unique physical sites 'almost in defiance of new technology' with its capacity to give audiences virtual access to their spaces (2014: 203). However, as Diana Taylor observes, the digital era requires reformulation of our understanding of 'site' alongside that of 'presence', the ephemeral, and embodiment (Taylor 2003: 4–5). The spatial dynamics which facilitate live theatre broadcast constitute new kinds of sites for performance. Whatever the set design of each show, the dimensions of the stage, its points of entry, and its surrounding audience configuration provide the broadcast's consistent starting point, the focus for what Pascale Aebischer terms the creation of 'a spatially extended atmosphere' that can be 'transactionally' shared with distant cinema audiences (Chapter 7).

If the decades of televisual remediation of Shakespeare largely constricted his plays within the studio's 'clearly designated and circumscribed space of production' (Wyver 2015c: 547), a tendency that in turn influenced the growth of studio-scale theatrical stagings of the plays, cinematic outside broadcasts from the open stage theatres of the RSC and National Theatre remediate Shakespeare through spaces that are simultaneously television studio, film set and performance locale. Live broadcast is turning what was a single-medium space – the stage – into a hybrid space accommodating multiple media. This spatial openness has become a determining factor in the 'expressive archiving' of Shakespearean performance, not only through the broadcast of repeated paratextual images of theatrical space but through the modes and styles of filming the architecture makes possible or excludes.

However, if open stage performance of Shakespeare has indeed been an essential element in the development of live broadcast theatre to date, such over-determined spatial self-definition may be on the verge of becoming as outmoded as the proscenium arch stage looked to Tyrone Guthrie when he advocated for the open stage in order to overcome the effect of the proscenium's analogies with the rectangular cinema screen (1963). Performance locale and cultural space realigned in new ways with the opening of Nicholas Hytner and Nick Starr's Bridge Theatre in October 2017. Funded by £12 million of venture capital investment, the theatre at Tower Bridge is the first large-scale commercial venue to open in central London since 1973. To the other South Bank institutions discussed by Aebischer in Chapter 7 it adds a flexible 900-seat space on a site earmarked by the developers for a 'world-class cultural facility' (Dex 2015), one designed to be 'a theatre that can be changed to suit ... the shows that people make in the 21st century' (Hytner in London Theatre Company 2017). With a promenade-style *Julius Caesar* in prospect as its second production, scheduled for broadcast by NTLive in 2018, the theatre has been designed to enable filming of all types of current staging. The hybridity of theatrical, televisual and cinematic space which has marked the entire history of filming Shakespeare on stage is now enshrined within a purpose-built theatre. What kinds of presence it will generate and capture remains to be seen.

Notes

1 Many of the surviving BBC recordings can be viewed online at the BBC Shakespeare Archive Resource (http://shakespeare.ch.bbc.co.uk/) by members of subscribed UK educational institutions.
2 On the development of NTLive, see Nesta 2011; Rosenthal 2013: 793–802; Sabel in Groves 2012; Hytner 2017: 270–3.
3 Two performances of the Almeida's 2017 *Hamlet* were filmed by Illuminations at the proscenium Harold Pinter Theatre, edited in post-production, and broadcast on BBC2 on 31 March 2018.

References

Adams, B. (1967), 'Much Ado', *Radio Times*, 2256, 2 February 1967, 11.
Anderson, A. (2012), 'Old Arts in New Media: Qualified Ontologies of "Live" in the Age of Media Casting', in C. Morgan and F. Malva (eds), *Activating the Inanimate: Visual Vocabularies of Performance Practice*, Oxford: Interdisciplinary Press, 185–95. Available online: https://ebookcentral.proquest.com (accessed 25 September 2017.
Auslander, P. (2008), *Liveness: Performance in a Mediatized Culture*, London: Routledge.
Beauman, S. (1982), *The Royal Shakespeare Company: A History of Ten Decades*, Oxford: Oxford University Press.
Brown, G. (1986), '"Sister of the Stage": British Film and British Theatre', in C. Barr, V. Lowe and A. Medhurst (eds), *All Our Yesterdays: 90 Years of British Film*, London: BFI, 143–67.
Buchanan, J. (2016), 'Being There: Shakespearean Event Cinema, 1964', 'Recreating Shakespearean Performance Cultures Worldwide: Live digital relay as creative

practice?' (seminar), World Shakespeare Congress, Stratford-upon-Avon and London.
Buhler, S. (2012), *Shakespeare in the Cinema: Ocular Proof*, New York: SUNY Press.
BUFVC (n.d.), *International Database of Shakespeare on Film, Television and Radio*, http://bufvc.ac.uk/shakespeare/.
Burnett, M.T. (2011) 'Shakespeare Exhibition and Festival Culture', in M.T. Burnett, A. Streete, and R. Way (eds), *The Edinburgh Companion to Shakespeare and the Arts*, Edinburgh: Edinburgh University Press, 445–66.
Calvo, C. and C. Kahn (2015), 'Introduction: Shakespeare and Commemoration', in C. Calvo and C. Kahn (eds) *Celebrating Shakespeare: Commemoration and Cultural Memory*, Cambridge: Cambridge University Press, 1–14.
Cavendish, D. (2010), 'Sir Nicholas Hytner on NT Live', *The Telegraph*, 24 May.
Cavendish, D. (2013), 'Should live theatre be shown in cinemas?' *The Telegraph*, 30 October. Available online: http://www.telegraph.co.uk/culture/theatre/10401993/Should-live-theatre-be-shown-in-cinemas.html (accessed 18 September 2017).
Clapp, S. (1999), 'Sher Heights', *The Guardian*, 10 January. Available online: https://www.theguardian.com/stage/1999/jan/10/rsc.artsfeatures (accessed 20 September 2017).
Crowther, B. (1966), 'The Screen: Minstrel Show "Othello": Radical Makeup Marks Olivier's Interpretation', *The New York Times*, 2 February. Available online: http://www.nytimes.com/movie/review?res=9D07E0D6163AEF34BC4A53DFB466838D679EDE (accessed 29 September 2017).
Dex, R. (2015), 'One Plan, Two Guvnors: National's Nicks to Open Tower Bridge Theatre', *Evening Standard*, 20 August. Available online: https://www.standard.co.uk/goingout/theatre/one-plan-two-guvnors-national-s-nicks-to-open-tower-bridge-theatre-a2917516.html (accessed 20 September 2017).
Dickson, A. (2012), '2008 Macbeth: Is this a Gun I see Before Me?', *The Guardian*, 12 August. Available online: https://www.theguardian.com/stage/2012/aug/12/macbeth-2008-tr-warszawa (accessed 5 October 2017).
Drazin, C. (2014), 'Film Finances: the First Years', *Historical Journal of Film, Radio and Television*, 34 (1): 2–22.
Gaudreault, A. and P. Marion (2015), *The End of Cinema? A Medium in Crisis in the Digital Age*, trans. T. Barnard, New York: Columbia University Press.
'Globe to Globe' (2012), *Shakespeare's Globe*. Available online: http://www.shakespearesglobe.com/uploads/ffiles/2011/10/326025.pdf (accessed 8 September 2017).
Greenhalgh, S. (2003), '"Alas Poor Country!": Documenting the Politics of Performance in Two British Television *Macbeths* since the 1980s', in P. Aebischer, E.J. Esche and N. Wheale (eds) *Remaking Shakespeare: Performance Across Media, Genres and Cultures*, Basingstoke: Palgrave Macmillan, 93–114.
Greenhalgh, S. (2007), 'Introduction: "True to You in My Fashion": Shakespeare on British Broadcast Television', in R. Burt (ed.), *Shakespeares After Shakespeare*, Vol. II, Westport, Connecticut: Greenwood, 551–74.
Groves, N. (2012), 'Arts Head: David Sabel, Head of Digital, National Theatre', *The Guardian,* 10 April. Available online: https://www.theguardian.com/culture-professionals-network/culture-professionals-blog/2012/apr/10/david-sabel-digital-national-theatre (accessed 6 October 2017).

Guthrie, T., R. Rapson and H. Frederick Koeper (1963), 'Architecture for the Stage: Tyrone Guthrie Theatre, Designed by Ralph Rapson, AIA', *Design Quarterly*, 58.

Hagerman, A.M. (2010), 'Monumental Play: Commemoration, Post-war Britain, and History Cycles', *Critical Survey*, 22 (2): 105–18.

Haill, L., ed. (2013), *National Theatre: 50 Years on Stage Programme*, London: Cantate Communications.

Hornby, R. (2011), 'National Theatre Live', *The Hudson Review*, 64 (1): 196–202.

Hunt, A. (1969), 'Arts in Society: Shakespeare: Pop Playwright', *New Society*, 17 April, 602.

Hytner, N. (2017), *Balancing Acts*, London: Jonathan Cape.

Kennedy Martin, T. (1964), 'Nats Go Home', *Encore*, 11 (2): 21–33.

London Theatre Company (2017), 'Press Release: The Bridge Opens', 19 April. Available online: http://www.theingeniousgroup.co.uk/media/321222/ltc-press-release.pdf (accessed 19 October 2017).

Marshall, R. (2012), 'Globe on Screen – or How to Build your Audience and your Archive', *The Guardian*, 2 November. Available online: https://www.theguardian.com/culture-professionals-network/culture-professionalsblog/2012/nov/02/globe-on-screen-streamed-theatre (accessed 12 September 2017).

McAuley, G. (2006), *Unstable Ground: Performance and the Politics of Place*, ed. Gay McAuley, Brussels: P. I. E. Peter Lang.

McCrum, R. (2016), 'Shakespeare Live! Was a Bold and Innovative Tribute', *The Observer*, 24 April. Available online: https://www.theguardian.com/culture/2016/apr/24/shakespeare-live-rsc-stratford (accessed 22 September 2017).

McLuskie, K. and K. Rumbold (2014), *Cultural Value in Twenty-first century England: the Case of Shakespeare*, Manchester: Manchester University Press.

Morley, S. (1969), 'Tony Richardson's New Theatre Venture', *The Times*, 3 February, 7.

Mullin, M. (1976), 'Tony Richardson's *Hamlet*: Script and Screen', *Literature/Film Quarterly*, 2 (4): 123–33.

NESTA (2011), *Digital Broadcast of Theatre: Learning from the Pilot Season: NT Live*, London: Nesta.

Osborne, L.E. (2006), 'Speculations on Shakespearean Cinematic Liveness', *Shakespeare Bulletin* 24 (3): 49–65.

Plunkett, J. (2013), 'BBC has "Downton Abbey Ratings Mentality", says National Theatre Chief', *The Guardian*, 7 March. Available online: https://www.theguardian.com/media/2013/mar/07/nicholas-hytner-criticises-bbc (accessed 29 September 2017).

Purves, L. (2013), 'Nicholas Hytner: The BBC Needs to Embrace the Arts', *The Times*, 7 March.

Richardson, T. (1993), *The Long Distance Runner: A Memoir*, London: Faber & Faber.

Rosenthal, D. (2013), *The National Theatre Story*, London: Oberon Books.

Scannell, P. and D. Cardiff (1991), *A Social History of British Broadcasting*, Oxford: Blackwell.

Shaughnessy, R. (2005), 'On Location', in B. Hodgdon and W.B. Worthen (eds), *A Companion to Shakespeare and Performance*, Oxford: Blackwell, 79–100.

Shaughnessy, R. (2006), 'Theatricality: Stage, Screen, and Nation: *Hamlet* and the Space of History', in D. Henderson (ed.), *A Concise Companion to Shakespeare on Screen*, Oxford: Blackwell, 54–76.

Sontag, S. (1966), 'Film and Theatre', *Tulane Drama Review*, 11(1): 24–37.
Spurling, H. (1969), 'Proved Most Royal', *The Spectator*, 28 February, 19.
Sullivan, E. (2014), '*Richard II* Performed by the Royal Shakespeare Company (RST)', *Shakespeare Bulletin*, 32 (2): 272–75.
Sullivan, E. (2015), 'Olympic Shakespeare and the Idea of Legacy: Culture, Capital and the Global Future', in P. Prescott and E. Sullivan (eds), *Shakespeare on the Global Stage: Performance and Festivity in the Olympic Year*, London: Bloomsbury, 283–322.
Taylor, D. (2003), *The Archive and the Repertoire: Performing Cultural Memory in the Americas*, Durham, NC: Duke University Press.
Tompkins, J. (2014), *Theatre's Heterotopias: Performance and the Cultural Politics of Space*, Basingstoke: Palgrave Macmillan.
Trueman, M. (2015), 'Small Screen, Big Audiences', *Financial Times*, 13 November.
Wade, L.A. (2011), 'The London Theatre Goes Digital: Divergent Responses to the New Media', in J.K. Curry (ed.) *Theatre Symposium Vol.19: Theatre and Film*, Tuscaloosa, AL: University of Alabama Press, 54–68.
Wardle, I. (1966), 'London's Subsidized Companies', *Tulane Drama Review*, 11 (2): 104–19.
'World Shakespeare Festival' (2012), *Royal Shakespeare Company*. Available online: http://www.worldshakespearefestival.org.uk/ (accessed 8 September 2017).
Wrigley, A. and J. Wyver, eds (2018), *Theatre Plays on Television*, Manchester: Manchester University Press.
Wyver, J. (2012), '*Julius Caesar* (BBC, 1959)', *Screenplays: Theatre Plays on Television*, 21 May, Available online: https://screenplaystv.wordpress.com/2012/05/21/julius-caesar-bbc–1959/ (accessed 19 July 2016).
Wyver, J. (2013), 'What's TV's Problem with Theatre?' *The Guardian*, 20 March. Available online: https://www.theguardian.com/stage/2013/mar/20/tv-problem-theatre (accessed 21 May 2017).
Wyver, J. (2014), '"All the Trimmings?": The Transfer of Theatre to Television in Adaptations of Shakespeare Stagings', *Adaptation*, 7 (2): 104–20.
Wyver, J. (2015a), 'Between Theatre and Television: Inside the Hybrid Space of *The Wars of the Roses*', *Critical Studies in Television*, 10 (3): 23–36.
Wyver, J. (2015b), 'Screening the RSC Stage: the 2014 Live from Stratford-upon-Avon Cinema Broadcasts', *Shakespeare*, 11 (3): 286–302.
Wyver, J. (2015c), 'Television and the Anti-Realist Theatricality of "Not Shakespeare"', *Shakespeare Bulletin*, 33 (4): 543–568.
Wyver, J. (2016), 'An Intimate and Intermedial Form: Early Television Shakespeare from the BBC, 1937–1939', *Shakespeare Survey*, 69: 347–60.

2

Shakespeare's New Marketplace: The Places of Event Cinema

Susan Bennett

In the still short history of Event Cinema, 'live' broadcasting of Shakespeare's plays has been a conspicuous success.[1] When, in 2014, Rentrak (a data measurement company supporting media industries) published its 'All-Time Top Ten at the UK Box Office' (Gant 2014: 15), seven of these Event Cinema screenings were of theatrical productions and four of those were Shakespeare plays: the RSC's *Richard II* (2013), the National Theatre's *Othello* (2013), the Manchester International Festival's *Macbeth* (2013) and the Donmar Warehouse's *Coriolanus* (2014). And, across these top-ranked broadcasts, earnings were, by any measure, impressive. The Donmar *Coriolanus* 'grossed £754,000 from a single night' and with Encore screenings the total rose to £952,000 (Gant 2014: 15).[2] To underscore the significance of these particular receipts, Charles Gant compared revenue generated by the broadcasts of the Donmar production with that of Ralph Fiennes's 2012 feature film version of the same play. Both were critically admired interpretations of *Coriolanus*, but Fiennes's film, with production costs reported at £5 million, earned only £901,000 for its entire UK cinema run (Gant 2014: 15). On 26 November 2015, the live broadcast of *The Winter's Tale* (production by The Kenneth Branagh Theatre Company at the Garrick Theatre in London) took £1.1 million at the box office, making it the highest grossing film in the UK for that day and relegating formidable competition in *The Hunger Games: Mockingjay – Part 2* to the number two spot. Yet even this level of success was eclipsed by Robin Lough's broadcast of Lindsay Turner's production of *Hamlet* at London's Barbican Theatre, with Benedict Cumberbatch in the title role: receipts for its premiere were a remarkable £2.9 million, paid by approximately 225,000 viewers across the globe (Gerard 2015), and total revenue after Encore screenings reached £6.32 million (Statista 2017b). In fact, in the history of Shakespeare on screen, only Baz Luhrmann's *Romeo + Juliet* (1997) has done better business at the cinema box office (Gant 2015: 15). There is already ample evidence, then, of the financial value of Shakespeare within the Event Cinema repertoire. Furthermore, the level of economic accomplishment achieved by these top-ranked Shakespeare performances demonstrates just how much the market has grown from the now modest-looking audience of 50,000 worldwide who watched *Phèdre* from the National Theatre in 2009 (Battersby 2016).

The extraordinary success of the Shakespeare–Event Cinema union exceeds the matter of box-office receipts, however. I will look here at the range of benefits, economic and otherwise, which accrue to the various stakeholders of Event Cinema and will consider how these benefits are delivered by staged Shakespeare extended to cinema screen. This is an account of a complex marketplace in which Shakespeare participates as a valuable instrument, a labourer on behalf of the Event Cinema brand. Daniel Sack, in *After Live*, astutely notes that 'capitalism continually feeds off the potentiality of another market, speculation, and the "futures market"' (2015: 21) and I will explore how these theatre-to-screen events pry loose the possibilities of other markets, further profits, and future audiences not just for Shakespeare or theatre, but for a larger range of interests.

New technologies and the promise of access

From its conception, Event Cinema has been promoted as a vehicle for increasing access. Worldwide distribution and increased capacity (far more available seats than in the single source auditorium) promised to boost the overall entertainment sector, specifically growing the audience for premium programming. Target consumers, wherever they might be situated in the world, had to be persuaded that this product gave them direct access to performers and productions considered among the very best, most famous and most highly regarded globally. Thus, not surprisingly, the mainstays of Event Cinema production have been dominant cultural brands: the National Theatre, the RSC, La Scala, the Royal Ballet and the Bolshoi Theatre among them. With statistical evidence from Event Cinema attendance in hand, these cultural institutions can report to their Boards and funders that, through participation in this new medium, they have delivered wider participation and more diversity – principles that have become common imperatives in mission statements for arts organizations in the twenty-first century. By 2008, more people saw productions by the Metropolitan Opera in cinemas than in New York. By 2016, more than 6 million viewers had seen an NTLive stage-to-cinema broadcast, and in that year (2016a), while 787,000 people saw a performance on a National Theatre stage, a seven-year record, 2.2 million people saw a NTLive production at one of 2,700 participating venues in fifty-five countries.[3] Indeed, as those audience figures suggest, NTLive has by now established itself as the field leader in the delivery of Event Cinema worldwide and its programming has swelled from six performances in the inaugural season of 2009 to fifteen in the most recent (season eight, 2016–17).

Stephen Purcell has suggested that NTLive 'exploited the increasing prevalence in cinemas of HD projectors and satellite equipment to "simulcast" a selection of their productions' (2014: 214). As cinemas introduced digital technologies, a market for premium content was created not simply because of what this new equipment could deliver, but also because it was required in order to produce a return on that investment for its developers. Installation of new digital-format equipment in cinemas and other venues also required increased profits so as to repay the capital investment and to legitimate its benefits through consumer uptake. Event Cinema emerged, then, as a new revenue stream at exactly the time one was needed. The shift to this new format was accelerated by the (now abolished) UK Film Council's funding of '240 screen projectors across the Digital Screen Network, including many of the country's independent cinemas' (NESTA 2011: 12) and statistics for the United States reveal an exponential growth in Digital (3D and non-3D) screens: 5,500 in 2009 and almost 40,000 in 2016 (Statista 2017a).

The relationship between technological innovation and an expanded cultural marketplace is not new, of course. As Adrian Curtin illustrated in his book on avant-garde theatre sound, the nineteenth-century creation of the *théâtrephone* (invented by Clément Ader and given its first public demonstration in 1881) was a precursor to 'live' broadcasting:

> Ader's invention allowed attendees of the exhibition to connect telephonically either to the Opéra or to the Théâtre Français, where, between the hours of eight and eleven o'clock at night, three evenings a week, they could listen to snatches of performances for a few minutes at a time. This was not simply an exhibition novelty. Less than a decade later, the *Théâtrephone* Company of Paris was selling the equipment for home use with more 1500 subscribers in place by 1893 and an expanded repertoire that included the Opéra, the Opéra Comique, the Comédie-Française and the Concerts Colonne.
>
> (2014: 88)

Curtin also tells us that coin-operated *théâtrephones* were also to be found in hotels, clubs, cafés and restaurants across Paris.

In London, the Electrophone Company was in operation from 1894 and counted Queen Victoria among its subscribers. Other countries, including the United States, had similar commercial ventures with subscription and casual users. The promise that new technologies created – to expand audience numbers in the late nineteenth and early twentieth centuries – is likewise recognized in an epigraph to the 2016 report, 'From Live-to-Digital', prepared by AEA Consulting for Arts Council England, UK Theatre and Society of London Theatre. It quotes the early twentieth-century inventor Lee de Forest (often called the 'Father of Radio' in America): 'It will soon be possible to distribute grand opera music from transmitters placed on the stage of the Metropolitan Opera House by a radio telephone station on the roof to almost any dwelling in Greater New York and vicinity.... The same applies to large cities. Church music, lectures, etc., can be spread abroad by the Radio Telephone' (Reidy et al. 2016: 18). Whether the *théâtrephone* subscription or the rooftop transmitter, these examples underscore a history where new advances in technology have relied on cultural products to demonstrate the new capabilities, to create a new consumer market and, thus, to prove economic viability. In effect, technology and culture have been intertwined for more than 100 years.

Equally true for today's Event Cinema or the earlier *théâtrephone*, developers, distributors, exhibitors and owners of the new media technologies recover costs only when that technology is harnessed to something a consumer is willing to pay to access. Market differentiation demands that the new product stand out from the usual offerings and deliver not just a novel, but also a superior, experience. Indeed, higher ticket pricing is an important strategy in convincing patrons that this is a premium experience. The more successful the launch, the sooner investors will be remunerated. Moreover, for the owners of venues that adopt new technology (whether that is a nineteenth-century Parisian café or a global conglomerate that controls thousands of twenty-first-century cinema screens), a potential upswing in contextual revenue generation can further boost their bottom line. Participation in Event Cinema provides much-needed revenue for the screening locations: tickets are generally bought ahead of the screening date (often resulting in a completely pre-sold house) and customer subscriptions to the full season means money banked whether or not the purchaser uses the tickets. Advance ticket sales also generate vital demographic data about those purchasers and venues and also benefit from advertising sent out to the patron lists held by the producing institution. As well, Event Cinema allows venues to operate at profit on off-peak evenings (week nights) and generates not just increased traffic but additional revenue from concessions (food and beverages). Some exhibitors reported that Event Cinema was effective in retaining leisure spending locally (rather than patrons travelling to a major city for their entertainment) (Abrahams and Tuck 2015: 8) and others – mostly smaller independent venues – suggested that this programming was nothing short of a lifesaver: the operator of the Strode Theatre in Somerset (England) indicated that it 'literally kept us open following loss of all local authority funding' (Abrahams and Tuck 2015: 27). NTLive estimate production costs for each broadcast at £250,000–300,000 (Abrahams and Tuck 2015: 8), but, with Event Cinema screenings of theatrical performances netting an average £550,000 in ticket sales in the UK alone (Abrahams and Tuck 2015: 15),[4] the gain for the National

Theatre's overall budget is equally important since its Arts Council England funding has dropped by 25 per cent since 2010 and will fall a further 3 per cent between 2018 and 2022 (National Theatre 2016b; Pickford 2017).

The first ventures into live programming (David Bowie's live-to-cinema performance of his album *Reality* in 2003 and the inauguration of 'The Met: Live in HD' in 2006) had instantly found enthusiastic, if niche, audiences, but it was only when London's National Theatre developed NTLive that Event Cinema became more widely recognized and built such a robust audience base. Indeed, not only has theatre emerged as the most popular genre of Event Cinema in Britain (generating, in 2015, 32.4 per cent of UK ticket sales compared to 19.8 per cent for its closest competitor genre, opera, with rock concerts at a mere 3.2 per cent [Statista 2017c]), the National Theatre's own technology has driven the theatre-to-screen market, demonstrated through its partnerships with other major cultural institutions such as the Barbican and the Donmar Warehouse. For this reason, I will focus on the relationship between NTLive and its Shakespeare broadcasts to consider how the consistent presence of Shakespeare within Event Cinema has fostered the success and dominance of the NTLive brand as well as how this programming has affected play selection within the overarching National Theatre repertoire.

NTLive and Shakespeare

At first, NTLive was underwritten by funding from NESTA (a UK innovation foundation) and Arts Council England, allowing crucial research and development as well as pilot programming.[5] If NESTA's contribution was driven by its innovation agenda, Arts Council England saw the NTLive initiative as a key contribution to its vision, 'Great art and culture for everyone' (2015)[6] – 'It aims to ensure more people experience and are inspired by the arts, and pledges to support organisations who want to achieve this through the use of digital technology' (NESTA 2011: 7). For the National Theatre, however, the Event Cinema project was not just about building new and more diverse audiences, but also the opportunity to create 'new sources of cultural and economic value' (NESTA 2011: 6). This was, as described in a NESTA-produced report written after the pilot season of NTLive, a particular challenge for the theatre since its name, although with 'a respected international profile', was not distinctive; since many countries have a national theatre, the National Theatre believed they would 'not have the same global reach as New York's Metropolitan Opera' (NESTA 2011: 7). In order to attract audiences internationally – and the National Theatre recognized from the outset that their broadcasts had to sell beyond the UK so as to at least meet operating costs – brand marketing was essential: 'the UK is well known for its excellence in theatre and NTLive used the "Live from London" hook as a way of building interest and awareness in the programme. In the second season, ... NTLive's strapline became "Best of British Theatre broadcast to cinemas around the world"' (NESTA 2011: 6).[7] And what could more easily and effectively connote the 'Best of British Theatre' than Shakespeare? That his plays were intrinsic to the construction and maintenance of NTLive identity is further perceptible from the shifts in the National Theatre's own repertoire, as well as from the collaborations forged within the NTLive brand.

From the outset, Shakespeare's plays have been a regular part of NTLive broadcasts. Only season six (2014–15), so far, has been without at least one Shakespeare performance and that absence might well be explained by the previous year's content when fully 50 per cent of the programming comprised plays by Shakespeare (*Othello* and *King Lear* from the National along with *Coriolanus* from the Donmar). Of the twelve productions of Shakespeare's plays broadcast by NTLive to date, eight have been original National Theatre productions. Yet in the decade before NTLive was launched, productions of Shakespeare's plays at the theatre were far from a regular occurrence. The only exception was 2003 when Trevor Nunn directed *Love's Labour's Lost*, his farewell production as Artistic Director, and Nicholas Hytner, Nunn's replacement, staged *Henry V* as his first show in the position. Otherwise, there were rarely Shakespeare plays at the National Theatre in this period (1999–2009). In effect, the task of establishing NTLive as a 'Best of British Theatre' brand has been undergirded by regular delivery of Shakespeare's plays that has, in turn, overdetermined the composition of the National Theatre's stage seasons.

Establishing brand recognition for NTLive has been more elaborate, however, than a simple equation of Shakespeare and 'Best of British Theatre': it has relied, too, on actors who will be recognized through their other work in theatre, television and/or film and who have national and/or international reputations. There are many examples of this model from the National Theatre's own Shakespeare productions: in season two (2010–11), Rory Kinnear starred in *Hamlet*; season three (2011–12), Lenny Henry in *The Comedy of Errors*; season four (2012–13), Simon Russell Beale in *Timon of Athens*; season five (2013–14), Simon Russell Beale again in *King Lear* as well as Adrian Lester and Rory Kinnear in *Othello*. Partnering with other theatres to screen their Shakespeare productions again illustrates the importance of high-profile actors in leading roles: Derek Jacobi in Donmar Theatre's production of *King Lear* (season two), Kenneth Branagh in the Manchester International Festival *Macbeth* (season four), Tom Hiddleston in Donmar Warehouse's *Coriolanus* (season five), Benedict Cumberbatch in the Barbican Theatre's *Hamlet* (season seven), Tamsin Greig in *Twelfth Night* (season eight) and, in one of two productions receiving advance promotion for season nine (2017–18), Ben Whishaw in the Bridge Theatre Company's *Julius Caesar*.[8] Star power benefits the NTLive brand through boosting audience appeal; worldwide circulation of NTLive showcases the actors in prestigious projects. While many of the 'stars' in these productions are best known to British audiences, they often have strong recognition internationally through ventures such as BBC Worldwide television (a £1 billion-plus business [BBC Worldwide 2015–16]), the Public Broadcasting Corporation's 'Masterpiece Theatre' or 'Masterpiece' (1971–2008) in the United States and, of course, from visits to London theatres so popular with tourists. Benedict Cumberbatch's *Hamlet* is the exemplary case, of course, with the more than £6 million in box office receipts generated by a global audience of more than 550,000 – many of whom would have been *Sherlock* rather than Shakespeare aficionados and younger than the typical average age of a NTLive audience (NTLive n.d.; Reidy et al. 2016: 28). The stronger the NTLive brand has become, the more exhibitors have signed up – by now extending well beyond conventional cinemas to include university campuses, cultural institutions such as museums, and community centres.

Perhaps inspired by (or jealous of) NTLive's sector-leading success with a Shakespeare-heavy repertoire, other theatre companies have participated in Event Cinema and, most often, replicated a reliance on the canonical playwright.[9] Shakespeare's Globe started broadcasting to screens in the UK, Australia, New Zealand and the US in 2012. The RSC launched RSCLive in November 2013 with a production of *Richard II* starring David Tennant. More than a dozen other RSC productions have now been screened in the UK and selected other countries, with Erica Whyman, Deputy Artistic Director of the RSC, reporting that the audience 'for a single live broadcast ... is about the same as an audience for an entire year at the Royal Shakespeare theatre [sic] in Stratford' (Gardner 2015). And, since 2014, the Stratford Festival in Ontario, Canada, has screened some previously recorded performances in cinemas across the United States and Canada – perhaps an initiative to respond to what theatre critic J. Kelly Nestruck described as the colonization of Canadian cinemas by Shakespearean productions from the National Theatre and the Royal Shakespeare Company (2013). In 2015, the Kenneth Branagh Theatre Company launched a season of three live broadcasts. The first two were Shakespeare plays, *The Winter's Tale* and *Romeo and Juliet*. In the first case, transmission underwrote a limited and expensive twelve-week run at the Garrick Theatre in London; as Jon Bath (Head of Production at Fiery Angel, partner in the live broadcast initiative) put it:

> *Winter's Tale* cost £1million up front, plus additional weekly costs in excess of £120,000 per week with little margin to be made from the theatrical presentation alone. We could only pull the company involved together for what totalled 53 performances due to availabilities and other commitments, not least those of key performers including Judi Dench and we could only sell 708 seats for each performance taking us to capacity at the Garrick Theatre. How could we extend the reach? We are a commercial venture that would otherwise struggle to make the figures

stack up and show a respectable potential margin to weigh up against the risks involved. We had to expand virtually.

(Reidy et al. 2016: 117)

In 2016, the second stage-to-screen performance, *Romeo and Juliet*, more than delivered on the Shakespeare and star power formula with Richard Madden and Lily James in the title roles – actors not just familiar from *Game of Thrones* and *Downton Abbey* respectively, but established as a romantic couple for the times from their roles as Prince Charming and Cinderella in Disney's 2015 remake (which, of course, Branagh had directed). Jon Bath stated:

> The live broadcasts of the Kenneth Branagh Theatre Company productions are a billboard for what's happening in the West End. We've agreed to show each of the three plays live over one month in Japan ... suddenly it's a trade mission. We won't make much money, but it's an exciting way of promoting and showing what we do – come to the West End and see it for real.
>
> (Reidy et al. 2016: 118)

Finally, in 2016, the small, but highly regarded, Almeida Theatre in London made its first venture into the medium with a performance of *Richard III* with Ralph Fiennes in the title role and Vanessa Redgrave as Queen Margaret (Almeida 2016a).[10] In short, Shakespeare has quickly been established as the 'super-brand' within Event Cinema, instrumental in building both demand and revenue.

If Shakespeare's plays, ideally with well-known and highly regarded actors in the leading roles, are the sweet spot for stage-to-screen production and critical to the delivery of a 'Best of British Theatre' identity, how those plays are curated for their remote audiences further suggests how Event Cinema promotes its brand and builds audience appetite for its products. Two example broadcasts will serve here to elaborate marketing practices within the medium, for Shakespeare and on behalf of other stakeholders: the Almeida Theatre Live's *Richard III* (2016b) and NTLive's *Twelfth Night* (2017c). In both cases, I saw these productions at a cinema in Calgary, Canada.

Insider knowledge and added value

From the outset, 'the National's key marketing expenditure has been on producing a cinema trailer. The trailer is created in-house at the National Theatre, and then formatted for distribution by a screen advertising agency. Trailers are usually shown five to six weeks prior to the broadcast' (NESTA 2011: 34). This is, no doubt, a smart strategy given the move into cinema space, to respect the conventional method of piquing audience interest in upcoming programming and prompting future visits. The first of the National's trailers – produced before a NTLive broadcast had been seen anywhere – oscillated between scenes of backstage preparations (the thirty-minute call, stage make-up being applied) and panoramic shots of London often seen in tourism marketing. The camera focused first on Tower Bridge and then zoomed along the Thames to a floodlit National Theatre where, it was implied, the performance was about to begin. The minute-long trailer ended with an actress making her entrance onto the stage that the viewer saw from behind, sharing the perspective of the technical crew watching from the wings. A voiceover, in 'Best of British' Received Pronunciation, announced: 'Live from the National Theatre in London comes a ground-breaking series of events – a season of plays broadcast live via satellite in high definition and shown in cinemas around the world' (NTLive 2010).

The modest budget of the NTLive's first few seasons prohibited the production of trailers for individual shows; rather, 'a season trailer promoted the whole range of shows and the concept of NTLive' (NESTA 2011: 34). Thus, the trailer for season two opened with a brand statement: 'For almost fifty years, Britain's National Theatre has been at the heart of theatrical excellence and innovation, then the curtain rose around the world on National Theatre Live,' followed by the promise of 'a brand new season of the very best of British theatre.' Visual components combine praise for season one (for example, 'A smashing success. *LA Times*.') with images from the upcoming productions, landing finally on an advertisement for NTLive's new sponsor, the British insurance and investment multinational, Aviva. By season three, Aviva had progressed to partnership with the National Theatre and was promoted at both the beginning and the end of the trailer. All three short narratives were designed to establish credentials – of London, of the National Theatre, of the individual productions and of the sponsoring company. All were shown to potential audiences as evidence of a premium offer: the trailers exhort the viewers to 'be part of the experience.' The challenge for the broadcast, then, was to create that experience – better than regular film, different from actual theatre attendance but imitating its special quality of liveness – as well as furnish value-added engagement with quality theatre at a location convenient to the ticket purchaser. Indeed, a distinctive attribute of Event Cinema has become this additional content, much of which is not available to those who buy an actual (and generally much more expensive) theatre ticket. Typically a theatre-to-screen broadcast now includes a pre-performance talk, interviews with the director and/or cast members as well as relevant contextual information, followed by another presentation in the intermission (see Aebischer, Chapter 7, and Osborne, Epilogue, for discussions of NTLive's paratexts). The information sheet for the Almeida Theatre Live *Richard III* supplied to exhibitors provides a specific breakdown: 'Event slides 15 minutes; Pre-show 15 minutes;

Introduction 5 minutes; Act One 1 hour 40 minutes; Interval 20 minutes; Act Two 1 hour 10 minutes' (UMS 2016).

In advance of the Almeida broadcast, their trailer (twice as long as a typical NTLive promotion) offered a simple hook: a single camera close-up of Ralph Fiennes as he delivered with characteristic intensity one of Richard's speeches not from *Richard III* but from *3 Henry VI*, an edited portion of the long soliloquy in Act 3 that ends 'Can I do this, and cannot get a crown? / Tut! were it further off, I'll pluck it down' (3.2.194–95; Almeida 2016b). Fiennes's performance, advertising Richard's frustration and ambition in anticipation of the play proper, was followed by foreboding music and three unadorned slides: one that named the theatre, the play and the director (Rupert Goold), a second with the cast list, and the last the date of the live screening. By contrast, the NTLive trailer for *Twelfth Night* used a compilation of many different moments from the play in performance, showing off the spectacular set on the Olivier's revolving stage and the use of contemporary dress and music, interspersed with text captured from reviews: 'Fabulously funny, dazzling and finely tuned', 'Masses of fun, a delicious crowd pleaser' – telegraphing that this NTLive Shakespeare brings no risk of boredom for the viewer (National Theatre 2017c). The final image promoted a new partnership for NTLive, with Sky Arts, a UK subscription TV channel dedicated to arts programming. This arrangement had been announced in March 2017: Sky Arts would become NTLive's 'headline sponsor' with Sky Arts content screened by NTLive before their broadcasts in the UK; Sky Arts described the partnership as part of their 'commitment to investing in, and facilitating wider access to, the arts' (Sky Arts 2017). (The pre-broadcast marketing for Sky Arts was in fact included when *Twelfth Night* was screened in Canada, although the channel is not available.)

Pre-show components to a live broadcast contextualize the performance by both situating it in the season of Event Cinema and emphasizing the uniqueness of the occasion. At my local Cineplex (in Calgary, Canada), a screening from NTLive typically begins with a series of their own upcoming productions (often five or six separate trailers within the pre-performance content), but also promotes other series such as the Bolshoi Ballet, classic films (newly digitized versions of films such as Billy Wilder's *Some Like It Hot* and Alfred Hitchcock's *North by Northwest*) and 'In the Gallery' (for example, the Katsushika Hokusai exhibition at the British Museum – a 'once in a lifetime opportunity' [Cineplex 2017]). The through-line is that these are all 'world-class' broadcasts, relayed in high definition and delivered by experts in their particular fields; in other words, the audience is affirmed in their good taste – all of these broadcasts are for them – even before the show proper.

How the actual broadcast begins is critical to constructing the audience's experience of a putative liveness. Typically the camerawork takes viewers into the theatre (often through doors into the lobby or the auditorium) and a presenter – almost always a woman familiar to British TV audiences[11] (Emma Freud, Kirsty Lang, Verity Sharp) – waits in the stalls as actual audience members take their seats to provide her remote audience with a critical introduction. For *Twelfth Night*, Kirsty Lang initially sent that audience on a virtual backstage tour of the National Theatre (the 'real' tour in the actual theatre comes with a £10 price tag[12]) where we learn about the 1,000 people who work there. A common strategy in Event Cinema, the backstage tour not only functions to promote the high production values behind the broadcast about to start, but also underscores the importance of the arts for job creation – a reminder to governments (and to voters) of the value of the creative industries to local and national economies. Since the transformation of Malvolio into Malvolia was the signature of this production (the poster, for example, featured only Tamsin Greig who played the role), it was not surprising to find the production's 'gender fluidity' the topic of Lang's critical introduction. Cameos from comedian Eddie Izzard, artist Grayson Perry, Eurovision Song Contest winner Conchita Wurst and blogger-activist Jack Monroe (all immediately recognizable to British audiences, but likely not at all to North Americans) showered praise on the production's gender-fluid exploration and added their own personal explanations of the term. The repetition of 'gender-fluidity' throughout the introduction suggested it was key to understanding this interpretation of *Twelfth Night*, no doubt trading on the term's very recent addition to the *Oxford English Dictionary* and making the Malvolio-Malvolia adaptation very much 'on trend'. Yet, in case this was a risk too far for the Shakespeare-'Best of British' brand, the introduction also had actor Daniel Ezra (Sebastian) defend a common humanity at the heart of the show, existing beyond differences in race, gender and sexuality. At the Almeida, the introduction concentrated on the parallels between *Richard III* and contemporary events – that the global recession in 2008 had produced politicians like 'Brexit'-architects, Conservative MP and former London Mayor Boris Johnson and then UKIP (United Kingdom Independent Party) leader Nigel Farage; that the war in Syria might be a modern-day equivalent to the Wars of the Roses; and that in 2012 the body of King Richard had been exhumed from underneath a car park in Leicester.

Mid-show, the illusion of liveness to remote audiences is again a focus, usually through audience chatter and movement either in the auditorium itself or, in the case of *Richard III*, as backdrop to an interview with director Rupert Goold, standing at the bar and offering a brief history of the Almeida as a community theatre that produces internationally significant work. A countdown clock on the bottom right of the cinema screen keeps the audience to theatre time, ironically so when it is an Encore screening (see Kirwan, Chapter 10, for further discussion). What theatre-to-screen does not offer, however, is the opportunity for a talkback with the cast and creative team, but audience participation through social media is the suggested substitute and actively encouraged: for *Richard III,* Facebook (almeidatheatrelive) and Twitter (AlmeidaLive_, #RichardIII).

Advance marketing and in-programme content serves, then, to persuade Event Cinema consumers that they are getting much more than a filmed performance. The provision of expert opinion serves not just to enliven the production, but also to recognize that among their audiences are certainly a significant number who are there in the context of Shakespeare-based curriculum in schools, colleges and universities.

More Shakespeare, bigger markets

The opportunity to screen Shakespeare's plays 'live' and worldwide was championed in the closing arguments of Greg Doran's Richard Dimbleby Lecture (first televised on BBC1, 16 March 2016). As Artistic Director of the RSC, one of his stellar accomplishments, he suggested, was that every production was now filmed and thus accessible to a much wider audience, and that screenings were available, free of charge, to every classroom in the country (UK). At first a co-venture between the RSC and the BBC ('Shakespeare Unlocked' [2012]), *Romeo and Juliet, Macbeth, A Midsummer's Night's Dream* and *Julius Caesar* – four of Shakespeare's plays commonly taught – were made available as extracts in digital format (BBC). In 2013, a stand-alone RSC initiative, Schools' Broadcasts, was launched to provide performances 'as live' on a single day and time to a special website in a student-friendly format. The Schools' Broadcasts come with a live introduction and suggested student activities and with a Q & A with actors at the end of the broadcast. Virgin Media and the Sidney E. Frank Foundation (an American charitable organization) are the programme's funders. The National Theatre has also created a digital platform for school use, 'National Theatre: On Demand. In Schools' (2017b). Their productions, supported by teachers' lesson plans and video resources for student use, are available on demand to registered schools in the UK. Four of the seven available productions are of Shakespeare's plays. For older students (Key Stage 3 and above), there is *Othello*, *The Comedy of Errors* and *Hamlet* (repurposing productions already seen at NT Live screenings), while students in Key Stage 2 can access a filmed version of Ben Power's production of *Romeo and Juliet* for young audiences. The Sidney E. Frank Foundation and the Stavros Niarchos Foundation (one of the world's largest philanthropic organizations) support the NT's school programme.

Doran's argument in the Dimbleby Lecture was that everyone deserves access to Shakespeare and to Shakespeare done well. While this may well be true, his rather innocent claim masks the fact that culture is an industry and it constantly requires, as Sack has noted, new audiences and new markets. What the RSC Schools' Broadcasts and 'National Theatre: On Demand. In Schools' projects are invested in, surely, is an exercise in lifelong brand recognition. How far are these broadcasts to schools from the kinds of marketing methods perfected by the Disney Corporation to establish an early affiliation that can be extended and developed through a viewer-consumer's lifetime? The KBTCLive broadcast of *Romeo and Juliet* (discussed by Osborne, Epilogue) suggests not far at all. And for theatre to thrive, on stage and on screen, a sufficient percentage of the occupants of today's classrooms must become tomorrow's paying audiences. Moreover, the commitment to contribute to the school curriculum is also an efficient strategy for extending its market congruent with public and donor funding requirements.

News in 2016 that GCSE drama courses no longer required students to attend a theatre performance, but offered the option instead 'to analyse a digital recording' prompted a letter from some of the UK's 'top actors' to the *Sunday Times* to protest this change: 'Recordings of live productions', they wrote, 'are valuable teaching tools but they should be in addition to the experience of live performance, not a substitute for it' (Lark et al. 2016). The defence, offered by Karen Latto (subject specialist at Oxford, Cambridge and RSA Examinations), was hardly surprising, that it was 'an option designed to expand access to live theatre' (Press Association 2016). The proposed move to digital recording was expedient and in line with substantially reduced budgets for both live arts organizations and schools:[13] it recognized that theatre is expensive to produce and asked why should governments fund theatres locally and regionally when the RSC can deliver 'the best' Shakespeare to 'everyone' via a digital recording? But the Department for Education has since changed its mind and reinstated the requirement to attend a live show (Busby 2017). Nonetheless, the concern illustrated risks identified with Event Cinema's dramatic growth: that institutions like the National Theatre and the RSC will cut back on touring where costs are high (Reidy et al. 2016: 78), and that smaller theatre companies will lose their audiences to digital delivery (including, of course, those school audiences for Shakespeare's plays). The 2016 'Live-to-Digital' reports warned that 'the barrier for entry [for local theatres] remains too steep' since 'a well-known brand, stars or expertise may be a prerequisite for staging Event Cinema' (Reidy et al. 2016: 78).

It is hardly new to observe that the dissemination of Shakespeare's plays and cultural institutions like the National and the RSC work to establish a particular kind of British identity for its citizens and Event Cinema has proven an asset in this ongoing project. But its global distribution also serves to educate a wider and more diverse audience in what comprises that identity: worldwide broadcast is instrumental in selling a much larger range of British products, cultural and otherwise. The foreword by the then Minister of State for Culture and the Digital Economy, Ed Vaizey, to a 2016 British Council report, 'All the World's: How Shakespeare is viewed around the globe and the role his work can play to support the UK's soft power' talks about Shakespeare as 'promoting the best that Britain has to offer' and that 'his legacy helps Britain to shine in the global arena' (British Council 2016: 2). Investment in the digital recording capacity is, among other things, investment in the marketing of Britain worldwide – as Jon Bath put it, 'a trade mission' (Reidy et al. 2016: 118). Shakespeare on the live broadcast screen promotes tourism and not just to the major theatres: the archaeological dig at the beginning of the Almeida's *Richard III* might not just be reference to the recent discovery of Richard's body, but equally a trailer for the newly opened King Richard III Visitor Centre in Leicester. And it promotes business – not just the suppliers of digital technology, but sponsoring companies like Aviva, Sky Arts and Virgin Mobile.

Event Cinema is a medium that has thrived in a global market. It sells an experiential engagement that asks the audience to want more. It rehearses what David Harvey has described as essential to neoliberalism, 'that the social good will be maximized by maximizing the reach and frequency of market transaction, and it seeks to bring all human action into the domain of the market' (2007: 3). The assiduous promotion of Shakespeare's cultural capital within Event Cinema programming obscures the work the medium does for actual capital. David Hancock, cinema analyst at IHS Technology, predicts that sector revenues will reach $1 billion by 2019 and that 'the true extent of programming flexibility will become apparent' (IHS 2015). Theatre, he notes, 'has become the new hot genre in the event cinema world, replacing the early drivers of opera and ballet' (IHS 2015) and, as I have shown here, Shakespeare's place in that growth is unmatched. What new markets his plays will open for Event Cinema and its stakeholders, only time will tell.

Notes

1. My first use of 'live' is in quotation marks to indicate the tenuous condition of liveness for these kinds of broadcast. 'Live' often applies only to the first screening for audiences in the GMT time zone. All other broadcasts are delayed; some may have never been shown live in the first place.
2. 'Encore' is a suitably theatrical term for the repeat performances that happen after the date on which the event is screened 'live' – the NTLive rights model allows for up to four Encore performances; some other Event Cinema providers offer a more flexible arrangement – as many Encores as the exhibiting venue deems viable.
3. Information from the National Theatre Annual Review 2015–16 and from previous National Theatre annual reports: the 2012–13 report notes that by 2013, 1.275 million people had seen an NTLive broadcast, the 2013–14 report indicates an audience 1.49 million, the 2014–15 report 1.2 million and the 2015–16 report a 700,000 UK audience and 1.5 million elsewhere in the world.
4. By contrast, average UK receipts for an opera screening are only £150,000.
5. Research and development was multi-dimensional – they needed to develop production logistics (NESTA 2011: 24–7) and a system of rights allocation

(NESTA 2011: 20–3) as well as choose productions for the first season. The rights model is particularly innovative, creating two paid rehearsals ahead of a live broadcast as well as profit sharing for all rights holders and artists. The timing of NT Live performances – a premiere and up to four Encore screenings within four weeks of the first showing – is established by this rights model (NESTA 2011: 22).

6   This is taken from their 2015–20 Mission Statement (Arts Council 2015); an earlier iteration (2010–15) was similar, 'Achieving great art for everyone'.
7   The 'Best of British Theatre' strapline has since been dropped. With a more established history for NTLive in particular and Event Cinema in general, marketing across the event series now champions the 'world class' stature of the repertoire.
8   Founded by Nicholas Hytner and Nick Starr after they left the National Theatre, the Bridge Theatre's inaugural season opened in October 2017. Their production of *Julius Caesar*, to be broadcast under the NTLive banner in March 2018, was their second show.
9   See also Pascale Aebischer and Susanne Greenhalgh's introduction to this volume.
10 For this event, the Almeida hired John Wyver, producer of RSC Live from Stratford-upon-Avon, to produce the cinema broadcast. The theatre has not, at time of writing, announced any further Almeida Theatre Live productions.
11 In effect, these live broadcasts have redeployed what John Wyver described as a 'televisual' element in his survey of stage-to-television transfers of Shakespeare. performance. See his '"All the Trimmings": The Transfer of Theatre to Television in Adaptations of Shakespeare Stagings' (2014: 105–6).
12 The tours are promoted (as they were in the case of the 'virtual' tour during the preliminary phase of the Event Cinema broadcast) as a chance to see the 'unseen': see National Theatre (2017a).
13 On schools funding, see Belfield and Sibieta (2017a).

References

Abrahams, M. and F. Tuck (2015), 'Understanding the Impact of Event Cinema,' 2 November. Available online: http://www.artscouncil.org.uk/sites/default/files/download-file/Understanding_the_impact_of_event_cinema.pdf (accessed 31 August 2017).

Almeida Theatre (2016a), 'The Almeida Theatre Announces the Launch of Almeida Theatre Live with a Live Broadcast of *Richard III* to Cinemas Around the World, in Partnership with Picturehouse Entertainment', 26 May. Available online: https://almeida.co.uk/index.php?option=com_docman&view=download&alias=302-almeida-theatre-live-richard-iii-live-cinema-broadcast&category_slug=pressreleases&Itemid=133 (accessed 31 August 2017).

Almeida Theatre Live (2016b), '*Richard III* trailer', video recording, YouTube, 10 June. Available online: https://www.youtube.com/watch?v=HOWfQkFphI8 (accessed 31 August 2017).

Arts Council England (2015), 'Our Mission and Strategy'. Available online: http://www.artscouncil.org.uk/about-us/our-mission-and-strategy (accessed 31 August 2017).
Battersby, M. (2016), 'Live Theatre On the Big Screen: The Fear that Streaming Plays in Cinemas Would Cannibalise Theatre Sales Has Largely Been Disproven', *The Independent*, 12 December. Available online: http://www.independent.co.uk/arts-entertainment/theatre-dance/features/no-mans-land-patrick-stewart-ian-mckellen-national-theatre-live-harold-pinter-a7469726.html (accessed 31 August 2017).
BBC (2012), 'Shakespeare Unlocked'. Available online: http://www.bbc.co.uk/programmes/b01dtvpl/episodes/guide (accessed 31 August 2017).
BBC Worldwide (2016), 'Annual Review, 2015–16'. Available online: https://www.bbcworldwide.com/annual-review (accessed 31 August 2017).
Belfield, C. and L. Sibieta (2017), 'The Short- and Long-Run Impact of the National Funding Formula for Schools in England', *Institute for Fiscal Studies*, 22 March. Available online: https://www.ifs.org.uk/publications/9075 (accessed 31 August 2017).
British Council (2016), 'Shakespeare: All the World's'. Available online: https://www.britishcouncil.org/sites/default/files/all_the_worlds.pdf (accessed 31 August 2017).
Busby, E. (2017), 'Exclusive: Schools Will Have to Take GCSE and A-level Drama Pupils on Theatre Trips, Following DfE Intervention', *Times Education Supplement,* 9 February. Available online: https://www.tes.com/news/school-news/breaking-news/exclusive-schools-will-have-take-gcse-and-a-level-drama-pupils (accessed 31 August 2017).
Cineplex (2017), 'In the Gallery'. Available online: http://www.cineplex.com/Events/InTheGallery (accessed 31 August 2017).
Curtin, A. (2014), *Avant-Garde Theatre Sound*: *Staging Sonic Modernity*. Basingstoke: Palgrave.
Gant, C. (2014), 'The Numbers: Event Cinema', *Sight and Sound* 24.6 (June): 15.
Gant, C. (2015), 'The Numbers: Shakespeare', *Sight and Sound* 25.12 (December): 15.
Gardner, L. (2015), 'To Beam or Not to Beam: How Live Broadcasts Are Changing Theatre', *The Guardian,* 6 May. Available online: https://www.theguardian.com/stage/theatreblog/2015/may/06/effects-of-live-satellite-broadcasts-national-theatre-rsc (accessed 31 August 2017).
Gerard, J. (2015), 'Benedict Cumberbatch Draws Record Audience for NT Live "Hamlet" Screenings', *Deadline Hollywood*, 16 October. Available online: http://deadline.com/2015/10/benedict-cumberbatch-hamlet-record-screenings-nt-live-1201585579/ (accessed 24 November 2017).
Harvey, D. (2007), *A Brief History of Neoliberalism*, Oxford: Oxford University Press.
IHS Markit (2015), 'Event Cinema Revenues to Hit $1 Billion by 2019, IHS Report Says', 1 July. Available online: http://news.ihsmarkit.com/press-release/technology/event-cinema-revenues-hit-1-billion-2019-ihs-report-says (accessed 31 August 2017).
Lark, A. et al. (2016), 'Pupils Need Live Drama,' *Sunday Times*, 17 April: 26.
National Theatre (2016a), 'Press Release: Annual Review 2015–16.' Available online: https://www.nationaltheatre.org.uk/sites/default/files/national_theatre_annual_review_press_release_2015–2016.pdf (accessed 6 September 2017).

National Theatre (2016b), *Annual Report 2015–16*. Available online: http://review.nationaltheatre.org.uk/#2016/finance/74 (accessed 31 August 2017).

National Theatre (2017a), 'Backstage Tours'. Available online: https://www.nationaltheatre.org.uk/shows/backstage-tours (accessed 6 September 2017).

National Theatre (2017b), 'National Theatre: On Demand. In Schools'. Available online: https://schools.nationaltheatre.org.uk/app/os#!/home (accessed 31 August 2017).

National Theatre (2017c), 'Twelfth Night – National Theatre Live'. Available online: http://ntlive.nationaltheatre.org.uk/productions/60537-twelfth-night (accessed 26 January 2018).

NESTA (2011), *NT Live: Digital Broadcast of Theatre, Learning From the Pilot Season*, 1 June. Available online: http://www.nesta.org.uk/publications/nt-live (accessed 31 August 2017).

Nestruck, J.K. (2013), 'Stratford Festival to Film Productions for Worldwide Theatre Distribution', *Globe and Mail*, 7 November. Available online: https://beta.theglobeandmail.com/arts/theatre-and-performance/stratford-festival-to-film-four-productions-each-season-for-worldwide-theatre-distribution/article15309859/?ref=http://www.theglobeandmail.com& (accessed 6 September 2017).

NTLive (n.d.), 'About Us'. Available online: http://ntlive.nationaltheatre.org.uk/about-us (accessed 31 August 2017).

NTLive (2009), 'First Season – Trailer', YouTube, 16 September. Available online: https://www.youtube.com/watch?v=8Bt4njIYoFo (accessed 31 August 2017).

'NTLive – Trailer' (2010). Available online: https://www.youtube.com/watch?v=JQjUYsDt6_k (accessed 26 January 2018).

Pickford, J. (2017), 'Arts Council Cuts Funding for Four Biggest Recipients,' *Financial Times*, 27 June. Available online: https://www.ft.com/content/56f832d8-5b3e-11e7-b553-e2df1b0c3220 (accessed 31 August 2017).

Press Association (2016), 'Actors Criticise New GCSE Drama Courses that Cut Out Live Theatre', *The Guardian*, 17 April. Available online: https://www.theguardian.com/education/2016/apr/17/actors-david-harewood-zoe-wanamaker-criticise-gcse-drama-courses-that-cut-out-live-theatre (accessed 31 August 2017).

Purcell, S. (2014), 'The Impact of New Forms of Public Performance', in C. Carson and P. Kirwan (eds) *Shakespeare and the Digital World*, Cambridge: Cambridge University Press, 212–25.

Reidy, B.K., B. Schutt, D. Abramson and A. Durski (2016), 'From Live-to-Digital: Understanding the Impact of Digital Developments in Theatre on Audiences, Production and Distribution', Arts Council England, 11 October. Available online: http://www.artscouncil.org.uk/publication/live-digital (accessed 31 August 2017).

Sack, D. (2015), *After Live: Possibility, Potentiality and the Future of Performance*, Ann Arbor: University of Michigan Press.

Statista (2017a), 'Number of Movie Screens in the United States from 2008 to 2016, by Format'. Available online: https://www.statista.com/statistics/589627/event-cinema-highest-grossing-releases-uk/ (accessed 31 August 2017).

Statista (2017b), 'Ranking of the 10 Highest Grossing Event Cinema Releases in the United Kingdom (UK) in 2015'. Available online: https://www.statista.com/statistics/255355/number-of-cinema-screens-in-the-us-by-format/ (accessed 31 August 2017).

Statista (2017c), 'Share of Box Office Revenues from Event Cinema Screenings in the United Kingdom (UK) in 2016, by Type'. Available online: https://www.statista.com/statistics/589241/cinema-events-box-office-revenue-share-by-type-uk/ (accessed 31 August 2017).

Sky Arts (2017), 'Sky Arts and National Theatre Live Announce Partnership', 9 March. Available online: https://corporate.sky.com/media-centre/news-page/2017/sky-arts-and-national-theatre-live-announce-partnership (accessed 31 August 2017).

UMS (2016), 'Almeida Theatre Live, *Richard III* cast list'. Available online: https://ums.org/wp-content/uploads/2016/08/Almeida-Live-Richard-III-cast-sheet.pdf (accessed 6 September 2017).

Wyver, John (2014), '"All the Trimmings": The Transfer of Theatre to Television in Adaptations of Shakespeare Stagings,' *Adaptation* 7.2: 105–6.

3

The Audience Is Present:

Aliveness, Social Media, and the Theatre Broadcast Experience

Erin Sullivan

In the spring of 2010, Marina Abramović staged an event that captivated the art world. Over the course of ten weeks, for 736 hours, she sat silently in the atrium of the Museum of Modern Art in New York while visitors took turns sitting in a chair facing her and experiencing the power of pure, embodied, focused presence (Cotter 2010). The impact of the show, 'The Artist Is Present', took many by surprise, with several participants breaking into tears during the minutes they spent with Abramović. In an age of distracted, distributed and increasingly virtual ways of being, it turned out that just looking into someone's eyes, and really being there with them, could prove a powerfully exposing and even transcendent experience.

In many ways 'The Artist Is Present' exemplifies the essence of theatre as it has often been defined: concentrated co-presence, both in time and place, which has the power to move, overwhelm and transform. And in this sense it is an odd place to start in an essay interested in broadcast theatre and its audiences, who are increasingly spread across the world. But as rooted as Abramović's marathon performance was in the physical here and now, it also enjoyed a vibrant life on screen that can help us begin to think about what it means for audiences to experience theatre in places and times distant from its inception. During the entire run of 'The Artist Is Present', a webcam live-streamed the project on the MoMA website, while photographs of its 1,545 sitters were uploaded to Flickr. These portraits then became material for the playful yet surprisingly poignant fan Tumblr, 'Marina Abramović Made Me Cry', which featured a steady stream of the pictures of sitters who were moved to tears. Two years later, an HBO documentary about the project brought it to even wider attention, with one clip in which Abramović is visited by her former lover and collaborator, Ulay, making its way to YouTube and going viral. More than 15 million people have viewed it to date, with thousands leaving comments in the discussion thread below. Several note the emotional impact of the mediated scene, despite its now distant time and place: 'I cried', one online spectator wrote in 2016, 'but I don't understand why. Why was I so moved?' ('Marina Abramović e Ulay' 2012).

Abramović's extraordinary project, and its remarkable afterlife online, begin to suggest the power of digital technologies to engage audiences in moments of startlingly captivating performance on screen. What's more, through the capacity they give to audiences not just to watch performance but also to respond to it, they begin to make spectatorship visible in a way that has not previously been possible. Although audience members are no longer physically located in the same performance venue, many are using social media to voice their presence in new ways and create their own communities of reception. Performance scholars have typically explored the impact of technology on theatre through a consideration of what it means for an artistic event to be 'live', but in this chapter I want to shift our focus slightly to the question of what it means for an audience's experience of it to be 'a-live', or animated with a sense of shared occasion, affect and absorption. Though I think that there are many ways for such 'a-liveness' to come into being, in this essay I am particularly concerned with how geographically dispersed audiences bring broadcast theatre to life by sharing their experiences of it with one another on social media. In such contexts, 'aliveness' takes the form of a collective audience practice rooted in the appreciation, celebration and discussion of an artistic event. By looking first at the idea of aliveness itself, and then by examining how it can be created through exchanges on social media before, after and even during a theatre broadcast, I consider how the nature of audience presence is being reimagined in a digitally distributed age.

Aliveness

Investigations into the meaning of liveness, and its crucial role in the production and reception of theatre, have been at the heart of debates about performance and technology for decades. At the end of the twentieth century, Philip Auslander famously contended that there is no such thing as pure, unmediated liveness, in which technology plays no part. Writing in response to Peggy Phelan's argument that 'Performance's only life is in the present', with its fundamental nature firmly fixed in the immediacy of co-presence ([1993] 2005: 147), Auslander countered that our modern conception of liveness is actually dependent on the rise of technology and that, as such, 'it is not realistic to propose that live performance can remain ontologically pristine' (1999: 40). Highlighting how the first usages of the word 'live' arose with the development of radio in the early twentieth century, he argues that liveness and mediation always exist in a 'historical and contingent' partnership, with each helping to define and produce the other (1999: 51–3).

With the coming of the new millennium and the rapid expansion of digital technologies in everyday life, the relations between liveness and mediatization have become even more intertwined. While Erika Fischer-Lichte has followed Phelan in arguing that 'the specific mediality of performance consists of the bodily co-presence of actors and spectators' ([2004] 2008: 38), others have attempted to resist 'essentialist assumptions' by navigating a middle way between the absolute necessity of physical presence and its total rejection (Balme 2008: 81). In the revised edition of his book and a follow-on article about digital culture, Auslander suggests that 'the experience of liveness' in the twenty-first century might be as much about being part of a community as it is about sharing the same time and place. In a digitized world, he writes, 'liveness is not limited to specific performer–audience interactions but to a sense of always being connected to other people, of continuous, technologically mediated co-presence with others known and unknown' (2008: 61; 2012: 6).

Martin Barker has similarly emphasized the importance of connectedness in the creation of a new kind of liveness, though for him the term 'eventness' proves more useful in understanding what excites audiences about a digitally mediated event like a live broadcast (2013: 57). Here, the 'live' in liveness has less to do with something that is 'heard or watched at the time [and place] of its occurrence', and more with an experience that is 'characterized by the presence of life, lively; busy, active, bustling' (*OED* 10a, 4a). Liveness or eventness in such contexts is about being part of an event that is 'a-live' with experience, engagement and possibility – and while other people are certainly part of that process, they don't necessarily have to be physically co-present actors on the stage. They might be an audience that assembles at a local cinema, as in Barker's examples, or they might even be a group of like-minded people who are physically remote from one another but who produce a feeling of connectedness through enthusiastic interaction online.

Such a view of liveness directs the term away from technical requirements about time and place and towards a particular kind of phenomenological experience that foregrounds interactivity and a feeling of togetherness. In this sense, 'aliveness' possesses a deep affinity with what Mikhail Bakhtin called 'the event-ness of Being', or a state of existence produced by the contingency and 'transitiveness' of the present moment (1993: 1). In moments of 'event-ness' and 'becoming', individuals are at once situated in a very specific, never-to-be-repeated time, and infinitely open to influences that arise in the instant. For Bakhtin, 'event-ness' is about individuality and potentiality coming together to produce a radical form of presence and present-ness (Morson 1991a, 1991b). Thinking back to Abramović, we might imagine that the experience of such labile receptivity is precisely what was being tested in each encounter between artist and visitor.

In the case of cinema broadcasts, discussions of how such eventness is created for audiences have typically focused on two factors: the real-time relay of the performance event and the collective, co-present gathering of people at different cinema venues. In such contexts, a more traditional conception of liveness as a function of time and place has been able to remain intact, even if embodied co-presence is now distributed across several points of reception rather than concentrated in a single theatre. But as broadcasting initiatives have diversified, liveness as a temporal and spatial entity, and aliveness as an experiential and affective quality, have begun to uncouple. This has been due both to practical constraints on the part of theatres and cinemas and to positive experiences of audiences at temporally asynchronous, or 'as live', showings (see Kidnie's discussion of Canadian contexts, Chapter 8). Indeed, while Barker previously stressed simultaneity as a core element in audiences' enjoyment of broadcasts (2013: 40), in 2016 he revised his views, commenting that '"live-ness" no longer seems so important for audiences' (quoted in Wyver 2016). The same year, Arts Council England's 'From Live-to-Digital' report similarly concluded that temporal '"liveness" does not drive demand for Live-to-Digital, nor affect the quality of the audience experience' (Reidy et al. 2016: 13).[1] More significant for the 1,200 audience members they surveyed were the convenience and lower overall cost of attending a screening, irrespective of whether it was relayed in real-time or at a later date.

Such findings point to the possibility that, while experiential aliveness at broadcasts is often enhanced by the liveness of shared time and place, one factor is not necessarily dependent upon the other. While producers of programmes like NTLive might have originally conceived of their projects as predicated on the temporally live experience, audiences have discovered other ways of creating a shared sense of occasion and producing aliveness through it. The physical co-presence of fellow spectators, irrespective of the original time and location of the performance, is certainly one important factor. And yet, just as temporal synchronicity is helpful but not essential in the generation of aliveness, physical proximity to other audience members is not indispensable either. Broadcasts from smaller theatres are increasingly being distributed online, with spectators typically watching from home, and while this almost always leads to a more physically solitary viewing experience, it is not necessarily a less socially involving one. Through social media, and in particular Twitter, some broadcast audiences are finding ways to connect with one another online and create new kinds of experiential aliveness. Even at cinema broadcasts some spectators can be seen using social media to extend their presence beyond their physical location and contribute to a geographically distributed, 'un-present' community online.

In the remainder of this chapter I want to explore how some spectators are using Twitter to generate a sense of aliveness that transcends physical co-presence. Using the Web-based tool Netlytic, I have collected 4,633 tweets from spectators at two broadcasts in 2016: Kenneth Branagh Theatre Company's *Romeo and Juliet*, directed by Rob Ashford and Branagh himself and transmitted to cinemas in July, and Shakespeare's Globe's *A Midsummer Night's Dream*, directed by Emma Rice and streamed online in September.[2] It should be noted at the outset that these tweets come from a small proportion of the broadcasts' spectators, so it is not my intention to generalize about audience experiences as a whole. Rather, in focusing specifically on those who freely embrace Twitter as a way of engaging with broadcast theatre, I explore one example of how aliveness as an audience practice can work.

Such an investigation contributes to the ongoing effort to understand what it means for an experience to be 'live' in a digital age. Geoffrey Way has suggested that the incorporation of interactive elements into broadcasts may be the key to generating a sense of lively eventness among audiences (2017: 399), while Auslander has pointed to the importance of emotional engagement, speculating that 'The emerging definition of liveness' in an increasingly digital landscape 'may be built primarily around the audience's affective experience' (2008: 62). In the examples that follow, we will see how central the sharing of emotion is to Twitter communities that form around live broadcasts, and furthermore how opportunities for self-generated interaction among audiences, especially during online streamings, can deepen the engagement that spectators experience while watching along from home.

Both case studies look at audience activity that occurred as stage performances were transmitted live, meaning that my analysis focuses more on what happens when physical co-presence is unsettled than when experiences of time and simultaneity are reconfigured. It is my hope, however, that some of the ideas explored here might be relevant to future studies of 'as live' audience communities, particularly in terms of aliveness as an experiential, rather than essentialist, concept. Through a mix of traditional close reading and more 'distant', computer-aided analysis, I consider what audience tweets during these broadcasts can tell us about presence and togetherness in a digitally distributed world. While such materials may seem far from the 'event-ness of Being' that Bakhtin originally imagined, in their celebration of shared experience they gesture towards a new kind of festivity that one hopes he might have appreciated.

At the cinema: Kenneth Branagh Theatre Company's *Romeo and Juliet*

On the evening of 7 July 2016, the recently formed Kenneth Branagh Theatre Company (KBTC) broadcast its star-studded production of *Romeo and*

Juliet, directed for screen by Ben Caron, to audiences around the UK, mainland Europe and eventually the world. Featuring the Hollywood actors Lily James and Richard Madden in the title roles (not long after they had co-starred in Branagh's feature film *Cinderella*), as well as Meera Syal as the Nurse and Derek Jacobi as an elder Mercutio, the production was largely sold out in the West End and generated excitement among theatre- and filmgoers alike. As the second instalment in the KBTCLive programme, which had begun in November 2015 with *The Winter's Tale* starring Branagh and Judi Dench, this broadcast adopted a 'top end' model of production in line with that established by the National Theatre and RSC in previous years (Reidy et al. 2016: 117). This meant that it involved a large and experienced filming team, who rehearsed their shots and cues in advance of the broadcast; that on the night it relayed the team's work directly to international cinemas, with further 'as live' showings to follow; and consequently that it necessitated a major financial investment from the company and its partners – around £500,000 in this case (ibid.). In this sense, the KBTCLive producers possessed, and wagered, all the forms of prestige highlighted in the 'Live-to-Digital' report: 'a well-known brand, risk capital to invest, star casting and expertise' (ibid.: 85).

A casual scroll through Twitter on the night might have left some readers wondering what, if anything, could be gleaned from a series of very excited though rather vague remarks about the experience of watching a live-to-cinema transmission. Looking at them in aggregate, however, can reveal some important insights into how audiences are engaging with and deriving meaning from broadcasts (a question further explored by Nicholas, Chapter 4).[3] In the case of KBTCLive's *Romeo and Juliet*, tweeting began well before the show actually commenced, with the official Twitter accounts for the theatre company and many participating cinemas sending out enthusiastic reminders on the day. 'Tonight's the night! #RomeoAndJuliet is broadcast to cinemas around the world!' @KBTCLive posted, and many ticketholders soon followed suit: 'SO excited for @KBTCLive screening of #RomeoAndJuliet tonight', 'Almost time for #RomeoAndJuliet! Can't wait for my night in fair Verona'.[4] On the day of the broadcast, institutions and individuals alike generated anticipation for the evening's entertainments to come.

Tweeting of this kind intensified considerably in the half-hour before curtain up, helping produce a sense of concentrated, shared time akin to the countdown clock described by Peter Kirwan (Chapter 10). During these thirty minutes, spectators used Twitter as a way of announcing their arrival at cinemas and creating a feeling of communal occasion. 'Settling in to watch #RomeoAndJuliet at the cinema. So excited! #BreakALeg', one spectator commented, and several others did the same from venues across the UK and Europe: 'ready in Worthing for #RomeoAndJuliet', 'At the Electric Cinema in Birmingham', 'Looking forward to #RomeoAndJuliet here in Belfast!', 'Best of luck from Barcelona!' As tweets continued to appear, a mental map of the geographically dispersed but experientially united broadcast audience began to take shape alongside the physical reality of each individual group assembling in person at local cinemas. Those using Twitter would have been aware of two kinds of presence materializing simultaneously: that of an embodied proximity at their local cinema and that of a digital connectedness spread across the country and continent. Particularly savvy social media users might also have been conscious of a third presence being created through the tweets themselves, which one-by-one helped establish a more lasting written record of a seemingly ephemeral event.

While each tweet was an announcement of presence in and of itself, frequent references to specific locations within them helped physically situate spectators' experiences and give them a material reality, even as they were relayed online. Of the tweets collected in the half-hour before show time, at least 16 per cent contained the name of a town, city or country, and at least 23 per cent mentioned the name of a cinema. In such instances, members of the broadcast audience actively drew attention to the places in which they had assembled, and in doing so helped create a sense of international reception that nevertheless foregrounded the local. Alongside information about cities and cinemas, many tweeters also included explicit reference to the family and friends who had joined them for the evening. At least 14 per cent of their pre-show messages did this in the text of the tweet – 'On my way to the cinema, date night with my Mum', 'watching with school gonna be amazing', '#RomeoAndJuliet with Hayley at the Harlequin' – while others accomplished this visually by sharing group selfies from the cinema. As with the announcement of location, these tweets helped inject the experiences of the physical, co-present audience into the distributed, virtual one. Rather than drawing audience members away from the community immediately around them in the cinema, tweeting offered many spectators a way of celebrating co-present togetherness while also participating in the wider production of aliveness online.

Once the broadcast commenced, tweeting absolutely ceased, with remote audiences observing a no phones policy that is still strictly enforced in theatres, even if it has relaxed in cinemas in recent years. During the interval, however, messages quickly reappeared, and with them lively expressions of appreciation and enjoyment. The vast majority of posts collected during these twenty minutes exuberantly commended the production and its actors: 'a brilliant experience', 'fabulous', 'AMAZING', 'genius!', 'GORGEOUS!!', '@_richardmadden is incredible', 'Lily James is magical!' – and the list could go on. Indeed, one thing that immediately becomes apparent when reading through audience tweets, whether written before, during, or after a performance, is just how positive they tend to be. Though some dissenting voices can usually be heard – and more on this soon – they typically amount to whispers amidst a boisterous chorus of celebration.

The extreme positivity of the *Romeo and Juliet* tweets can be further illustrated through a sentiment analysis of the messages collected. Such analyses involve the computational processing of emotional content in tweets, with key words like 'excited', 'happy', 'frustrated', or 'annoyed' being coded by an algorithm as either positive or negative feeling. Of course, this kind of automated breakdown has many pitfalls: a tweet along the lines of 'I am so *not* excited about this event' would still register as positive in a rudimentary sentiment analysis due to the word 'excited', despite the clearly opposite feeling expressed in the statement. But provided we approach the results of these analyses with caution, spot-checking distant reading methods with more traditional, close reading practices, then the information they provide can be helpful and even illuminating.[5] In the case of the *Romeo and Juliet* tweets, a sentiment analysis in Netlytic yields 461 instances of positive feeling versus 26 negative ones – or a ratio of nearly 18:1. Closer examination of individual comments in each category suggests that, if anything, the results may swing more dramatically in the direction of undiminished praise, with several false negatives quickly appearing but virtually no false positives. Whether considered together or more anecdotally, responses on Twitter to this broadcast of *Romeo and Juliet* were overwhelmingly happy.

For some, such a uniformly positive response to a theatrical event might confirm a suspicion that Twitter is not a particularly rich place for communal cultural debate – or, as Gabriel Egan has provocatively put it, that this social media platform 'is inherently a non-reflective, off-the-cuff medium for sound-bite anti-intellectualism' (comment after Reisz 2016). Indeed, with so many audience members uniformly 'on message', the kind of theatrical aliveness produced on Twitter might seem worryingly close to marketing hype. It would be wrong, however, to assume that all this positivity stemmed from mindless flattery of institutional and commercial idols, or that such behaviour is unique to social media. For one thing, most tweeters did not use KBTCLive's institutionally branded hashtag, #BranaghTheatreLive, opting instead for the community-generated and Shakespeare-focused #RomeoAndJuliet. Such a choice suggests that their messages were intended more for one another than as lip-service to an institution. Furthermore, audience researchers working in a number of contexts, both online and off, have shown how spectators regularly report their experiences in positive terms. Such tendencies, they argue, are due to a complex mixture of social etiquette, a 'sense of ownership' for the success of the event, and a desire to be a part of a mutually affirming, 'collective experience' (Johanson and Glow 2015: 264; Bennett 2012: 551). That said, such positivity can never be taken for granted: as Kitamura Sae's essay for this collection clearly illustrates (Chapter 11), online reception can certainly go the other way.

Most telling of all, then, are the tweets themselves, which quickly reveal their individual texture and personality when examined in detail. Many include comments indicating that participation in the broadcast help mark the evening as a particularly special one for the tweeter, whether in terms of celebrating a personal achievement or of embracing art's ability to inspire and uplift. 'Celebrating getting a distinction in my first year at uni', one excited spectator tweeted alongside a picture of her ticket stubs, while another reflected more sombrely, 'In the current world & domestic political mess, a trip to see the fantastic live broadcast of #RomeoAndJuliet was v welcome. #TheArts #Love'. Others commented on the powerful impact the production had on them, in some cases suggesting the kind of metamorphosis that Fischer-Lichte locates at the heart of performance: 'I never expected such a brilliant experience ... Can't wait for the 2nd act', 'Completely in tears at the end of #RomeoAndJuliet', 'Never been moved as much by a piece of Shakespeare in my life', 'Jesus, I'm shocked, amazed and speechless. Fantastic, utterly fantastic #RomeoAndJuliet'.

Of course, a 140-character tweet can rarely capture all the nuance and depth of a truly transformative encounter with art, but it would be short-sighted to reject the validity of such comments simply because they come to us through social media. By listening more carefully to these expressions of engagement, we can hear audiences telling us in their own words how a broadcast has affected them. When they do this publicly on a platform like Twitter, we can also see how very personal instances of transformation through art help generate a wider, more collective sense of presence and aliveness. Audience members may be spread across the UK and Europe, but through social media they make visible a feeling of community and shared experience. The fact that these messages live on after the event only heightens their power to generate aliveness: not only do they produce a sense of connectedness during the performance itself, but they continue to tell that story after other traces of the event have faded from view. In this sense, they reflect Pascale Aebischer's argument about the reciprocal relationship between the temporally *'live'* experience and its digital records, which allow an event to go on *'living'* for spectators, researchers and students who encounter it in the future (2013: 146) – an issue also explored by Susanne Greenhalgh (Chapter 1).

While the majority of tweeters at the *Romeo and Juliet* broadcast responded to the production with glowing positivity, among these celebratory missives we can also find more detailed and sometimes critical commentaries on specific performance choices. Several tweeters discussed KBTCLive's decision to broadcast the performance in black and white, creating a distinctive difference between the in-house and at-a-distance viewing experience. 'Very much enjoying @KBTCLive #RomeoAndJuliet though would prefer to have the same experience as in the theatre (rather than b& w)', one spectator wrote, while another countered, 'broadcast in 16:9 black and white looks great – good choice'. Others discussed filming techniques ('why do they keep panning off the person who's talking?'), as well as the cultural politics of casting ('really not here for the only named character played by a Black actor being Tybalt'). Indeed, the more we dig, the more we find specific reactions to particular elements of the broadcast, helping us understand the performance in finer detail and get a better sense of its varied reception. At the same time, the post-hoc nature of these tweets, which were written either during the interval or after the performance finished, means that they tend to function more as miniature, after-the-fact reviews than as in-the-moment comments that lead to further discussion. In order to find examples of more sustained, interactive dialogue, we need to look to broadcasts in which tweeting doesn't just happen before and after the performance, but also takes place throughout it: something that can increasingly be seen during online streams that audiences watch from home.

At home: Shakespeare's Globe's
A Midsummer Night's Dream

Two months after the KBTCLive *Romeo and Juliet* broadcast, on 11 September 2016 Shakespeare's Globe in London embarked on its own high-profile theatre relay. Although the Globe had for many years distributed live recordings of its summer productions through its Globe on Screen programme, these films were typically screened 'as live' in UK cinemas a year after the stage run and then released internationally on DVD and by download (for more Globe broadcasts, see Aebischer, Chapter 7). In contrast, the Globe's Sunday evening broadcast of Emma Rice's *A Midsummer Night's Dream*, directed for screen by Ian Russell, involved streaming the production live online for anyone in the world with an internet connection. This colourful and unabashedly populist *Dream*, which was Rice's first production as artistic director, featured the Australian burlesque performer Meow Meow as Titania; incorporated electric sitar, Beyoncé and David Bowie into its heavily amplified soundscape; and, most controversially, projected a vivid lighting design into a space long known for a more historically unplugged aesthetic. As part of the BBC and British Council's year-long 'Shakespeare Lives' festival, which commemorated the 400th anniversary of Shakespeare's death in 2016, the broadcast was distributed for free and remained online for six months. This meant that while it began as a temporally live event – much in the fashion of the Globe's *Richard II* starring Mark Rylance, which in 2003 had aired live on the television channel BBC4 – it evolved into a more disparate, 'as live' experience as time went on (Purcell 2014: 213–14).

In many ways, the Twitter activity leading up to this *Dream* was much the same as it was with KBTCLive's *Romeo and Juliet*.[6] Festival organizers heavily promoted the event on social media, and would-be spectators contributed to the excitement by voicing their support: 'Can't wait!', 'How happy am I?', 'So excited!!!', 'TODAY'S THE DAY!' As the broadcast began, many others eagerly name-checked the locations around the world from which they were watching, including Australia, Canada, Denmark, Finland, France, Germany, Norway, the Philippines, Spain, Switzerland, Turkey, the US and, of course, the UK. The fact that the broadcast occurred on the final night of this popular production's run added to the sense of occasion: having debuted nearly five months earlier in April, this largely sold-out *Dream* was enthusiastically recommended online by many who had already seen it. As with *Romeo and Juliet*, positive feeling was strong; although audience members were not physically gathered together in local cinemas, many participated in the creation of community through the lively exchange of tweets online.

What was different about this broadcast, however, was the ability of audience members to continue to tweet freely once the performance began. Live-tweeting has grown in popularity over the last decade alongside the proliferation of smartphones in daily life. Television has become a particular focus, with audience members who are physically distant from one another producing a '"group viewing" experience' by tweeting about a programme in real-time (Wohn and Na 2011). While such activity is still unusual in the theatre, the built-in hybridity of online streaming has tempted some spectators to carry it over from other media and see what the results might be. Not everyone would see this as a good thing, of course, particularly since tweeting tends to split spectators' attention between the performance and their phones. This potential for distraction is one reason why some fans of cinema broadcasts are sceptical about streaming. 'Event Cinema is uninterrupted. Streaming you can get interrupted', one respondent in the 'From Live-to-Digital' report commented; 'It's not the same experience, not a communal experience, not an event. It cheapens it' (Reidy et al. 2016: 55).

Looking at the tweets of *Dream* audiences on the night, however, we can quickly see that many spectators risked distraction in order to discuss their responses to the performance as it occurred. The very first scene – in which the mechanicals appeared as Globe ushers and talked the on-site audience through a series of humorous health-and-safety measures – inspired multiple remarks from spectators online. This was due at least in part to the provocative nature of this tongue-in-cheek prelude, which playfully sent up the historically oriented approach to performance that had characterized work at the Globe before Rice's arrival. A new regime at the theatre was being established from the start, and online spectators responded with both delight and disdain.

@BBCShakespeare kicked things off with its own post, 'This is like no safety briefing we've seen before!', and in doing so implicitly granted permission for other would-be live-tweeters to join in. 'This preshow speech is giving me life. #NoSyphillis #NoLunging #NoDreaming #Breasts #RylancesTambourine #DreamLive', one enthusiastic viewer replied, with each hashtag referring either to one of 'Rita' Quince's self-important decrees or to the character's brandishing of a hallowed tambourine that she claimed came from Rylance himself, the Globe's first artistic director. Other spectators likewise repeated and riffed on Quince's instructions, which wove together jokes about what a show at the original, sixteenth-century Globe might have been like ('No spreading of syphilis? I'm out!'); about the revered status of Rylance and historical reconstruction at the theatre ('"Mark

Rylance gave me this tambourine!"'); and finally about amateur dramatics in both *Dream* and the present day ('The stewards are crack ups!', 'LOVE. Captures that very British am dram officiousness').

Not all the comments were positive, however, with more critical viewers objecting to Rice's irreverent take on the history of the Globe or to the overall effect of this newly scripted scene. 'Man, that intro is the opposite of funny #cringing', one spectator wrote, reflecting the scope for sharply contrasting perspectives within the online conversation. Indeed, before the production even began, some who had seen it in person countered the build-up of excitement on Twitter by questioning Rice's use of the Globe stage. 'Sam Wanamaker built @The_Globe for the specific purpose of performing Shakespeare's plays without stage lighting', one person commented, and once the broadcast got going others likewise took issue with Rice's interpretation: 'A mess of a dream. Horrible design', 'This mishmash is not my cuppa', 'As a show it's really entertaining, as Shakespeare it's a bit of a mess. Verse speaking is poor would be so much better if sorted'. This controversial production, which in many ways set out Rice's vision for the new direction of the Globe, generated significant criticism from those who were unimpressed by the artistic approach of the incoming regime.[7]

Although such comments were not reflective of the overall tone of the online conversation, which like that of *Romeo and Juliet* was generally very positive, in their force and specificity they illustrated how alternative viewpoints existed and might spark additional debate online. In several cases, these live-tweeters engaged in conversation with more enthusiastic spectators, helping produce something akin to genuine discussion. Running a chain network analysis in Netlytic, which illustrates back-and-forth exchanges between tweeters, is telling: as can be seen in the visualizations in Figure 3.1, the *Dream* tweets are far denser and more interconnected than those for *Romeo and Juliet*. This is because the *Dream* network of tweeters involved much more interaction among individual profiles, with audience members responding directly to one another in addition to engaging with big institutional accounts. Netlytic's 'reciprocity' score for the *Dream* tweets, which provides a measure 'of ties that show two-way communication ... in relation to the total number of existing ties', comes in at 0.01165, whereas *Romeo and Juliet*'s is 0.00749 ('Network Analysis' 2017). What such numbers tell us is that audience members live-tweeting during *Dream* were more likely to engage in direct exchange with one another than those posting messages before, after, and during the interval of *Romeo and Juliet*.

Such interactivity also allows for a more sustained investigation into how audience members responded to certain performance choices within a production. In the case of the Globe *Dream*, its focus on issues of sexuality and gender proved especially compelling for tweeting spectators. Several commented on Rice's decision to change the female character Helena into a male 'Helenus', thereby introducing a same-sex relationship into the plot. 'Changing Helena to Helenus is a pretty brilliant move. Gives the story

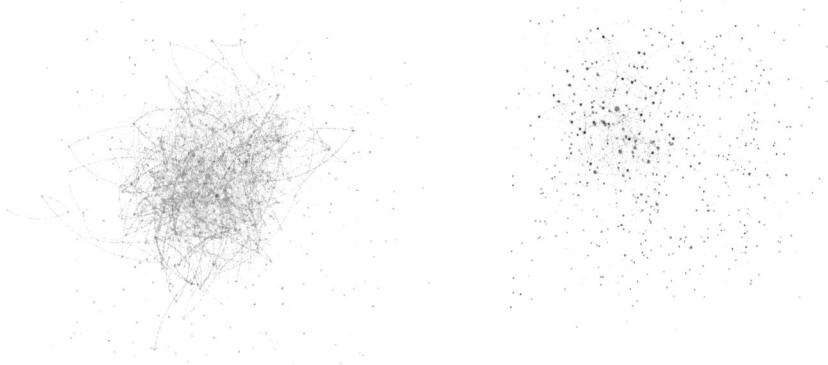

FIGURE 3.1 *Netlytic analysis of* A Midsummer Night's Dream *(Shakespeare's Globe, dir. Emma Rice, 2016) (left) and* Romeo and Juliet *(KBTC, dir. Rob Ashford and Kenneth Branagh) (right).*

another layer', one spectator remarked, while others added, 'Love the gender swap', 'The first time I've ever BOUGHT the Hermia-Helena friendship', 'Loving the casting of a chap as Helena – Helenus is fabulous and feels natural'. This did not mean, however, that responses were blithely uncritical: one tweeter commented that although she liked Helenus, it was still 'a shame that one of the best female parts [got] taken from the grasp of female actors', and another asked why it is that 'Helena/Helenus's behaviour' in the woods – specifically her unyielding commitment to Demetrius – seems 'less acceptable when it comes from a woman?' For others this textual intervention reinforced a wider commitment to inclusive representation under Rice's artistic directorship: 'Oh the beautiful colours of a diverse stage! :)', one person exclaimed, while another commented, 'I adore the way the Globe actually stages diversity of race, gender, possibility, and world'. Through such posts, spectators used Twitter to begin to work through some of the thorny questions that the production raised concerning gender, sexuality and cultural representation. The ability to discuss such issues online allowed participants to engage collaboratively in the process of meaning-making around the production and, in doing so, to animate their communal experience of this theatre broadcast.

For some attendees such discussion proved a particularly enriching form of spectatorship – even more so, in fact, than that achieved by attending a production in person. In her review of the *Dream* broadcast, Heidi McElrath reflected on the sense of community that she felt during the stream: '[W]e weren't alone. Thanks to social media, I watched the livestream in an audience of Shakespeare-lovers from around the world' (2016). The fact that this audience was able to debate the interpretive choices of such a 'bold', 'provocative' and 'unapologetic' production in real time added to McElrath's experience of engagement and togetherness: 'I've never connected so deeply with an audience, even those I could touch and see.' Such comments suggest that, for some, interactivity may be as powerful a factor as physical presence in the creation of aliveness among audiences. It may also be the case that interaction that foregrounds conversation is particularly enhancing: as audience researchers Anja Mølle Lindelof and Louise Ejgod Hansen have shown, 'when participants share their experiences and their proposals for interpretations they become more aware of what the performance is about to them' (2015: 250).

Lindelof and Hansen's work focuses on the way *post*-show discussions can enhance an audience's 'understanding of the theatre experience', allowing it to grow 'after the performance through dialogue with others', but McElrath's reflections suggest that such enrichment can also occur *during* a production through participation in an activity like live-tweeting. While such a practice might not be for everyone, the positive experience of it among some spectators helps illustrate how there is more than one route to theatrical aliveness. Sitting in the same theatre as the performers and other audience members may remain the preferred mode for many, but gathering at a distance in cinemas, interacting online with others before and after a show, and conversing on social media as the performance takes place may prove even more powerful pathways for others.

Such an emphasis on the diversity of audience experience may be the most important lesson we can take away from this investigation into the nature of experiential aliveness. Several years ago, the sociologist Sherry Turkle argued that technology was contributing to greater social isolation and the troubling phenomenon of being 'alone together' (2011), but the tweets considered here suggest an alternate possibility: that social media, when embraced enthusiastically, can help create opportunities for being 'together alone'. Not all audience members will feel the same way, of course: to return to the beginning, and Abramović's remarkable piece of performance art, it's worth noting that alongside the many positive engagements with this work online are thoughtfully articulate reservations such as those of Amelia Jones, who felt that the highly mediated nature of the project made it 'anything but energizing, personal or transformative' (2011: 18). For many, screens can prove a disruptive and disconcerting presence, and that must be acknowledged. For others, however, digital transmission and the forms of engagement it allows may indeed open up new and enlivening opportunities for experiencing art together, even at a distance.

As we have seen, for McElrath and many other audience members, social media provided a way of sharing their individual experiences of aliveness and turning them into something more collective. The fact that Branagh's production included such high-profile actors, and that Rice's was implicated in a wider debate about the future of the Globe, no doubt stimulated interest among viewers around the world. But this doesn't mean that other companies can't generate their own forms of aliveness during broadcasts, whether large or small. During its 2017 streaming of *The Winter's Tale*, Cheek by Jowl invited audience members to use Twitter to ask questions about the ideas and techniques underpinning the production, which director Declan Donnellan and designer Nick Ormerod then answered. The same year, Yorkshire Dance collaborated with researchers on the development of 'Respond', an online platform that 'encourage[s] audiences to slow down and dwell' on artistic experience by talking about it with others (Walmsley 2017). And as we've seen with Abramović's show and the documentary based on it, discussion threads following online clips allowed geographically dispersed audiences the opportunity to share their experiences of engagement, emotion and even transformative change. In each case, we can see artists, producers and audiences exploring new ways in which aliveness as an experiential force can be sustained, and perhaps even deepened, as theatre and performance find their way in an increasingly digital world.

Notes

1 Wyver's conference report (2016) summarizes the main points of Barker's as yet unpublished keynote lecture.
2 I am grateful to Beth Driscoll, Danielle Fuller and DeNel Rehberg Sedo for teaching me how to use Netlytic, and to Elaine Goodfellow for helping me analyse these tweets.
3 Tweets for *Romeo and Juliet* were collected from noon to 4am GMT on the day of the broadcast using the official event hashtag, #BranaghTheatreLive, and the most popular alternative, #RomeoAndJuliet.
4 Tweets from audience members have been anonymized; see Fazel (2016) for more on the ethics of citing social media.
5 Netlytic provides a standard set of emotion-related words for which its algorithm will search, but users can edit this list to suit their particular query. Of course, emotional response is a complex issue, and seemingly negative words such as 'disturbed' or 'upset' can in fact reflect desirable affective reactions, particularly in the context of audiences watching a tragedy. This is one of many reasons why close reading and human interpretation remain important elements in computer-assisted analysis.
6 Tweets for *Dream* were likewise collected from noon to 4am GMT on the day of the broadcast using two hashtags: the Globe's official one, #DreamLive, and the most popular alternative, #MidsummerNightsDream.
7 See Aebischer, Chapter 7, for the controversy surrounding Rice's short-lived artistic directorship.

References

Aebischer, P. (2013), *Screening Early Modern Drama: Beyond Shakespeare*, Cambridge: Cambridge University Press.

Auslander, P. (1999), *Liveness: Performance in a Mediatized Culture*, 1st edn, Abingdon: Routledge.
Auslander, P. (2008), *Liveness: Performance in a Mediatized Culture*, 2nd edn, Abingdon: Routledge.
Auslander, P. (2012), 'Digital Liveness: A Historico-Philosophical Perspective', *A Journal of Performance and Art* 32 (3): 3–11.
Bakhtin, M. (1993), *Toward a Philosophy of the Act*, trans. V. Liapunov, ed. V. Liapunov and M. Holquist, Austin: University of Texas Press.
Balme, C. (2008), 'Surrogate Stages: Theatre, Performance and the Challenge of New Media', *Performance Research* 13 (2): 80–91.
Barker, M. (2013), *Live to Your Local Cinema: The Remarkable Rise of Livecasting*, Basingstoke: Palgrave.
Bennett, L. (2012), 'Patterns of Listening through Social Media: Online Fan Engagement with the Live Music Experience', *Social Semiotics* 22 (5): 545–57.
Cotter, H. (2010), '700-Hour Silent Opera Reaches Finale at MoMA', *New York Times*, 30 May. Available online: http://www.nytimes.com/2010/05/31/arts/design/31diva.html (accessed 4 April 2017).
Fazel, V. (2016), 'Researching YouTube Shakespeare: Literary Scholars and the Ethical Challenges of Social Media', *Borrowers and Lenders* 10 (1). Available online: http://www.borrowers.uga.edu/1755/show (accessed 4 April 2017).
Fischer-Lichte, E. ([2004] 2008) *The Transformative Power of Performance: A New Aesthetics*, trans. S.I. Jain, London: Routledge.
Johanson, K. and H. Glow (2015), 'A Virtuous Circle: The Positive Evaluation Phenomenon in Arts Audience Research', *Participations: Journal of Audience and Reception Studies* 12 (1): 254–70.
Jones, A. (2011), '"The Artist Is Present": Artistic Re-enactments and the Impossibility of Presence', *TDR: The Drama Review* 55 (1): 16–45.
Lindelof, A.M. and L.E. Hansen (2015), 'Talking about Theatre: Audience Development through Dialogue', *Participations: Journal of Audience and Reception Studies* 12 (1): 234–53.
'Marina Abramović e Ulay – MoMA 2010' (2012), uploaded by MiticoMazz, *YouTube*, 15 December. Available online: https://www.youtube.com/watch?v=OS0Tg0IjCp4 (accessed 4 April 2017).
McElrath, H. (2016), 'Digital Groundlings', *Blogging Shakespeare*, 18 September. Available online: http://bloggingshakespeare.com/digital-groundlings (accessed 4 April 2017).
Morson, G.S. (1991a), 'Bakhtin, Genres, and Temporality', *New Literary History* 22 (4): 1071–92.
Morson, G.S. (1991b), 'Bakhtin and the Present Moment', *The American Scholar* 60 (2): 201–22.
'Network Analysis / Visualization' (2017), *Netlytic*. Available online: https://netlytic.org/home/?page_id=2 (accessed 4 April 2017).
Oxford English Dictionary (2017), Oxford: Oxford University Press. Available online: http://www.oed.com/ (accessed 4 April 2017).
Phelan, P. ([1993] 2005), *Unmarked: The Politics of Performance*, London: Routledge.
Purcell, S. (2014), 'The Impact of New Forms of Public Performance', in C. Carson and P. Kirwan (eds), *Shakespeare and the Digital World: Redefining Scholarship and Practice*, Cambridge: Cambridge University Press, 212–25.

Reidy, B.K., B. Schutt, D. Abramson and A. Durski (2016), 'From Live-to-Digital: Understanding the Impact of Digital Developments in Theatre on Audiences, Production and Distribution', Arts Council England, 11 October. Available online: http://www.artscouncil.org.uk/publication/live-digital (accessed 4 April 2017).

Reisz, M. (2016), 'Shakespeare Scholar Vents 500-Tweet "Bitterly Sarcastic" Attack on Book', *Times Higher Education*, 6 June. Available online: https://www.timeshighereducation.com/news/shakespeare-scholar-vents–500-tweet-bitterly-sarcastic-attack-book (accessed 4 April 2017).

Turkle, S. (2011), *Alone Together: Why We Expect More from Technology and Less from Each Other*, New York: Basic Books.

Walmsley, B. (2017), 'Meaningful Audience Relations', *Arts Professional*, 4 May. Available online: http://www.artsprofessional.co.uk/magazine/article/meaningful-audience-relations (accessed 7 May).

Way, G. (2017), 'Together, Apart: Liveness, Eventness and Streaming Shakespearean Performance', *Shakespeare Bulletin* 35 (3): 389–406.

Wohn, D.Y. and E. Na (2011), 'Tweeting about TV: Sharing Television Viewing Experiences via Social Media Message Streams', *First Monday* 16 (3). Available online: http://firstmonday.org/ojs/index.php/fm/article/viewArticle/3368/2779 (accessed 4 April 2017).

Wyver, J. (2016), 'Live Cinema – live!', *Illuminations* blog, 27 May. Available online: http://www.illuminationsmedia.co.uk/live-cinema-live/ (accessed 4 April 2017).

4

Understanding 'New' Encounters with Shakespeare:

Hybrid Media and Emerging Audience Behaviours

Rachael Nicholas

In the first book-length investigation of theatre broadcast audiences in cinemas, Martin Barker proposed that broadcasts constitute a whole new 'mode of participation' (2013: 70). This chapter explores how such new modes of participation have since evolved by focusing on two personal experiences of Shakespeare broadcasts in 2015: the Encore cinema screening, with audio commentary, of the NTLive *Coriolanus* recorded at the Donmar Warehouse the year before, and the live-stream, from Berlin, of Forced Entertainment's *Table Top Shakespeare*. Both broadcasts harnessed the possibilities of personal digital technology to engage their remote audiences, with NTLive making use of smartphones to augment the cinema experience, and Forced Entertainment bypassing the cinema altogether by streaming directly to the audiences' digital devices. The incorporation of conventions and technologies belonging to several media forms within these digital experiences fits with Michael D. Friedman's argument that theatre broadcasts 'constitute a new postmodern pastiche of the media forms in which Shakespeare has taken shape in the past' (2016: 458). Importantly however, as the broadcasts themselves become more hybrid, increasingly diverse ways of participating in theatre broadcasts of Shakespeare emerge. Beyond imitating existing media forms, the expansion of theatre broadcasts outside of the cinema creates new sites for experiencing theatre and enables fresh approaches to viewing. The approaches to spectating involved in watching *Complete Works* online and listening to the *Coriolanus* audio commentary reveal the tangible impact of such hybridity on audience experience. In each broadcast, the specific mix of technologies employed determined how audiences approached and engaged with the work.

In particular, I argue, digital technologies can affect how viewers perform as audiences. For Caroline Heim, the audience attending live theatre constitutes another troupe of performers, co-creators who actively contribute to the event by performing in multiple ways. Heim claims that audience performance relies on the co-presence between the audience and actors, and that it is produced by 'the audience's kinetic, paralingual and verbal expressions' (2016: 20). She contends that 'it is the encounter with others that... initially constructs the individual as performer' (3). Although Heim specifically discusses physical encounters between actors and audience, I contend that even without such co-presence, both theatre broadcast experiences I focus on in this chapter created multiple opportunities for 'encounters' with others that allowed audiences to perform a diverse range of roles. While some of these encounters, as I will show, were unintentional and prompted the confrontation of different modes of spectating within the space of the cinema in which *Coriolanus* was screened, others were sought out and encouraged by the creative teams themselves, as when Forced Entertainment's artistic director Tim Etchells took part in live tweeting with the audience during the streaming of *Complete Works*. In such a set-up, as Erin Sullivan points out in Chapter 3, Twitter can make 'spectatorship visible in a way that has not previously been possible'. Digital spaces can thus become conduits through which a proportion of the audience may perform consciously and deliberately *as* an audience: as individuals voice their reactions, read those of others, and talk back to the production, a sense of community develops around the broadcasts.

The performances a broadcast elicits from its audiences depend on the hybrid media spectatorship practices it enables, as well as on the context of the production and the audiences it attracts. These two broadcasts mixed together media conventions and formats including serialization, durational performance, the DVD and live online video. The resulting hybridization influenced the practices that audiences drew on and performed as part of their broadcast experience. Some of these practices, such as listening to DVD commentaries and watching online videos, were integrated into the broadcasts and their paratexts at the point of production, whilst others, including tweeting and commenting online, were driven by audiences at the point of reception, happening alongside, but mostly independent of, the broadcast itself.

Exploring these practices as, respectively, 'strategies' and 'tactics' is a useful way of understanding the power relationships underpinning the audience performances that the broadcasts provoke. Michel de Certeau distinguishes between 'strategies', which are set out by those whose power is derived from being located in a specific place, and 'tactics', i.e., the actions taken by the dislocated in order to create space for themselves within a 'strategy'. The ways of viewing determined by production companies and the etiquettes of cinemas and theatres work as 'strategies', which are met with a range of audience approaches or 'tactics'. In the types of broadcast experience I analyse here, audience performances often disrupt the distinction between strategy and tactic. Whilst de Certeau's tactics 'circulate without being seen' (1984: 35), here audience approaches are visible in the cinema, and responses are voiced online, sometimes resulting in tensions between different tactical approaches. These audience performances are also capable of being appropriated to become part of the 'strategies' of theatre companies: both NTLive and RSCLive regularly co-opt audience responses on Twitter, collating and retweeting positive comments as part of their publicity campaigns. In reaction to the hybrid range of practices enabled by broadcasts, audience performances continue to change, and their function as tactics can potentially alter the power relationships of the networks that 'delimit the circumstances from which [audiences] can profit' (1984: 34). It is because media hybridity affects the roles performed by audience members and the forms of power they exert that it has an impact on the theatre broadcast experience.

Headphones in the cinema: an audio-commentary of *Coriolanus*

> *I enter the cinema, sit down and get out my phone. As I pull out my headphones, another audience member walks past and says something about me to her companion, just loud enough for me to hear. It's about my phone and it isn't complimentary. I open the National Theatre Backstage app and navigate to the* Coriolanus *digital programme, swiping across to find the 'audio-commentary' section. Obeying the 'Notes on Use' I switch my phone to flight mode. Before the features begin, the cinema screen displays instructions that app users should start their commentaries. I press play. If I'm honest, I feel a little bit smug.*
>
> Coriolanus, Encore Screening, Donmar Warehouse/NTLive,
> 24 September 2015, Personal Account

The Donmar Warehouse production of *Coriolanus* had an extended run from December 2013 to February 2014 and was first screened to cinemas by NTLive on 30 January 2014, selling out both in the theatre and cinema. This level of success can be in part attributed to the headline casting of British actor Tom Hiddleston, whose popularity had recently surged after his appearance as Loki in the high-profile superhero movie *Thor* (2011, dir. Kenneth Branagh, Marvel Studios; see Blackwell 2014: 344). The broadcast's Encore cinema screening in September 2015 was accompanied by the release of a digital programme, available to download via the *National Theatre*

Backstage app.[1] As well as production and rehearsal photographs, trailers, and programme notes, the programme contained an 'audio commentary', designed to be listened to through the user's personal device alongside the Encore screening. The first time such a feature had been made available, the app invited audiences to join in with the 'experiment' and described the commentary as 'a world first for stage and screen'.

Despite the emphasis on novelty, the commentary drew on the established form of the DVD director's track, which offers an optional extension of a film beyond the main feature in private, domestic situations. It thus embodied what Heim, relying on Erving Goffman's concept of frontstage and backstage behaviours, might describe as a 'backstage' audience performance, more appropriate to a home setting (2016: 119). Engaging with the private audio commentary as part of a public cinema screening therefore constituted a hybrid performance of the 'backstage' behaviour of watching a DVD while sitting in the 'frontstage' space of the cinema auditorium.

As Deborah Parker and Mark Parker argue, the DVD commentary track is a 'form of exposition, blending reminiscence, anecdote, close reading, and criticism' (2011: 36). Commentaries involving directors tend to focus on the practicalities of filmmaking, exploring the rationale behind how shots were created and edited together. Perhaps because this feature was produced by the Donmar Warehouse rather than NTLive, the commentary for *Coriolanus* did not feature screen director Tim van Someren, and only a few of the conversations focus on the practicalities of creating the NTLive broadcast, such as shot choices, or the negotiations involved in translating the production to film. Instead, it was the theatre director, Josie Rourke, who led the discussion with cast members Tom Hiddleston, Deborah Findlay, Peter de Jersey and Hadley Fraser. Rourke was a constant throughout the commentary, accompanied occasionally by Associate Director Rob Hastie, with actors commenting on scenes in which they appeared.

The resulting emphasis on the theatrical production rather than the broadcast implied that the feature's implied audience would be interested primarily in hearing from performers and the stage director. This perception reflects the responses to a question in Arts Council England's 2016 *Live-to-Digital* report, which asked audiences to select the type of supplementary content they would like to see as part of 'Event Cinema' screenings (Reidy et al. 2016: 83). Out of 1,001 respondents, 62 per cent selected 'Interviews with actors' and 59 per cent selected 'Interviews with directors' – much higher than the demand for documentary material. Fifty-one per cent of respondents also selected 'Digital programme sent before the performance', indicating an appetite for digitally accessible material that engages with the processes of theatre production.

In addition to information regarding production decisions and acting choices, the *Coriolanus* audio commentary prominently features discussions about Shakespeare's text. Insights into production choices and the backstage workings of the theatre are almost equally balanced with plot descriptions and character analysis. The constant slippage in the conversation between the fictional world of the play and the 'real' world of theatre production is particularly evident when Hiddleston and Rourke discuss the battle of Corioles. As the screen Hiddleston disappears over a ladder at the back of the stage, Rourke asks, 'what happens to you now?' Hiddleston begins his answer in character, explaining that he is 'shut inside the city gates of Corioles alone'. He then switches to actor-mode to describe in detail what is *actually* happening behind the scenes – that he is 'crawling along the lighting rig, down the lighting and fire ladder, stripping off my armour as fast as [he] can, and standing in a small paddling pool whilst being doused in blood'. This piece of commentary provides information on a number of levels, on the one hand helping the audience navigate Shakespeare's plot, and on the other, providing privileged access to backstage information.

In this small section of the commentary, Hiddleston performs the roles of character and actor. Later in this same scene, he additionally performs the role of literary critic. Singling out the line 'O me alone! Make you a sword of me!' (1.6.76) as one of his favourites in the play, he goes on to interpret it as expressing Martius' isolation as the result of his physical bravery and political ideology. Such remarks, frequent throughout the commentary, participate in the construction of Hiddleston's public identity. Noted for his Eton and Cambridge education, Hiddleston's star persona 'has been founded upon reinforcing the features of performance, class and Englishness conventionally tied to the "Shakespearean"' (Blackwell 2014: 344). If, as Anna Blackwell argues, Hiddleston's physical portrayal of Coriolanus was a move away from previous roles that foregrounded this 'Shakespearean Englishness', then the audio commentary provides a space for him to perform and, more importantly, for audiences and fans to access and enjoy, the aspects of his persona that the production itself minimized.

If DVD commentary tracks enable viewers to 'achieve a keener sense of the medium' (Parker and Parker 2011: 24–5), in the *Coriolanus* audio commentary the appreciation and understanding of the medium gained is not of the theatre broadcast, but of the theatre production, its actors, and of Shakespeare's text. Moreover, because listening to the commentary during the Encore screening was a public and 'necessarily communal' act (Friedman 2016: 458), the assimilation of this knowledge turned into an audience performance as theorized by Heim. Anxiety over the smartphone's potential to disrupt the experience of non-participating audience members was evident in the 'Notes on Use' in the digital programme, which asked users to put their phones on flight mode and to keep light and noise from devices to a minimum. Prescribing 'instructions for use' is a strategy in de Certeau's terms, one which here attempted to reduce the impact of the smartphone in the cinema at the point of use (1984: 30). A further strategy – the on-screen announcement that alerted users to press play on Part One of the commentary – also worked to legitimize the presence of headphones and smartphones to other audience members. My feeling of smugness at seeing this announcement demonstrates how my audience performance transformed from interloper into insider. If listening to the commentary was a tactic to assimilate knowledge that was in harmony with the strategy deployed by the Donmar Warehouse, performing this tactic was a source of further empowerment through acquiring, and demonstrating, a deeper understanding of the production.

In hybridizing modes of media spectatorship, the *Coriolanus* audio commentary, when used in the cinema, thus created new, and sometimes awkward, encounters between audience members, which in turn changed how those audiences performed as audiences. While it was an experiment, the analysis of how it influenced audience performance may extend to the broadcast's other paratexts (or 'paradocumentation'; see Abbott and Read 2017: 175). Even for viewers not equipped with the audio commentary, the *Coriolanus* broadcast, in the manner of all NTLive productions, included supplementary features around the main production, including a live introduction by presenter Emma Freud, a pre-recorded video about the history of the Donmar Warehouse, and a live interview in the interval with Josie Rourke.[2] As Friedman argues, these paratexts partly work to 'prompt cinemacast spectators to imagine themselves [...] as participants in the theatrical event' (2016: 460–1).

The negative critical reception of these paratexts, however, indicates that they also affected and framed spectatorship in other ways. The reviews of this broadcast focus heavily on both the form and content of the paratextual features, with the *Guardian* reviewer advising that NTLive 'cut the chat and get on with the show'. Ryan Gilbey (2014) explicitly compares the features with 'DVD extras', which he argues 'can get in the way of our interpretation rather than enhancing it' and, evoking yet another media form, describes the features as 'bad arts television'. Peter Kirwan's review echoes concern that the interval features work to direct interpretation and audience response, describing NTLive's major weakness as an 'anxiety over reception' which leads to 'explanatory interviews and features' that 'attempt to ensure interpretation is as homogenous as possible' (2014: 276). Both reviewers take umbrage at a moment in the interval interview with Rourke, where Freud mentions Hiddleston's recent award of the title of 'MTV's sexiest man alive' for 2013. Kirwan describes how Freud and Rourke 'giggle (literally)' (2014: 276) over Hiddleston's casting, while Gilbey sees this moment as an affront to his own preferred mode of viewing, writing that they were 'hardly the words you want ringing in your ears as Act Two begins'. The reminder that a different (read: young and predominantly female) audience with divergent values and motivations is also watching the broadcast is articulated as interfering in Gilbey's broadcast experience.

In his far more considered reading of the broadcast, Kirwan points out that the 'acknowledgment of the enthusiasm for Hiddleston's casting wasn't entirely gratuitous', since the reference to Hiddleston's body mirrored the camera's focus on it throughout the broadcast (2014: 276). Blackwell further argues that whilst the production 'capitalizes on the physicality of its star', the focus on the body throughout the production works as a dramatic device that makes the audience 'complicit in the Romans' clamour to view and possess Coriolanus's body' (2014: 349). In the interval feature, Rourke herself goes some way to explain the importance of the body in the play, brushing off Freud's 'sexiest man' comment (which was actually relatively insignificant within an overall straight-faced interview) and launching into a discussion about the impact a younger, more athletic Coriolanus has on the interpretation of the play.

The fact that out of the varied material included in the interview it was the 'giggling' that stuck in these reviewer's minds implies that some audience members shared an anxiety over reception. As Gilbey's 'ringing in my ears' comment infers, this is less a concern about reception as a whole than about the kind of reception that values Hiddleston over Shakespeare. Some of the diverse approaches to viewing and valuing the broadcast, and its paratexts in particular, are demonstrated in the 199 comments left by readers of Gilbey's *Guardian* article online. At one end of the scale audience members appreciated the features for illuminating the text, and at the other they deemed them offensive and patronizing.

In general terms these responses fall into Barker's categorization of 'livecast' audiences in the cinema as either 'immersive' or 'expert'. 'Immersives' welcome 'all the bonus materials, because [they] allowed them to become audiences in a way that previously they had not been able to', while 'experts' display 'a feeling that the event was almost being misappropriated', seeing themselves as 'holding expertise which the livecasts undercut' (2013: 66). In relation to the *Coriolanus* broadcast, commenters tended to qualify their positions by aligning themselves with a particular kind of knowledge, experience or authority – 'I'm a big Hiddleston fan', 'I'm a Shakespeare lover' – thus staking their claim over different aspects of the performance.

The way that these different types of 'expertise' are pitched against each other complicates Barker's distinctions. As Daisy Abbott demonstrates in her consideration of fan responses to the production and its broadcast, Hiddleston fans, offended by the reduction of Hiddleston's appeal to his physicality, were just as likely as the Shakespeare lovers to regard the mid-show interview as 'undercutting' their expertise (2015: 25). This sense of entitlement and ownership from different audience groups also played out throughout the run of the show, fuelling online arguments over ticket availability, filming in the theatre, stage-door behaviour, and demands for a DVD release. Whereas Hiddleston fans exerted their right to perform as fans, 'theatre aficionados demonstrated anger in reaction to what they saw as the undermining of their rights to access Shakespeare' (Abbott 2015: 25). Despite its mixed reception from Hiddleston fans, the mid-show interview reinforces 'Hiddleston fandom' as a legitimate viewing position, one that viewers focused on Shakespeare saw as demeaning of their own values and expertise.

Barker's categories are further extended by other comments which lay claim to 'expertise' about the theatre broadcast form and its agenda of increased access. For example, one *Guardian* response describes the 'sexiest man alive' comment as 'cheesy' but then goes on to say that 'the younger ladies in the audience absolutely loved this bit [...] this put a smile on my face'. The writer concludes by saying 'if the intention was to open Shakespeare to a wider audience then NTLive succeeded'. Although this audience member didn't personally value the interval features, the comment acknowledged the enjoyment other kinds of audience members ('the younger ladies') got from it, and found a way of appreciating the interval material by proxy.

The interplay between the 'strategies' of NTLive and the 'tactics' of its audiences is thus evident in the paratexts of *Coriolanus*. The mid-show interview and the audio commentary worked as adaptive strategies, which attempted to respond to the tactics of the Hiddleston fan base, with varying levels of success. The fact that these audience tactics, as well as NTLive's strategies, were publicly performed fuelled the tactic/strategy interaction. As strategic 'backstage' media modes, such as the director interview, became part of the 'frontstage' experience, audiences voiced their views online tactically to create their own 'backstage' performances. The reliance on digital media for audience performances demonstrates that theatre broadcasts operate firmly within a network of contemporary media practices. The strategic employment of the smartphone for the dissemination of the Encore audio commentary illustrates the impact that operating within this media network had on the shifting power relationships between NTLive and the various audiences for *Coriolanus*.

Watching live online: *Complete Works: Table Top Shakespeare*

I get home from work and rush to open my laptop. I'm a little late for the first play but I quickly work out where we are in the plot. I sit and watch for a while, captivated by the storytelling style and amused by the choice of household objects used to represent characters. On another tab of my browser I check the official hashtag #completeworks on Twitter to see what people are saying and tweet a couple of responses. Half an hour later, I pull up a livestream from the Wimbledon Tennis tournament on another tab, but keep it on silent, listening to the audio from the Shakespeare stream. I spend the rest of my evening watching the two remaining hour-long plays, flicking between the three tabs and even managing to make my dinner.

Complete Works: Table Top Shakespeare, Online Broadcast, Forced Entertainment, 25 June 2015, Personal Account

The audience behaviours described in relation to NTLive's *Coriolanus* arise from a hybridity which results from the collision of audiences, digital technology and theatre in the physical space of the cinema. However, theatre broadcast experiences in which audience members are physically absent not only from the actors, but from each other, also create new ways of enacting the role of audience member. In the UK, companies including Cheek by Jowl (see Kirwan, Chapter 10), Tara Arts (see Rogers, Chapter 9), Belarus Free Theatre and Shakespeare's Globe (see Sullivan, Chapter 3, and Aebischer, Chapter 7) have all broadcast their work live online for free, with the recordings sometimes remaining available for a limited period of time after the livestream. As well as reaching a larger, and typically younger, audience (Reidy et al. 2016: 11), these livestreams have also had an impact on how audiences approach and engage with these productions. The lack of physical spaces for communal reception in these experiences mean that modes of audience engagement closely resemble those associated with social media. In the *Coriolanus* audio commentary, the incorporation of 'private' digital technologies within the public space of the cinema shaped audience performance; in Forced Entertainment's *Complete Works* livestream, audiences watched in private spaces and on personal devices, but the use of social media allowed them to perform publically as audiences.

Since its first run at the Berlin Foreign Affairs Festival in June 2015, the production has been live-streamed twice: once from its first run in Berlin, and again from the Theaterfestival in Basel in September 2016.[3] Shot on a single, static camera facing a narrator sitting at a large wooden table, the stream was stripped back in comparison to the high-quality, high-definition aesthetic of NTLive or RSCLive multiple-camera broadcasts. This, along with the single narrator and the use of objects as a means of illustration – rather than as crucial elements of the performance – meant that the focus was on the aural rather than the visual. Much like radio, this strategy allowed a greater degree of audience flexibility, both physically and virtually, whilst watching and listening to the production. My account of the 2015 livestream above demonstrates how this scope for increased mobility enabled certain audience tactics and performances, which in my case included entering at a random point, switching between streams, preparing food, and engaging in live-tweeting.

The ability to toggle between the stream and other Web applications without necessarily missing much of the performance encouraged the sharing of responses and the engagement with other audience members on Twitter. As Erin Sullivan explains in Chapter 3, live-tweeting can build a sense of community during a streamed performance. This was enhanced in *Complete Works* as, unlike the stream of Cheek by Jowl's *Measure for Measure* which remained online for five days (see Kirwan, Chapter 10), it was only available to watch online live, so that audience members had to watch simultaneously. This increased the opportunity for audiences to engage with each other and to respond to the performance on social media during the stream, with the stream's 'liveness' contributing to a sense of community building.

Echoing Sullivan's analysis of other live broadcast experiences, the reactions on Twitter were largely positive. The tweets composed between 25 June 2015 and 3 July 2015 that used the official hashtag #completeworks show varied levels of engagement that ranged from praise ('R+J was pretty spellbinding. Even my parents liked it') to appreciative comments on the relevance of the objects to the characters ('Throat spray=Apothecary @ForcedEnts R&J #completeworks – genius'). Unable to applaud the performers directly, some audiences took to Twitter to perform this applause ('Applause, applause to the fabulous Terry O'Connor! @ForcedEnts #completeworks'). Others tweeted pictures of their screens or viewing situations to let other audience members know their location ('Watching @ForcedEnts collectively in Warsaw'). Social media thus facilitated both communication and audience performance during the production and helped sustain a sense of community as it unfolded across the nine days of performances. Through Twitter, spectating became a collaborative act, with reception inflected by audience observations and analyses in real time.

Whilst live-tweeting was a tactical way for audiences to overcome geographical separation, the company also deployed it as a deliberate strategy. Tweeting was encouraged by the Forced Entertainment Twitter account, which tweeted updates, and re-tweeted audience comments to their sixteen thousand followers to drum up interest in the stream. The tweeting was furthermore propelled by high-profile theatre critics such as *The Guardian*'s Lyn Gardner, with their own significant Twitter followings, as well as scholars and practitioners, who were also noticeably present on the hashtag. Countering negative reviews of the live show that had voiced concerns about oversimplification and loss, such as Michael Coveney's comparison of the productions to 'badly edited prose digests' (Coveney 2016), these tweets offered detailed moments of analysis that worked to legitimize the simple format as worthy of study and attention. For example, theatre critic Matt Trueman's tweet – 'these objects seem to play every possible version of these characters at once. Every Hamlet. Every Romeo. Every Rosalind' – initiated a chain of replies from his network of followers. Theatre researcher Jack Belloli responded: 'but aren't these #completeworks making specific, often political, interpretations too – as if uneasy with Shake's universality'. The production's artistic director Tim Etchells then joined the conversation to suggest that 'no 1 "inhabits" the characters – narrator describes their actions/text, while objects stand in for them', following up with 'well the spectator is always an imaginative co-author, we're just shifting the percentages/margins'. Unlike the one-way information given in the *Coriolanus* audio commentary or in director interviews, Twitter here opened up a two-way interaction between the production and its audiences that blurred the lines between company strategies and audience-driven tactics.

Forced Entertainment's *Complete Works* stream participates in a wider proliferation of 'live' online videos that privilege multiple interactions between audiences and performers or companies. Between 2015 and 2017, YouTube, Instagram, Facebook and Twitter all integrated the capability for live broadcasting into their platforms, capitalising on the popularity of the Web applications Periscope and Meerkat, which were designed to enable users to broadcast live to other users from anywhere in the world.[4] Live content maximizes prospective advertising revenue by keeping users on the platform for as long as possible. Comment sections, which are visible to the broadcaster, play a large part in keeping audiences engaged. On Facebook Live, for example, the comments are just below the live video, and viewers can interact by posting responses, replying to other viewers, and clicking reaction buttons which then become visible to the person broadcasting. The broadcaster can react to these responses in real time, creating a two-way interaction between audience and broadcaster.

The importance of these exchanges to the 'live' online experience was demonstrated by one of the first majorly successful Facebook Live videos. On 8 April 2016, media outlet Buzzfeed livestreamed two employees stretching rubber bands around a watermelon until, after forty-five minutes, it eventually exploded. The stream attracted 800,000 live viewers at its peak, and in the following days the saved video had over ten million subsequent views. The live comments on the stream displayed a particular fascination with the other audience members, with comments oscillating between judgement (e.g. 'Over 700,000 people have nothing better to do with their lives') and reflection (e.g. 'it's a Friday night and I'm watching this. What is life[?]'). There were over 320,000 comments in total, with the top comments generating high numbers of responses and likes. A number of the comments stated that the audience discussion was the most entertaining part of the stream for them, and others went so far as to pose the possibility that the stream was a 'social experiment' of which they and their fellow audiences were the subject. Performing as an audience member, and being a spectator of this audience performance, was an integral element of the broadcast experience for this stream, indicating how central audience interaction is to this developing form of online media.

Forced Entertainment's stream of *Complete Works* strategically drew on these emerging viewing practices, enabling new kinds of audience performance through Twitter. Additionally, the stream drew on other modes of performance and spectating. In a *Guardian* interview, Tim Etchells speaks of the connection between *Complete Works* and previous livestreams of the company's durational works *Quizoola* (2013) and *Speak Bitterness* (2014). Etchells describes *Complete Works* as 'durational episodically' (2015a). He thus evokes both durational theatre, a form associated with performance art that runs over an extended continuous period (Etchells 1999; Kalb 2011), and the media format of serialization, which is usually associated with episodic television drama. Elsewhere, he links the production to other practices of offline and online spectatorship: *Complete Works*' wooden table, he suggests, 'finds a close mirror in the camera shot presenting the action to the online audience', and he compares it both to the 'how-to space of so many Internet tutorials', and to 'the "wooden O" invoked by Shakespeare in *Henry V* as the arena for the audience's collective imagination' (2015b).

Etchells' hybridization of theatre, film, televisual and online modes of engagement in the stream creates opportunities for multiple approaches to the work, as durational performances and television series invite distinctive types of audience performance. While theatre scholar Jonathan Kalb explicitly distances durational theatre from media participation, arguing that it constitutes 'a broad-based resistance-response to the glib and trivialising tendencies of the media age' (2011: 192), Etchells posits that durational performance works are well suited to mediatized reception. Stating that during their live durational works audience members would drop in and out to chat to their friends at the bar, he claims that livestreaming and Twitter have 'amplified that double track of the work and the social space/conversation' (2015a). This assessment of the suitability of durational work for online distribution is echoed in media journalist Brian Feldman's analysis of Buzzfeed's watermelon stream. He describes a successful live video as being 'immediately arresting, visually and narratively, so that people can enter at any moment [...] and understand immediately what's happening'. Feldman also cites the relatively long duration of the video, its build towards a collectively expected release, its ephemerality and its liveness as features of the stream's appeal (2016). The familiar plot lines, narrative structure and live distribution of *Complete Works* fit Feldman's criteria for successful online reception.

Since the stream of *Complete Works* was less expensive and easier to access than the live production, viewers could opt to experience it durationally. However, since each play was a discrete production, audiences could alternatively choose which 'episodes' to watch across the nine days, inviting an approach more like that of watching a television series. 'Serializing' the plays is a strategy that Emma Smith argues can be traced back to the publication of the 1623 Folio (2008: 147). As Susanne Greenhalgh has charted, serialization has been seized upon in television adaptations of Shakespeare since the 1960s (2017: 425). Seen from this vantage point, *Complete Works* participates in a 'completist' tradition of works that cover Shakespeare's dramatic canon, including the BBC Television Shakespeare (1978–85). Moreover, in positioning itself as an accessible form of Shakespeare, *Complete Works*' narrative style, delivery, and condensed plots were reminiscent of series of Shakespeare for children from the Lamb's *Tales from Shakespeare* (1807) to *Shakespeare: Animated Tales* (1992–94).

In using the strategy of serialization in a durational structure, *Complete Works* opened itself up to flexible audience approaches – audiences could choose what and how much to watch, crafting their own experience. However, because each streamed 'episode' was only available to watch live, the production also frustrated the ability of viewers to watch in a fully durational or serial way. 'Completing' the whole series as a viewer would have required a significant time commitment. In order to overcome this, some audiences deployed collaborative tactics – for example, three members of staff of the theatre review website *Exeunt* attempted to produce live written responses to the plays (Jankovic et al. 2015). Twitter also facilitated a shared labour of spectating: shared comments and screenshots became archives of each play after its stream, allowing viewers to engage in some way with the material they had missed.

Twitter was utilized as a tactical tool by audiences to approach the durational and serial strategy of the production, facilitating viewers' participation in cultural and social conversations. A number of the tweets praised the potential of the livestream to open these conversations out to new audiences (e.g., '#completeworks has been a wonderful way to open access to experimental theatre through live streaming') but the high proportion of 'expert' responses suggests that this potential may not have been fully realized. As Romano Mullin warns, the algorithmic set-up of Twitter can result in users operating in 'cultural or political silos' in which they mostly encounter like-minded individuals (2017: 224). The overwhelming positivity of the tweets quoting '#Completeworks' indicate that this 'echo-chamber' effect is likely to have shaped who was aware of the livestream and the subsequent interactions between audience members. Moreover, the audience performances on Twitter may also have worked against the aim of increased access: viewers performed their knowledge of Shakespeare and theatre by making in-jokes, thus creating 'cliques' and potentially alienating those less familiar with the plays from the critical conversation (Matrix 2014: 127).

Forced Entertainment's co-option of the tactic of tweeting therefore introduced a two-way dialogue that worked to engage their audiences, but threatened to exclude non-expert audience members, potentially undercutting the initial strategy to make the work genuinely accessible. This increasingly complex relationship between strategies and audience tactics demonstrates how audience performances can exert pressure on the broadcast experience, changing how theatre companies interact with their audiences, as well as determining how other audience members approach and relate to the work.

Engaging with Shakespeare: performing participation

These two very different encounters with Shakespeare demonstrate the widening spectrum of theatre broadcast experiences. Theatre broadcasts operate within a complex network of historic and contemporary media practices, within which each broadcast occupies a distinctive position.

Paying attention to how broadcast experiences hybridize different media and the impact this has on reception, and particularly on how audiences perform, provides some insight into how theatre broadcasts and their audiences are developing. Overall, broadcasts multiply the opportunities for audience performances that range from wearing headphones, tweeting photos of their computer screens, engaging in discussions with the artistic director, to commenting on online reviews. Additionally, audiences may also perform by sharing pictures or illegal links to copies of the broadcasts, creating fan fiction (Abbott 2015), or by being captured on screen as an audience member at a filmed production (as happened to Raby, Chapter 6).

Such audience performances are neither neutral nor irrelevant to an understanding of the production and distribution of broadcasts. Rather, they constitute tactics that operate within, and sometimes disturb, power structures and cultural hierarchies. As evident in the *Coriolanus* broadcast, these performances are often expressions of expertise and entitlement. Viewers attempt to claim ownership over aspects of the performance and its performers, setting different approaches and value systems against one another. These performances and tensions can feed back to the broadcast, influencing the shape of its paratexts, distribution strategies and afterlives. The reciprocal relationship between audience and broadcast looks set to evolve further as theatre broadcasts branch further out into online distribution and as two-way interaction becomes a strategy of live online video to the point where audience performance is an integral part of the experience.

Heim sees the increase in audience performance in the twenty-first century as a largely positive move, and many of the audience performances I have described are deliberate tactics that challenge power dynamics or seek to overcome the dislocation of being an audience of a theatre broadcast. However, the encounters created by the two broadcasts discussed here were not always comfortable ones, and some of the performances they elicited from audiences were reluctant or reactionary. As well as celebrating audience performance, we should therefore also ask how online platforms and networks shape audience performances and which constituencies these new forms of audience performance might exclude or ignore. Non-participation in audience performance is also a valid approach, and we should consider how to account for audience responses that are not so visible or accessible: though hard to document, just because some forms of audience performance remain private, this does not mean that they are not taking place.

As theatre broadcasts continue to expand and multiply across media, with some companies now experimenting with Facebook Live as a method of distribution, the voice and performance of the audience becomes an increasingly significant aspect of the theatre broadcast experience. If broadcasts achieve their stated aim of reaching wider and more diverse audiences, then we can expect these performances to mirror this diversity. In turn, we might expect theatre and broadcasting companies to react and respond to these performances. Because of the symbiotic relationship between broadcasts and their audiences, it is essential that we consider the dynamics at work in their reception along with the production and distribution of theatre broadcasts. Critical attention must extend beyond the broadcasts themselves to the multiple, complex and creative performances by audiences of Shakespeare broadcasts as they use digital media to make themselves seen and heard.

Notes

1 The app was first released on 28 July 2015 and was available to download for free on iPhone and iPad with in-app purchases for each digital programme. As of 14 July 2017, the *Coriolanus* digital programme (at a cost of £2.99) is the second most popular in-app purchase, the first being the digital programme for *Hamlet* starring Benedict Cumberbatch (2015, dir. Lyndsey Turner).
2 For a full description of these features, see Abbott (2015: 25).
3 In the 2015 livestream discussed here, Robin Arthur, Claire Marshall, Cathy Naden, Terry O'Connor, Richard Lowdon and Jerry Killick performed the plays in rotation.
4 Periscope was acquired by Twitter in 2015; Meerkat was shut down in 2016.

References

Abbott, D. (2015), '"Cut me to Pieces" Shakespeare, Fandom and the Fractured Narrative', in A. Maragiannis (ed.), *Proceedings of the Digital Research in the Humanities and Arts Conference DRHA 2014*, London, 24–8. Available online: http://www.drha2014.co.uk/wp-content/uploads/2015/08/LOW_res_final_paper_proceedings_drha2014.pdf (accessed 1 August 2017).
Abbott, D. and C. Read (2017), 'Paradocumentation and NT Live's "CumberHamlet"', in T. Sant (ed.), *Documenting Performance: The Context and Processes of Digital Curation and Archiving*, London: Bloomsbury, 165–87.
Barker, M. (2013), *Live to Your Local Cinema: The Remarkable Rise of Livecasting*, Basingstoke: Palgrave.
Blackwell, A. (2014), 'Adapting *Coriolanus*: Tom Hiddleston's Body and Action Cinema', *Adaptation,* 7 (3): 344–52.
Buzzfeed (2016), 'Watch Us Explode this Watermelon One Rubber Band at a Time', *Facebook Live,* 8 April. Available online: https://www.facebook.com/BuzzFeed/videos/10154535206385329/ (accessed 1 August 2017).
de Certeau, M. (1984), *The Practice of Everyday Life*, trans. S. Rendall, Berkeley: University of California Press.
Coveney, M. (2016), 'Complete Works: Table Top Shakespeare', *What's on Stage*, 2 March. Available online: http://www.whatsonstage.com/london-theatre/reviews/forced-entertainment-table-top-shakespeare_39870.html (accessed 30 June 2017).
Etchells, T. (1999), *Certain Fragments: Contemporary Performance and Forced Entertainment*, Abingdon: Routledge.

Etchells, T. (2015a). 'Wherefore Art Thou Pepper Pot? Shakespeare's Plays Retold with Household Objects', interview with Andrew Haydon, *The Guardian*, 24 June. Available online: https://www.theguardian.com/stage/2015/jun/24/shakespeare-plays-retold-with-household-objects-forced-entertainment (accessed 30 June 2017).

Etchells, T. (2015b), 'Table Top Shakespeare: Nowhere to Run, Nowhere to Hide.' *Exeunt*, 2 July. Available online: http://exeuntmagazine.com/features/table-top-tim-etchells/ (accessed 30 June 2017).

Feldman, B. (2016). 'This is What Facebook Live is For: Blowing Up Watermelons With Rubber Bands', *New York Magazine*, 8 April. Available online: http://nymag.com/selectall/2016/04/this-is-what-facebook-live-is-for.html (accessed 4 June 2016).

Friedman, M.D. (2016), 'The Shakespeare Cinemacast: Coriolanus', *Shakespeare Quarterly*, 64 (4): 457–80.

Gilbey, R. (2014), 'Coriolanus at National Theatre Live: Cut the Chat and Get on With the Show', *The Guardian*, 31 January. Available online: http://theguardian.com/stage/2014/jan/31/coriolanus-national-theatre-live (accessed 4 June 2016).

Greenhalgh, S. (2017), 'Sticky or Spreadable?: Shakespeare and Global Television', in J.L. Levenson and R. Ormsby (eds), *The Shakespearean World*, Abingdon: Routledge, 418–30.

Heim, C. (2016), *Audience as Performer: The Changing Role of Theatre Audiences in the Twenty-First Century*, Abingdon: Routledge.

Jankovic, B., A. Märten and D. Ralf (2015), '#completeworks: Live Written Responses to Forced Entertainment's *Table Top Shakespeare*', *Exeunt*, 30 June. Available online: http://exeuntmagazine.com/features/completeworks/#author-info (accessed 1 August 2017).

Kalb, J. (2011), *Great Works: Seven Works of Marathon Theater*, Ann Arbor, MI: University of Michigan Press.

Kirwan, P. (2014), '*Coriolanus* Performed by the Donmar Warehouse (Review)', *Shakespeare Bulletin*, 32 (2): 275–78.

Matrix, S. (2014), 'The Netflix Effect: Teens, Binge Watching, and On-Demand Digital Trends', *Jeunesse: Young People, Texts, Cultures*, 6 (1): 199–238.

Mullin, Romano (2017), 'Tweeting Television/Broadcasting the Bard: @HollowCrownFans and Digital Shakespeares', in S. O'Neill (ed.), *Broadcast Your Shakespeare: Continuity and Change Across Media*, London: Bloomsbury, 207–26.

National Theatre (2017), '*Coriolanus* Digital Programme', *National Theatre Backstage*, Mobile App, Version 1.9.1. Available online: https://itunes.apple.com/gb/app/national-theatre-backstage/id1006110950?mt=8 (accessed 29 Jan 2017).

Parker, D. and M. Parker (2011), *The DVD and the Study of Film: The Attainable Text*, New York: Palgrave.

Reidy, B.K., B. Schutt, D. Abramson and A. Durski (2016), 'From Live-to-Digital: Understanding the Impact of Digital Developments in Theatre on Audiences, Production and Distribution', Arts Council England, 11 October. Available online: http://www.artscouncil.org.uk/publication/live-digital (accessed 30 June 2017).

Smith, E. (2008), 'Shakespeare Serialized: *An Age of Kings*', in R. Shaughnessy (ed.), *The Cambridge Companion to Shakespeare and Popular Performance*, Cambridge: Cambridge University Press, 134–49.

PART TWO

In the Theatre

5

A View from the Stage: Interviews with Performers

Beth Sharrock

The Royal Shakespeare Company's (RSC) engagement with live broadcasting theatre productions from the Royal Shakespeare Theatre (RST) reached its fourth season in 2017. Although the tagline 'RSC Live from Stratford-upon-Avon' (RSCLive) assures cinema audiences that their experience will be as 'faithful' to the theatre performance as possible, the practicalities of broadcasting can have a number of effects on an attempt to replicate theatrical performance. Reflecting on the fledgling live theatre broadcast productions of 2014, John Wyver (Director, RSC Screen Productions) details how actors were 'reassured ... that they should not attempt to change or modulate their performances for the cameras'. 'They were', as he recalls, 'asked to play to the house just as on every other night' (2015: 294). This notion of actors' performances being replicable overlooks the protean and responsive nature of theatre, and Wyver has acknowledged elsewhere that actors are 'either unconsciously or consciously' influenced by being filmed for a broadcast (Wyver qtd. in Stone 2016: 640). Nonetheless, actors' reflections suggest that an ethos of acting 'just as on every other night' still firmly underlies the process of theatre broadcasting.

In this chapter, I consider actors' experiences of rehearsing and performing for a live theatre broadcast in light of the mandate not to alter their performances for the broadcast cameras. I draw on interviews with RSC actors in the 2017–18 'Rome season' productions of *Julius Caesar* and *Antony and Cleopatra* and on an interview with Natalie Simpson, who performed in the RSC's 2016 *Hamlet*, *Cymbeline* and *King Lear*. Each actor has varying degrees of film, television and live-broadcast experience. Taking account of this range of individual experience, I explore how the increased pressure of recording, acting for a global audience, the presence of cameras, and a reduced theatre audience may modify an actor's performance.

The RSC's practice of committing their broadcasts to DVD invests actors with a permanent and public record of their performance, unlike NTLive's avowedly ephemeral cinema screenings. The nerves that may accompany RSC broadcasts are palpable in a description from James Corrigan (Mark Antony in *Julius Caesar* and Agrippa in *Antony and Cleopatra*) of the process as 'a one-take film'.[1] Broadcast filming is perhaps even more problematic than Corrigan allows. The multi-camera setup and live-mixing of shots comes with risks for the performer such as momentarily blocking a shot or accidentally disrupting the sound feed. The presence of backstage monitors can also be unsettling; although several actors unanimously expressed embarrassment at watching themselves on DVD, the live-feed monitors backstage mean that the actors can watch other members of the company being filmed in real time (Wyver 2015: 295).

The potential for increased pressure on broadcast night has diverse effects on actors' performances, as the actors interviewed described reactions either of nerves or of exhilaration. Whereas some regarded the pressure either as equal to that of any other night or, as will be discussed, an opportunity to experiment by incorporating their screen acting experience into their stage performance, others responded to the broadcast with trepidation. Committing to DVD and to performance archives just one night out of a run of perhaps a hundred can prompt an actor to modify the spontaneity of her performance, as Natalie Simpson elaborates:

> There is definitely a huge amount of pressure added when you know you are being filmed and broadcast live around the world. You know it will go in the archives, so you feel the need to stick to the well-rehearsed and less adventurous version of your performance to ensure that you are serving the narrative in the best way possible. I wouldn't feel comfortable trying completely new things for a recorded performance.[2]

Simpson's preference for a more tried-and-tested performance style resonates with Corrigan's view that 'where on a normal night you might be relaxed and respond in the moment', the awareness of the broadcast makes it hard not to 'settle into going through the motions because something worked well last night'. Likewise, Amber James, playing Charmian in *Antony and Cleopatra*, reflected that she 'stuck to certain choices that I know have worked in the past because it made me feel safer'.[3] While other nights of the production's run may be characterized by instinctual moments, the awareness of a recorded performance before a global audience drew Simpson, Corrigan and James toward performances they felt had been successful with previous audiences.

Playing safe is not a universal effect of the broadcast, nor is it a consistent technique even for the same actor. After reflecting on her choice of a less adventurous performance for the *Antony and Cleopatra* broadcast, James stated that for the next live broadcast she intended to treat the performance 'exactly as normal'. Similarly, Andrew Woodall (in the roles of Caesar in *Julius Caesar* and Enobarbus in *Antony and Cleopatra*) compares the process explicitly to performing on any other night. Although he noted that the pressure of broadcasting set the company 'on their best behaviour', Woodall's trust in the skill of the broadcast's creative team led him to describe the experience as 'risk-free'.[4] Indeed, for Woodall, 'the pressure you might have in a one-take situation isn't there because in theatre that's what you do every night anyway'. The ability of multi-camera shooting to respond in the moment and smooth over any errors by switching shots instantaneously resembles the way an actor may improvise to cover a missed cue or a technical error.

Some actors responded to the broadcast performance as a unique chance to utilize techniques of film and television acting, including more understated movement and intimate voice projection, modifying their theatrical performances for the cameras and thereby responding to the hybrid medium of live theatre broadcasts. Though the cameras remain intentionally hidden for a cinema audience (Wyver 2015: 296; Greenhalgh 2014: 259), for the actor the presence of cameras and crew makes a marked difference to the atmosphere of that night's performance. In preparation for the live broadcast, RSC acting companies undertake a broadcast-specific rehearsal process which is structured so as to offer two 'runs' with the cameras: one with no audience and, importantly, a second camera rehearsal recording watched by paying and guest audience members (usually filmed the day before the broadcast) which is kept in the event of any major disruptions on the live night. To accommodate the four mobile cameras including one on a crane (an additional two are fixed on the lower circle), a significant number of seats are removed from the centre of the stalls and others from the sides of the RST's thrust stage.[5]

That cameras replace a segment of the audience is a decisive factor in actors' motivation for changing their performance. This decision is often, as was the case for Martin Hutson, playing Cassius in *Julius Caesar*, taken as a result of the RSC's two-stage rehearsal process for the broadcast:

> There's lots of direct address ... to the audience, but we were asked not to look into the camera, albeit not being able to see the cameras. I would catch something and think, 'Did I just look down the lens?' So [the second camera rehearsal] was completely disruptive.[6]

Where for Hutson the camera rehearsals in particular challenged his usual method of addressing the stalls audience, the practical consequences of mounting broadcasting equipment in the theatre space often affected an actor's performance in smaller ways. Simpson notes that while she tried not to 'intentionally change [her] performance in any way', ignoring the cameras for all her soliloquies, 'in some intimate and quiet moments', the sound of the crane camera moving closer was 'a bit off-putting'. However, for Simpson and Hutson the disruptive effects of the cameras were neither catastrophic nor enduring; both asserted that the accustomed desire to inhabit their respective roles quickly took priority. As Hutson concludes, the distractions provided by the camera ultimately had a positive effect on his performance as 'a reminder to pull back to the basic principles of telling the truth, suiting the action to the word and the word to the action'.

Alex Waldmann, however, reshaped his performance of Brutus in *Julius Caesar* 'completely' in response to the visible cameras, and this represented a milestone on his 'journey over the run to feeling more secure in [his interpretation of] the role'[7]. Waldmann affirms that his performance of the traditionally pensive Brutus benefitted from the close proximity of cameras, allowing him to communicate Brutus' introspection more vividly than to a distanced audience on a normal night. This was particularly the case during soliloquies: 'to do some thinking to the top of the audience feels unnatural, but when the cameras were on I could just think as anyone else would and the camera would pick it up.' Waldmann's emphasis on soliloquies reflecting the moment-to-moment process of thought suggests this is a form which is apt for balancing theatrical and filmic acting techniques, with cameras able to capture minute details of emotion and expression that may not register when 'performing ... to reach the top' of the theatre (Lester 2016: 14). In light of the removed stalls seats and the cameras which take their place, Waldmann and Woodall considered there was a tendency to deliver these soliloquies in a more intimate, filmic style (see Raby, Chapter 6, for a matching account from the theatre audience's point-of-view). As Woodall explains, reflecting on his performance of Enobarbus's Cydnus 'barge' speech (2.2.200–28), the case may be the same for set-piece speeches as well:

> I was very aware of the crane creeping in on me, but it was rather nice. The temptation, of course, was to make my performance very filmic. Enobarbus has a number of minor soliloquies and when it was only me on stage I made it as intimate as possible, using the techniques I've learnt from working on film – but for both [Enobarbus and Julius Caesar] I didn't change anything radically.

Waldmann and Woodall's shift in performance techniques to accommodate different forms of address in soliloquy and longer speeches illustrates how an actor's relationship with the cameras cannot be generalized even for the same actor. Rather, different roles and different modes of speech allow actors to draw upon their experience in filmed mediums and utilize – or ignore – the cameras accordingly.

Woodall illustrates the necessity to tailor a broadcast performance both to the cameras *and* to different modes of address in his reflections on playing Julius Caesar. Compared with the intimacy afforded by the cameras in playing Enobarbus, Woodall notes that his performance of Caesar demanded very little recalibration. 'Stage gestures and movements', Martin Barker comments, 'almost inevitably remain larger and broader than would seem appropriate for cinema or television' (2013: 18). Though Woodall was conscious how the gestures and movement he had adopted for the role might look inappropriately 'theatrical' on camera, he recalls how his instinct not to 'stand there declaiming speeches' because of the cameras was countered by the fact that Caesar is 'slightly more declamatory anyway'. Where Woodall may have felt self-conscious about his gestures or delivery looking overblown on film, the cameras instead highlighted Caesar's intentional grandiosity. Adrian Lester, also an experienced film actor, has reflected similarly on his own balancing of theatrical delivery with an awareness of the effects of filming. In conversation with Ayanna Thompson, Lester noted that on camera, the scale of movement and projection required by the National Theatre's vast Olivier stage makes it look 'like you're pretending'. Lester's solution, like Waldmann's, was consciously to modify his performance to accommodate the focus of the cameras. Such alterations came at the expense of projecting to the audience in the upper levels of the theatre, whom Lester admits he 'completely ignored' during the broadcast night (2016: 14). Woodall made a similar judgement, noting that to perform 'as I would do in the theatre, particularly to the audience in the top circles, would just look stupid on camera'. The experiences and choices of Lester, Waldmann, and Woodall suggest that the hybrid form of live theatre broadcast makes contrasting demands of an actor: to act for a live theatre audience whilst simultaneously tailoring the end result to look believable through a camera lens.

As well as being conscious of how their performance will translate on screen, actors are aware that the performance will have two separate audiences (one with a global reach) and that this may impact on their broadcast performance. The RST's thrust stage allows actors very few spaces to hide, offering what Peter Hall once termed a 'vast diving board' into the audience (Billington 2010). The substitution of camera equipment for stalls seating can therefore dramatically transform the dynamics of performing to and amongst the audience. The impact this may have on performance is hinted at in Hutson's comment that the audience are the 'last major part of the puzzle' in an actor's performance of character. While rehearsing for the broadcast of *Julius Caesar*, Hutson realized that a diminished audience presence in the stalls was leading him to 'stare into the middle distance, to self-generate, which is the worst type of acting'. While audience numbers fluctuate over a run of any production, a reduced audience presence, particularly in the stalls, is an impactful necessity of broadcasting from a space like the RST or the National Theatre. The solution devised by Hutson for the broadcast, following an informal request to the RSC's front of house staff, was to have an usher sit alongside the cameras in the stalls to whom he would play his moments of audience address.

Hutson's recruitment of an usher to substitute for the missing stalls audience highlights that acting for the cameras, even though they denote a wider audience watching in cinemas, is never tantamount to acting for a theatre audience. Here the disparity between the 'shared audience' rhetoric of broadcasts and the reality in the theatre emerges; whereas the emphasis on a shared 'liveness' in marketing and paratexts often invites the cinema audience to experience themselves as vicariously part of the theatre audience, the lack of eye contact and engagement with cameras means actors typically experience not a communal audience but what Hutson recalled as 'just a big black space, with machines hovering in the darkness'. Hutson also details how responses from the cinema audience are almost exclusively retrospective: 'I've just joined Twitter and to read strangers talking about an event who weren't in the room with you, perhaps not even in the same country, that's sort of peculiar. It makes it, after the event, real.' The encouragement for cinema audiences to share their experiences on social media networks provides, for actors, a distinct and novel type of audience feedback; not immediately perceptible as with a theatre audience, but delayed and predominantly digital.

The presence of cameras in the stalls also has a noticeable impact on the theatre audience. Simpson notes that the cameras actually had the effect of galvanizing the theatre audience; although the stalls felt 'a little empty', the rest of the house was 'more lively' on the night of the broadcast. The extra energy evident in the theatre audience, presumably due to the exciting prospect of being filmed themselves (despite having been exhorted to ignore the filming, as Julie Raby discusses in Chapter 6), allowed Simpson to retain her usual performance style and 'ignore the cameras and, as normal, address the audience'. Simpson's approach is distinctly at odds with those of Lester, Waldmann, and Woodall, who modified their performances in order to prioritize the cinema audience.

Such differences, even within the same theatre and the same production, also reflect the relative novelty of the live theatre broadcast medium and the varied demands it makes of performers. Indeed, Woodall commented that each individual actor must negotiate the practicalities of a medium which, particularly for the RSC, is relatively nascent: 'There is no threat involved, but [the broadcasts are] a slightly odd thing to do because, in truth, no-one is quite sure what you should do. As an actor you just have to use your own instinct.' Woodall's reliance on 'instinct' confirms the general impression that acting for the cameras requires a performance balanced on the medium's own threshold between film, television and theatre. It also recognizes that an actor's decision to alter her or his performance can be instantaneous, an immediacy that is perhaps lost in Alison Stone's otherwise apt view that acting on a live broadcast night 'requires a profound mental recalibration for actors' (2016: 640). A recalibration does indeed characterize the experience of many of the actors interviewed; however, even within the same company, the same production and the same night, experiences cannot be generalized. The instruction to 'play to the house just as on every other night' seems to assume that an actor's theatrical performance is something static and fixed. While this is true of certain interpretations of character and directorial choices, Simpson highlights the necessity for an actor to always remain responsive, to 'always stay alive and listening' in the moment. Crucially, this dichotomy is true of acting for the 'one-take' broadcasts. What the experiences of these actors highlight is that while the three-stage rehearsal process emerges as a playing space for reinvention as well as trial and error, broadcasts constitute just another challenge – or perhaps another opportunity – to respond to sometimes drastically altered playing conditions with an attempt at performing 'just as on every other night'.

Notes

1 All quotations from Corrigan are from the panel, 'Q & A with RSC Actors', British Graduate Shakespeare Conference, 2 June 2017.
2 All quotations from Simpson are from personal email communication, 31 May 2017.
3 All quotations from Amber James are from personal email communication, 14 June 2017.
4 All quotations from Andrew Woodall are from personal communication, 26 May 2017.
5 The typical layout of cameras for an RSC broadcast is detailed in Aebischer (forthcoming).
6 All quotations from Hutson are from personal communication, 23 May 2017.
7 All quotations from Waldmann are from the panel, 'Q & A with RSC Actors', British Graduate Shakespeare Conference, 2 June 2017.

References

Aebischer, P. (forthcoming), *Shakespeare, Spectatorship and Technologies of Performance*, Cambridge: Cambridge University Press.
Barker, M. (2013), *Live to Your Local Cinema: The Remarkable Rise of Livecasting*, London: Palgrave Macmillan.
Billington, M. (2010). 'Sir Peter Hall: "Politicians don't grasp the case for the arts"', *The Guardian*, 1 November. Available online: https://www.theguardian.com/stage/2010/nov/01/sir-peter-hall-at-80 (accessed 12 July 2017).
Greenhalgh, S. (2014), 'Guest Editor's Introduction', *Shakespeare Bulletin*, 32 (2): 255–61.
Lester, A. (2016), 'In Dialogue with Ayanna Thompson', *Shakespeare Survey* 70: 10–18.
Stone, A. (2016), 'Not Making a Movie: The Livecasting of Shakespeare Stage Productions by The Royal National Theatre and The Royal Shakespeare Company', *Shakespeare Bulletin*, 34 (4): 627–43.
Wyver, J. (2015), 'Screening the RSC Stage: the 2014 Live from Stratford-upon-Avon Cinema Broadcasts', *Shakespeare,* 11 (3): 286–302.

6

A View from the Stalls:

The Audience's Experience in the Theatre During the RSC Live from Stratford-upon-Avon Broadcasts

Julie Raby

In an interview in *The Telegraph* in 2013, the RSC's Artistic Director Gregory Doran suggested that the cinema audience for 'RSC Live from Stratford-upon-Avon' broadcasts (RSCLive) would share 'the thrill of sitting in the audience and experiencing theatre live; familiar from the company's "one-room spaces"'. This chapter explores the impact of the recording process on the theatre audience's experience during the broadcasts of *Richard II* (2013), *Two Gentlemen of Verona* (2014), *Love's Labour's Lost* (2015), *Othello* (2015), *Henry V* (2015), *Julius Caesar* (2017) and *Antony and Cleopatra* (2017), drawing on my experiences as a theatre audience member in the Royal Shakespeare Theatre (RST) in Stratford-upon-Avon on the nights of these broadcasts and during other performances in the course of the productions' runs. Even though the theatre audiences are led to believe that their experience is (or should be) the same as any other night, their normal viewing behaviour is disrupted by a number of factors, of which altered sightlines and directors' addresses to the audience are the most obvious. I also explore the impact of the theatre's geographical location in Stratford-upon-Avon, and the audience's positioning in the theatre.

Writing of performance practices in the early modern Globe, Evelyn Tribble develops the concept of cognitive scaffolding and explains how players used 'the physical environment of the stage' and 'cognitive artefacts' in that environment to shape their performance (2011: 25). The cognitive prompts in their environment, combined with learned conventions of theatre-going, similarly shape the performances of present-day theatre audiences. Entering the theatre, finding seats, and understanding the mechanisms of intervals and applause at the curtain call are behaviours directed by a series of codes and instructions, including marked entrances, seat numbers corresponding with ticket information, and announcements. As I will show, in the run-up and during a broadcast, additional help is provided through environmental and cognitive prompts such as signage, camera placements, and explicit instructions by the director that affect the experience of the theatre audience and direct it into performing its role differently on that particular night.

The RST's location in Shakespeare's home town is evidently as key to the broadcasts' identity as Shakespeare is to the RSC brand (Rumbold 2011: 34). By virtue of their branding as 'Live From Stratford-upon-Avon', the broadcasts are presented as embedded in their authentically Shakespearean environment. This embeddedness is felt with particular force by the theatre audience, for whom a visit to the RSC in Stratford-upon-Avon may not just consist of viewing a performance in one of the three theatres, but may also include visits to the Shakespearean heritage sites close by. As Barbara Hodgdon explains, a visitor to Stratford-upon-Avon is a pilgrim, heritage tourist or scholar in search of Shakespeare (1998: 191). A visit to the RSC includes an array of para-experiences that can be sampled before and after the performance: the walk through Stratford to and from the theatre, visits to the gift shop (which is cunningly placed adjacent to the Box Office so that ticket collection and souvenir hunting are presented as organically connected activities), the café, the Rooftop Restaurant, and possibly even backstage theatre tours. Writing of the similar set-up in Shakespeare's Globe, Farah Karim-Cooper notes how '[w]hat audiences ought to know can be made subordinate to what ... consumers need to know in order to purchase their tickets, food and beverages, and the wide range of offerings in the gift shop' (2012: 55). This division between what audiences 'ought to know' and 'need to know' is also at work in the RSC's audience spaces, in which signs to bars and instructions on ordering interval drinks guide the movement of the audience through the building.

On broadcast nights, however, the 'need to know' aspect of the experience is heightened and another layer of para-experiences connected with the filming is added. Theatre audiences will notice the outside broadcast vans outside the theatre, will have to step over the thick bundles of cabling connecting the vans to the foyer and the auditorium, and will be intensely aware of the cameras in the stalls which may partly obstruct their sightlines. Additionally, notices are placed at auditorium entrances and even in the toilets to remind the audience that the interval will only be fifteen minutes (instead of twenty), that food may not be consumed in the theatre (a standard expectation that clearly is considered to require explicit reinforcement on this occasion) and that while the broadcast is being filmed, the audience may not be readmitted if they leave the auditorium. For broadcast performances, too, spectators are directed to take their seats a quarter of an hour before the start time. This results in several false starts as the audience anticipates the performance is about to begin. There is a buzz, which then descends into a hushed silence, before the buzz starts up again, and this can be repeated several times before the actual start at 7.15 pm.

Even ticket sales are organized differently for broadcast performances, though the pricing of public sales remains the same. While tickets for the run of *Richard II* went on sale in January 2013, tickets for the broadcast performance only went on sale in mid-August 2013, with the stalls kept off public sale. The same happened in the 2017 season, when no stalls seats were sold to the public for broadcast performances. For the broadcasts of *Two Gentlemen, Love's Labour's Lost, Othello* and *Henry V*, however, some stall seats were sold during the week of the broadcast. Rather than relying on the public sale of tickets and a lottery approach to its audience make-up, the RSC casts its own stalls audience. Just before the performance starts, ushers move audience members to empty seats in the stalls which might be visibly unoccupied for cinema audiences. I saw this happen just before the broadcasts of *Caesar, Antony* and *Richard II*. As a result, the audience in the front of the stalls on the broadcast night for *Richard II* was visibly younger than it would normally be, since these are among the most expensive tickets in the house (habitually, school and college parties are seated further back in the stalls).

In *The Experience Economy*, Joseph Pine and James Gilmore use theatre-going to describe how companies interact with their consumers by selling an experience alongside the product: 'When a person buys a service, he [*sic*] purchases a set of intangible activities carried out on his behalf. But when he buys an experience, he pays to spend time enjoying a series of memorable events that a company stages – as in a theatrical play – to engage him in an inherently personal way' (2011: 2). On broadcast nights, this experience includes an exclusive address to the theatre audience by the broadcast presenter and sometimes even the director *before* the cameras start recording. Addressing the spectators in the RST before the broadcast of *Henry V*, Doran, who had directed this production, instructed them to 'remember to breathe'. For the broadcast of *Two Gentlemen of Verona*, he requested that the audience respond to the performance as they would to any other performance in the RST and imagine that the cameras were not there (an injunction bound to make those audience members *more* aware of their presence). Before the broadcast of *Antony and Cleopatra*, director Iqbal Khan asked the audience to continue to talk while his interview with presenter Suzy Klein was being broadcast to the cinema audience, thus ensuring that they acted out the expected behaviour of a theatre audience before a performance starts. Since the ringing of mobile phones interrupted filming of both *Julius Caesar* and *Othello*, he also reminded the audience to switch off their mobile phones. These directions to the audience on the evening of a recorded broadcast remind them of theatre conventions, which become conscious behaviours in response to a unique event.

Once the performance begins, the experience of watching the play is affected by the presence of the cameras placed around the theatre's thrust stage, with cameras on tracks at the rear of the stalls on either side of the stage. In the *Othello* broadcast, one camera was situated downstage under the proscenium arch and was able to capture audience members in the front rows. I was particularly aware of the camera's positioning as I was sat in the front of the stalls, and was selected for a lengthy close-up. For the theatre audience the cameras are visible both because of how they are positioned and because of the lights on the camera monitors, which emit a faint glow; a red light additionally shows whenever a particular camera's feed is being used in the live mix. The cameras can even inadvertently light parts of the auditorium in a manner that affects the focus of a scene. Thus, Brutus's (Alex Waldmann) soliloquy to the audience in Act 2 of *Julius Caesar*, 'It must be by his death...' was normally directed to the audience in darkness (2.1.10–34). On the night of the broadcast, however, this area of the auditorium was visible to the theatre audience as it was lit by the cameras, revealing how only a few members of the audience were seated in this part of the auditorium (see Sharrock, Chapter 5, for a matching account from Waldmann's point-of-view). Furthermore, the cameras are audible when they move on the tracks. At the back of the stalls, one can also hear the calls made by the broadcast director and production assistant from the main broadcast operations van. It is the crane camera, however, which is the most noticeable, both visually and aurally (see Figure 6.1). The extendable camera arm can sweep across the stage, making a slight noise in the process of moving into a close-up from a vantage-point inaccessible to the theatre audience. For example, in the broadcast of *Richard II*, the boom moved into a close-up of Richard II (David Tennant) and Aumerle (Oliver Rix) on an upstage gantry at a significant distance from all members of the theatre audience.

It is therefore evident to theatre audiences that what the cameras re-mediate for the benefit of broadcast audiences does not correspond to their own experience of the performance or their own ability to see specific parts of it close up. RSCLive producer John Wyver explains how, '[w]ith only the most minimal changes to the stage work, the productions under[go] a process of what might best be called "translation". This suggests both a strong degree of fidelity to a pre-existing original as well as a recognition of inevitable and intentional creative mediation' (2015: 290). Such 'creative mediation' is particularly essential for those parts of a performance which cannot be quite captured by a broadcast simply because they take place beyond the temporal and spatial boundaries of the performance on the RST stage. The pre-shows that often blur the lines between an audience's settling-in time and the performance proper and which sometimes start in the foyer

FIGURE 6.1 *Track and crane cameras in the RST stalls.*

or even outside the theatre are a key example of how in the process of creative mediation a broadcast can affect the performance itself.

In the pre-shows for *Antony* and *Two Gentlemen*, for instance, the broadcast team and equipment physically got in the way of sightlines or stage business. The pre-show of *Antony* consisted of the Soothsayer (Will Bliss) sitting on the steps of a raised platform upstage left. On the night of the broadcast, the view of Bliss was partially obscured by Klein's interview with Kahn on the thrust stage in front of him, making it likely that they would not grasp the Soothsayer's significance in this production. Neither Klein nor Khan could be heard by the theatre audience, who were excluded from the interview experience while providing a backdrop to it. Klein's onstage position at a café table during the introductory broadcast interview for *Two Gentlemen* similarly impacted on sightlines and distracted attention away from the pre-show's portrayal of the goings-on on the terrace of an open-air Italian café on Valentine's Day. Habitually, this included Speed (Martin Bassindale) launching a paper airplane into the circle. On this night, however, the cameras obstructed this stage business. Meanwhile Lucetta (Leigh Quinn) always used the pre-show to make contact with a male audience member so as to direct stage business at him later in the performance. She always picked on someone downstage left, but as the cameras occupied this area, Quinn now had to direct this stage business to stage right, changing the blocking of her performance in response to the broadcast. Meanwhile, an element of the production that could not be observed by the cinema audience involved a flower seller (Johnny Glynn), who stood outside the theatre on the patio overlooking the Bancroft Gardens before the show began, and who entered the pre-show at its halfway point. The broadcast could not capture the flower seller outside the theatre even though he was part of the production, since for the broadcast team, the auditorium constituted the spatial boundary of the production.

A yet different problem arises when the pre-show is designed to blur the line between the pre-show and the start of the performance, as was the case in Doran's *Richard II*. There, theatre audiences settled down while the weeping Duchess of Gloucester (Jane Lapotaire) was sprawled beside the coffin of her dead husband. Only when trumpeters entered the auditorium via the circle and played a fanfare was there a clear signal of the start of the performance. On many nights, therefore, audiences were confused and did not know whether to talk or be quiet (Rogers 2014: 314). Only the five-minute bells ringing in the foyer and audience members still being shown to their seats signalled that the performance proper had not yet begun. This lack of clarity resulted in the audience quietening down prematurely and then talking again. For the broadcast, however, the pre-show was cut down to about five minutes from the original fifteen, considerably reducing the ambiguity and therefore also the fluctuation in the theatre audience's responses.

While the changes I have discussed so far principally affect a broadcast's framing by physical set-up, signage, directorial intervention and alterations to the pre-show, live-capture can also affect moments within the performance itself. In *Love's Labour's Lost*, for example, a globe was placed upstage as part of Simon Higlett's pseudo-Elizabethan manor house set. In previous performances, when the King of France (Sam Alexander) mentioned 'Navarre' in his opening speech, he would spin the Globe to show the kingdom's location in present-day Spain (1.1.12). For the live broadcast, this stage business was omitted and it did not return for the rest of the run. In the same production, Edward Bennett (Berowne), who had mastered the art of giving the impression that he was continually just about to corpse, toned this business down on the evening of the recording, with a consequent toning down of the metatheatrical jokes that might not work as effectively for a screen audience (for a discussion of successful theatrical corpsing in a broadcast, see Aebischer, Chapter 7).

Finally, the 'minimal' changes that Wyver refers to might be due to mishaps, as they can in any live performance. As Peter Kirwan notes, all live broadcasts benefit from 'the frisson of knowledge that something may go wrong' (Chapter 10), and glitches can signal theatrical immediacy and 'liveness' for a remote audience as they do for the theatre audience. For example, Mossop, playing Crab the dog in *Two Gentlemen*, whined in inappropriate places during the broadcast performance, possibly because she was disturbed by the lights from the cameras (she did whine in odd places on other nights, too). In the second half of the same performance, the bandit's netting caught on the proscenium arch. The camera caught how Elliot Barnes-Worrell, playing one of the bandits, attempted discreetly to remove it before giving up and leaving it there. More distractingly, during the *Othello* broadcast, a mobile phone was clearly heard ringing in the gallery as Othello was about to murder Desdemona. My distraction and unease at the intrusive sound was heightened by my awareness that the performance was being filmed.

Although RSCLive is committed to making only minimal changes in order to replicate the theatre audience's experience for cinema audiences, many of the normal conventions of theatre-going are thus disrupted for the broadcast performance. These transformations amount to a unique experience for the theatre audience, who, to return to Pine and Gilmore's formulation, enjoy 'a series of memorable events' staged for their benefit to 'engage [them] in an inherently personal way'. For the theatre audience no less than for the cinema audience, the night of the broadcast partakes of the excitement and uniqueness characteristic of events in the experience economy. Normal codes of learned behaviour are disrupted by the changes to the physical environment and the cognitive scaffolding provided by signs, objects and explicit guidance by ushers, presenter and director. For the theatre audience, the evening of the screening becomes one of Pine and Gilmore's 'memorable events', as their experience of the broadcast performance is enriched with extra content, focal points, and distractions. It is not only the actors' performance that is re-mediated as part of the broadcast: the theatre audience in the RST is also cast and directed, becoming a vital part of the performance on screen.

References

'David Tennant's Performance of Shakespeare's Richard II to Be Broadcast Live in Cinemas' (2013), *The Daily Telegraph*, 28 May. Available online: http://www.telegraph.co.uk/culture/theatre/10083402/David-Tennants-performance-of-Shakespeares-Richard-II-to-be-broadcast-live-in-cinemas.html (accessed 15 July 2017)

Hodgdon, B. (1998), *The Shakespeare Trade: Performances and Appropriations*, Philadelphia: University of Pennsylvania Press.

Karim-Cooper, F. (2012), 'The Performance of Early Modern Drama at Shakespeare's Globe', in P. Aebischer and K. Prince (eds), *Performing Early Modern Drama Today*, Cambridge: Cambridge University Press, 53–69.

Pine II, J. and J.H. Gilmore (2011), *The Experience Economy*, Boston: Harvard Business School Publishing.

Rogers, J. (2014), '*Antony and Cleopatra* Performed by the Royal Shakespeare Company (Swan), And: *Richard II* Performed by the Royal Shakespeare Company (RST), And: *Thomas of Woodstock* Performed by the Royal Shakespeare Company (Barbican Theatre) (Review)', *Shakespeare Bulletin* 32 (2): 310–19.

Rumbold, K. (2011), 'Brand Shakespeare', *Shakespeare Survey* 64: 25–37.

Tribble, E.B. (2011), *Cognition in the Globe: Attention and Memory in Shakespeare's Theatre*, Basingstoke: Palgrave Macmillan.

Wyver, J. (2015) 'Screening the RSC Stage: The 2014 Live from Stratford-Upon-Avon Cinema Broadcasts', *Shakespeare* 11 (3): 286–302.

PART THREE

Close-ups

7

South Bank Shakespeare Goes Global:

Broadcasting from Shakespeare's Globe and the National Theatre

Pascale Aebischer

In 2003, Shakespeare's Globe, in association with BBC4, was the first company in the UK to broadcast a 'live, uncut, theatre performance of Shakespeare' using HD digital video (Marr 2003). Since then, the Bankside theatre has been joined by its upriver neighbour, the National Theatre, in a game-changing endeavour to broadcast 'South Bank Shakespeare' to national and international audiences. The theatres' respective locations opposite Westminster's Houses of Parliament and the City of London, the seats of political and financial power, is crucial to their identity. As the National Theatre's former artistic director, Nicholas Hytner (2003–15), puts it: 'The South Bank in the 1590s and early 1600s was where almost the whole of London went at some point to see its fears, hopes, lives and politics anatomised. And I think if you've got something called the National Theatre, you have to try and reach for that again' (Wark 2017). Whereas their authority stems from their historical association with the early modern theatre industry, South Bank Shakespeares are shaped by the theatres' distinctive architectures and the types of performer–audience dynamics fostered by the buildings' affordances, as interpreted by their successive artistic directors.

Through their architecture, Shakespeare's Globe and the National Theatre adopt contrasting positions vis-à-vis the tension, in Shakespeare's plays, between illusion and theatrical self-consciousness or, in Bridget Escolme's words, between 'people who talk to themselves' and those who 'talk to the audience'

(2005: 9). In the Globe, the thrust stage and the daylight performers share with the surrounding spectators mean that 'imaginative complicity is essential for the creation of illusion' and the performance style is presentational (Purcell 2009: 150). The Shakespearean subjectivities (re)constructed through such complicity depend 'upon the potential for direct encounter between performer and spectator within a continually foregrounded theatre building' (Escolme 2005: 8). Integral to the experience of creative co-presence which William B. Worthen has dubbed 'Globe performativity' is the reconstructed building itself (2003: 110). The material re-imagining of the first Globe contributes to the generation of a powerful sensation of transhistorical presence in which past words, characters and conventions commingle with twenty-first-century subjectivities, objects and ambient noise. For the Globe, 'access' to its work 'draws together the related but very different ideas of physical, cultural and intellectual accessibility' that are all part of the Globe's mission to 'further the experience and international understanding of Shakespeare in performance' (Carson 2008: 115; Shakespeare's Globe 2017). Because the theatre does not benefit from government funding, its broadcasts have been dependent on partnerships with distributors and production companies. The four BBC broadcasts from the theatre (three 'live' from the Globe, one delayed from the Sam Wanamaker Playhouse), the recorded theatre DVDs of productions in 2007, 2009 and thereafter, the Globe on Screen cinema screenings of between 2011 and 2016, and the Globe Player streaming platform launched in 2014 all contribute to the theatre's mission to make the Globe experience global in reach.

By contrast, from the National Theatre's foundation, its Olivier stage, despite its 'open' shape and absence of a proscenium arch (see Greenhalgh, Chapter 1), has tended to portray Shakespeare as the inheritor of nineteenth-century realist performance practice, with the fourth-wall convention locking characters into a world separate from that of their audience – i.e., a theatre designed for 'people who talk to themselves'. Designed by Denys Lasdun as a brutalist layering of concrete boxes, the National Theatre's appearance proclaims its uncompromising modernity. In its main auditorium, the structure of the building itself recedes into the background, with attention focused instead on set design and sophisticated stage technologies, with excellent sightlines from all vantage points. Access to its productions is profoundly connected to the National Theatre's commitment to being 'as national as possible'. Arts Council funding supports the drive 'to keep ticket prices affordable, to reach a wide audience and to . . . maintain artistic risk-taking, accessibility and diversity' (National Theatre 2017). NTLive's cinema broadcasts are one further way in which this mission can be fulfilled, increasing the theatre's 'virtual capacity' to include nationwide audiences while generating additional income and brand recognition from international distribution (Bakhshi and Throsby 2010: 5; Groves 2012).[1] For the occasion of the live broadcast, each receiving cinema is reimagined as a satellite auditorium of the National Theatre, complete with printed cast list (a requirement by NTLive), downloadable e-programme, and a theatre-style interval which, together, act as cognitive prompts that invite broadcast audiences to experience the receiving venue as 'theatrical'.

There is, I argue, a clear (though not a necessary) connection between the theatre buildings, the performer-audience dynamics they foster in live performance, the companies' understanding of 'access', and the manner in which broadcasts from the two theatres engage with their remote audiences. Recognizing that broadcasts are shaped, to a significant extent, by 'established industry skillsets' of multi-camera live capture (Wyver 2017), I examine how broadcast directors create consistent house styles for NTLive and Shakespeare's Globe by deploying those skills when they adapt to the buildings and the productions' own engagement with the stage spaces and their audiences. Each house style remediates its own atmosphere, understood as, in Gernot Böhme's definition, 'the common reality of the perceiver and the perceived', an aura-like 'spatially extended quality of feeling' (1993: 122, 118). Whereas NTLive's Shakespeare broadcasts produce a predominantly illusionist Shakespeare attuned to the modern technologies and performance styles on display on the Olivier stage, broadcasts from Shakespeare's Globe between 2003 and 2016 reflect the company's predominantly presentational performance style under artistic directors Mark Rylance (1995–2005) and Dominic Dromgoole (2005–16). Most recently, the stylistic convergence of broadcasts from the two theatres has begun to blur the distinctions between illusionist and presentational styles.

This chapter shows how through paratexts, camerawork and the triggering of strong affective responses, broadcasts are able to generate atmospheres in which broadcast audiences experience a 'distributed presence' that transcends boundaries of time and place. A phenomenology of space and affect grounded in Michel de Certeau's work allows me to explain how broadcasts produce the experience of spatial inclusion or exclusion, which in turn contributes to the sensation of participation in the event. I argue that strong affects have the capacity to transcend spatial and temporal boundaries, connecting remote audiences with the performance in the here-and-now of their emotional response. The handling of strong affect, combined with a representation of space as transactional, is a catalyst of what Erin Sullivan describes as 'aliveness as an experiential and affective quality' (Chapter 3).

Shared affect and the creation of spaces

On 15 September 2011, the NTLive broadcast of Hytner's production of *One Man, Two Guvnors*, directed for screen by Robin Lough, opened not inside the National Theatre's Lyttelton auditorium, on whose proscenium stage the performance took place, but just outside, on an impromptu AstroTurf piazza framed by coloured party lights against the backdrop of the Thames riverside and the National Theatre's iconic concrete walls. There, a crowd had gathered for the free screening of the production on a giant pop-up screen. As night fell, broadcast viewers could see people milling around, sitting on the AstroTurf, or dancing to the sound of a skiffle band. The music acted as a sound bridge when the camera cut to the inside of the Lyttelton, where a packed audience was watching the band.

Fifty minutes later, James Corden's permanently ravenous servant Francis turned to his audience to ask if anyone had a sandwich for him. Promptly, somebody in the stalls offered up his sandwich. When Corden, helplessly cracking up with laughter, went wobbly in the knees and buried his head in his hands, a camera located at the side of the stalls picked out the owner of the sandwich. 'Of all the nights . . .,' spluttered Corden in recognition that this was the performance that was being broadcast live, as another shot showed the whooping, applauding front rows. If spectators had suspected that Corden's corpsing was a pre-scripted 'glitch' designed to generate the frisson of liveness for the theatre audience, Corden's interjection (which, in effect, was the only improvization that actually took place in this sequence) extended that frisson to the cinema audience.

The peripatetic mix of shots cutting between indoor and outdoor areas during the pre-show was also in evidence during the interval feature, which took broadcast viewers out onto the Piazza before leading them backstage. The curtain call, too, began inside the Lyttelton and ended on the Piazza. This mobile representation of the spaces in and around the auditorium meshed together with Corden's infectious laughter to transport broadcast viewers affectively into a performance space which reached beyond the boundaries of the theatre. Set off by Corden's wobbly-kneed giggles, the Lyttelton audience's responsive laughter acted 'as a sign that all members of the group [were] willing to enter into the play frame' (Ghose 2008: 6). Shared laughter could ripple across the physical boundaries of stage and stalls to encompass within that play frame London's South Bank and cinemas worldwide. Laughter, in combination with Lough's fluid representation of the theatre building's inside and outside, enabled the fixed and stable *place* of the National Theatre building to become an atmospheric *space* that became the common reality of production and viewers worldwide. In Michel de Certeau's influential formulation,

> A place (*lieu*) is the order (of whatever kind) in accord with which elements are distributed in relationships of coexistence. It thus excludes the possibility of two things being in the same location (*place*). The law of the 'proper' rules in the place: the elements taken into consideration are *beside* one another, each situated in its own 'proper' and distinct location, a location it defines.
>
> ([1984] 1988: 117; original emphases)

By contrast, a *space* is determined through operations and actions:

> A *space* exists when one takes into consideration vectors of direction, velocities, and time variables. Thus space is composed of intersections of

mobile elements. It is in a sense actuated by the ensemble of movements deployed within it. Space occurs as the effect produced by the operations that orient it, situate it, temporalize it. . . . In short, *space is a practiced place*.

([1984] 1988: 117; original emphases)

Corden's infectious laughter allowed the 'law of the "proper"' to be transgressed both spatially and temporally. Audience members were invited to laugh with Corden and, through that shared social practice, it became possible for separate entities – the theatre audience and the broadcast audience, the moments of performance and reception – to inhabit the same *space* as they experienced a shared affect in an emphatically marked present.

The 'distributed self' through which subjects can express their consciousness across different digital platforms via avatars (email addresses, Twitter handles, Facebook personas, etc.; Gilbert and Forney 2013: 26–7) can therefore be seen at play in broadcast situations (see also Sullivan's thoughts on 'distributed co-presence', Chapter 3). Remote viewers can experience a 'simultaneous mental occupation of two spaces' and time periods (Wardle 2014: 141). I felt this distributed presence, the experience of being both within the space of the broadcast and in a separate place and time, with disruptive vehemence when watching *One Man, Two Guvnors* six years later in the National Theatre archive: it translated into excruciating self-consciousness over the disconnection between my physical location in a place of silent study and the convulsion of suppressed laughter that, tears streaming down my face, bound me affectively into the remote space, time, and atmosphere of the broadcast. Affective responses potentially enable the viewer be present simultaneously in two temporalities via a shared space, irrespective of whether the broadcast is watched 'live' or asynchronously.

The National Theatre as a *space*: illusionist Shakespeare for NTLive

In view of Nicholas Hytner's recurring historical narrative regarding the South Bank location which anchors the National Theatre's mission in Shakespeare's holding up a mirror to contemporary politics, it is not surprising that Shakespeare featured prominently in the theatre's repertoire during his artistic direction. With Shakespeare known to 'nearly always [perform] well' (Flo Buckeridge, email, 24 July 2017), in total, over 20 per cent of NTLive's total output in those years was dedicated to Shakespeare and all eight Shakespeare plays staged in the Olivier between June 2009 (the date of NTLive's first broadcast) and July 2017 have been screened. An additional four were broadcast from other producing houses under the tagline 'the best of British theatre to a cinema near you' (see also Bennett, Chapter 2).

Just two multi-camera directors, Robin Lough and Tim van Someren, are (at the time of writing) behind all the NTLive broadcasts of Shakespeare's plays from the National Theatre. Between them, they have created a distinctive NTLive style of illusionist Shakespeare broadcast that immerses viewers in the stage space of the Olivier. Complex paratextual framing additionally establishes a strong sense of the theatre's structure, location and history, and the Shakespearean legitimacy that arises from these factors. Paratexts and camerawork use complementary strategies to portray the theatre as a space full of de Certeau's 'intersections of mobile elements' that spatially extend to the broadcast viewer an atmosphere of aliveness and the experience of illusionist immersion in a performance of Shakespeare in which characters 'talk to themselves'. Theatre audiences, consequently, tend to be elided from the broadcasts themselves even though they feature prominently as a backdrop for the broadcast presenters' introductions (Greenhalgh 2014: 259). Meanwhile, affective bridges connect cinema audiences with their invisible counterparts in the theatre, allowing broadcast viewers to experience their presence as distributed across the cinema and the theatre auditoria.

In the run-up to a recording, the broadcasting department liaises with the theatre's marketing department to create promotional materials, interview scripts and documentaries that are filmed in-house or farmed out to external producers (Buckeridge, personal interview, 11 March 2017). These paratexts are subsequently in part repurposed as promotional and educational material that is integrated on the National Theatre's website, to which broadcast viewers are repeatedly directed with pointers to the digital theatre programme. Within the broadcasts, these paratexts play a key role in orienting viewers in relation to the building, the specific auditorium from which the show is broadcast, the National Theatre's history, and its connection with and approach to Shakespeare.

A vivid example of NTLive's promotion of South Bank Shakespeare to mark the Shakespeare quatercentenary is the broadcast of Polly Findlay's *As You Like It* on 25 February 2016. The twenty-six minutes of introductory material started with the now standard loop of slides that invited audiences to access the theatre and its wares via a range of platforms. Broadcast viewers unable to physically enter the building could instead either project a part of themselves outwards to 'Join in the conversation' via NTLive's social media channels (Twitter, Facebook, email), or, conversely, have a part of the theatre, in the form of books and gifts, sent to them thanks to the international shipping available from the bookshop 'Inspired by National Theatre productions and our iconic building'. With NTLive positioned as a space full of potential transactional vectors into and out of the building, the next item worked to root that space in its geographical environment. To this purpose, a filmed tour through key London sites (St Paul's Cathedral, the London Eye, the Palace of Westminster) embedded the NTLive experience in London's tourist-destination environment before concluding with external night-time footage of people entering the brightly-lit National Theatre. Shots of auditoria, cameras and operating desk were then mixed with NTLive's slogans 'World class theatre ... Filmed live in high definition ... Now playing in over 2,000 cinemas worldwide'. This produced yet more vectors of movement into the building and back out towards worldwide audiences, though the emphasis on interaction was now toned down. A documentary film, produced in-house by the NTLive team, dedicated to 'Shakespeare at the National Theatre' zeroed in further to the core of the broadcast. Here, the Shakespeare Institute's Abigail Rokison reflected on the National Theatre's gestation as 'a house for Shakespeare', while Benedict Nightingale (a long-time theatre critic for *The Times*) enthused about the Olivier stage's ideal fit 'for the amplitude of Shakespeare'. Olivia Vinall, a veteran Desdemona and Cordelia at the National, gushed about the Olivier's 'intimate' feel and Shakespeare's continued relevance to audiences 'either emotionally or socially or politically or historically'. The theatre's recently appointed artistic director Rufus Norris concluded: 'I am sure that as long as people are speaking English, as long as people are listening to English, they'll be listening to Shakespeare. Nobody's done it better', while a slow fade-in superimposing Shakespeare's face over one of the concrete walls cemented the playwright's association with the very fabric of the building.

This, then, set the screen for the broadcast of *As You Like It*, live-mixed from the Olivier auditorium following two camera rehearsals. With the broadcast audience primed to appreciate the 'intimacy' of the vast Olivier stage, Tim van Someren's cameras eliminated the theatre audience from the visual field once the house lights went down. The single exception, the entrance of a character through the stalls in the final scene, was disorienting for broadcast viewers as a camera abruptly swivelled into the darkened auditorium to capture that arrival. Instead of being invited to experience spatial inclusion via a proxy theatre audience (as in *One Man, Two Guvnors*), cinema audiences were swiftly immersed in a broadcast that complemented theatrical modes of signification with conventions borrowed from film and television. In his mix, van Someren approximated the film style and speed of editing associated with professional wrestling for the arrival of the imposing figure of Charles the wrestler in the fighting ring.[2] The high-up crane camera rapidly zoomed down on Charles in his golden cape, receded just as fast, tracked left to right before cutting back to the crane camera, which zoomed-and-swivelled back down. The technological hype of this professional's entrance contrasted with Orlando's down-to-earth arrival, filmed with a simple stage-level tracking shot. The camerawork thus carried much of the burden of telling a story which opposed pastoral simplicity with the technological excesses and competitive violence of city life. When, in designer Lizzie Clachan's *coup de théâtre*, the court's office desks and chairs were raised to dangle halfway from the flies as the trees and branches of the Forest of Arden, a slow tracking shot encompassing the set and a closer-up view of chairs and tables swaying mid-air were followed by a crane shot revealing the rubble-strewn stage floor. The camera set-up conveyed, for remote audiences, the affective force of the Olivier's stage technologies that introduced a breath-taking verticality into the production. In what Sullivan describes as the crane camera's 'poetic view of seeing' (2017: 649), viewpoints unavailable to theatre audiences translated the vertiginous surrealism of Clachan's scene change into the medium of theatre broadcast. And when Oliver first arrived in the forest and had eyes only for Celia, the story of their budding love was told through narrative framing, as the cameras focused on the lovers-to-be and disregarded Rosalind.

Van Someren's camerawork thus remediated, for cinema audiences, the atmosphere of the Olivier stage's state-of-the-art stage machinery and its combination of vastness with a strong central focal point. If the Olivier's design had pushed performers towards an illusionist performance style, the absence of interaction between performers and spectators within the theatre was heightened by the broadcast. The theatrical 'intimacy' vaunted in the introductory paratexts was converted into cinematic 'immediacy': the illusion of immersion in and direct encounter with the performance (see also Way 2017: 395). While such immediacy does not 'commit the viewer to an utterly naïve or magical conviction that the representation is the same thing as what it represents' (Bolter and Grusin 2000: 30), it nonetheless generates a powerful sense of presence and mobility within the performance space. The cinema audience was wrapped in its own collective experience of a broadcast in which camera movement, framing and speed of editing generated a space brought to life 'by the operations that orient it, situate it, temporalize it'.

What nevertheless anchored the image in the 'live' theatrical context was the aural bridge of laughter on the soundtrack. Laughing with the theatre audience at, for instance, the absurdity of a human sheep keeling over after eating a Post-it note 'leaf' generated the final, crucial vector that allowed broadcast viewers to enter the play frame of the broadcast's atmospheric space. Without going to the lengths of *One Man, Two Guvnors*, the paratexts and camerawork of NTLive's *As You Like It* thus represented the National Theatre's Olivier auditorium as a geographically specific, historically Shakespearean, transactional space. By combining the screen equivalent of theatrical illusionism, immediacy, with an affective sound bridge, it offered broadcast viewers experiences analogous to those of the theatre audience, with whom they could laugh within the play frame that connected communities of viewers across 2,000 cinemas worldwide. The dynamics I have outlined in the *As You Like It* broadcast can also be found at work in NTLive's other Shakespearean comedies, *All's Well That Ends Well* (2009) and *The Comedy of Errors* (2012). If a satellite cinema audience refrains from laughing along, on the other hand, the affective disconnection between theatre and cinema can, as I will explain at the end of this chapter, result in an experience of emotional and spatial distance.

Laughter is not the only affective vector capable of contributing to the experience of distributed presence. This is clear when looking at the broadcast of Nicholas Hytner's sinister *Timon of Athens*, directed for screen by Robin Lough (2012), as an example of NTLive's Shakespearean tragedies. Here, too, the NTLive team's paratextual materials complemented the camerawork within the broadcast to create an illusionist Shakespeare in which the National Theatre was presented as a transactional space, even as they emphasized, with critical force, the geographical specificity of the theatre's location vis-à-vis its London environment. Two elements stood out from the standard paratexts that introduced the screening: a promotional feature produced by NTLive's sponsor Aviva and a documentary that contextualized Hytner's production.

The Aviva advert prominently included the National Theatre's concrete structure as a backdrop for an introduction to Aviva's 'Street-to-School' project in Calcutta. The mini-feature explained how NTLive's corporate sponsor was supporting 400,000 children in 17 countries. These figures rubbed shoulders with broadcast presenter Emma Freud's vaunting, straight afterwards, of the 'totally sold out production', which was being broadcast to over 600 cinemas worldwide: it was as if the theatre's success and its global expansion through broadcasting needed to be offset by the global charity work of NTLive's sponsor.

The corporate sponsorship underpinning NTLive came under indirect, but nonetheless robust, scrutiny in the subsequent documentary *A Timon for Our Times* about the context for the production.[3] There, Shakespeare became the meeting point of vectors bringing together the National Theatre, the City of London, the Parliament at Westminster and Shakespeare's Globe against the backdrop of the global recession of 2008. Standing inside the window of the Gherkin building overlooking the heart of London's financial district, Paul Mason (at the time Economics Editor for BBC2's *Newsnight*) spoke of the connections between wealth, arts sponsorship and privileged access to political power. Meanwhile, shots of then Prime Minister David Cameron and Mayor of London Boris Johnson entering an exclusive arts event illustrated Mason's reference to 'gift-giving and backscratching' in high-level politics. A view from Waterloo Bridge panning from the City of London on the North Bank towards the National Theatre on the South Bank then precisely located the theatre in relation to the production's thematic setting. Strikingly, Hytner's statement that 'what Shakespeare is *always* writing about is his own world' was accompanied by footage of 'Occupy' tents outside St Paul's Cathedral and a zoom in to Shakespeare's Globe across the river. Even as the feature ended with footage of the National Theatre, the neighbouring Globe thus became a shorthand for South Bank Shakespeare's historical authenticity, guaranteeing the broadcast's adherence to a Shakespearean model of relevance to contemporary politics.

That urgent sense of relevance was carried over into Tim Hatley's design for *Timon*, which incorporated in his naturalistic set several of the landmarks featured in the documentary. Consequently, the inside of the theatre bore a clear relationship to its outside, as multiple vectors connected the production to London's geography of power and wealth. With the auditorium darkened, Lough's crane camera in its establishing shot of a tent city on the Olivier stage immersed viewers in an illusionist environment which mirrored the historical 'Occupy' protesters in the documentary. A further link was created when the inauguration of 'The Timon Room' in an art gallery reflected the documentary's footage of real-life politicians, who were furthermore indexed by a scene set in a members' club with huge windows looking out on Westminster's Houses of Parliament. Much in the manner of van Someren, Lough's mobile use of the crane and cameras on tracks immersed the broadcast viewers within the production's illusionist space and blocked out the theatre audience even in moments when Apemantus, the play's cynical truth-teller, addressed that audience directly, looking past the camera into what the broadcast represented as a void.

In this misanthropic environment, it was disgust, not laughter, that acted as a visceral bridge uniting cinema and theatre viewers in the here-and-now of the production when Simon Russell Beale's Timon, disillusioned about his parasitical dinner guests, served them faeces on silverware. Repulsion sharpened into collective nausea when, in a revolting detail picked out by a long tracking shot, Timon circled the table before rubbing a handful of gloopy excrement into the bald pate of one of his guests. As queasiness united audiences, characters and performers, Lough cut to a shot from the rising crane camera to show Timon's dinner guests rushing off. Disgust functioned as the affective vector that enabled broadcast audiences to feel included in the space of the theatre.

NTLive's Shakespeare broadcasts thus typically deploy an illusionist form of South Bank Shakespeare that presents the National Theatre as a transactional space which wraps remote viewers in a spatially extended atmosphere. NTLive's paratexts begin by situating cinema viewers within their own environment but represent the theatre as an increasingly transactional space criss-crossed by multiple vectors (this is true especially of broadcasts from the Olivier, but is also true of NTLive broadcasts from other venues). Meanwhile, during the broadcasts themselves, the mobile camerawork immerses cinema viewers in a stage space that excludes the theatre audience. The distributed presence generated through these mechanisms is welded together through affects which have the potential to bind remote audiences into the here-and-now of the performance in an experience of aliveness. This is a broadcast experience which, thanks to the technological 'bravura' of crane camera and tracks (Barker 2013), is emphatically *not* theatrical, not identifiable with a possible audience viewpoint within the theatre, even as the medium is used to highlight the theatricality of its modern stage designs, technologies, and performances – and of the cinema audience's collective response to the production in a satellite auditorium.

Shakespeare's Globe as a *place*: presentational broadcasting

Broadcasts from Shakespeare's Globe have a long and complex history involving multiple partners, phases, artistic directors and broadcast directors. It is therefore the more significant that, nevertheless, a fairly consistent house style has emerged which once more takes a lead from the affordances of the theatre building. NTLive's Shakespeare broadcasts, we saw, invite cinema viewers into the *here-and-now* of the performance. By contrast, Shakespeare's Globe's strategy is to invite remote viewers, whether in a collective cinema setting or watching on their own on a small screen, to observe the *there-and-then* of an always already remote and separate place, time, and atmosphere. The building's history as a reconstruction generates a mode of engagement with the work produced within it which is at ease with the contradictory notions that there is a specifically Shakespearean, interactive Globe performativity accessible only by virtue of physical presence within the building, and that all performance within that building is essentially in a relationship of 'surrogation' vis-à-vis an early modern original (Roach 1996: 2). The fact that this original is at a significant temporal and even a small geographical remove exposes 'the obvious discontinuities, misalliances, and ruptures' between the 'previous Golden Age' of Shakespeare and performance practice in today's Globe. It is therefore easy for broadcasts from Shakespeare's Globe to tap into this dynamic and pitch themselves as a further level of surrogation: as a stand-in for an experience of Globe performativity which it 'must vainly aspire both to embody and to replace' (ibid.: 3).

De Certeau's 'law of the "proper" [which] rules in the place' determines that while broadcast audiences can see the Globe's 'groundlings' standing in the yard and might view them as their proxy, they can only with difficulty *experience* what it is like to stand shoulder-to-shoulder in an open-air arena. Instead, the light shared by performers and spectators in the Globe excludes broadcast audiences regardless of their viewing context: whereas the physical regime of the darkened cinema for NTLive broadcasts facilitates the elision of the similarly seated and darkened theatre audiences and hence the cinema viewer's immersion in the illusionist performance, no such elision is possible in Globe broadcasts. When the broadcasts re-mediate the profoundly transactional performance space of the Globe as a separate 'proper' place, they present the theatre audience as an integral part of the 'things, persons or their constellations' that constitute the atmosphere of a Globe performance (Böhme 1993: 122). Broadcast audiences remain in their own, separate places. Broadcasts from Shakespeare's Globe offer viewers the ability to *observe*, rather than *experience*, the spontaneous generation of Globe performativity in the there-and-then of the Globe, which itself is a surrogate for an authentic Shakespeare who is both a constitutive part of the building and always already at multiple removes. Without producing affective aliveness, the live-capture of a performance nonetheless allows it to continue '*living* . . . even as the live event to which it is related has receded into the past' (Aebischer 2013: 146).

This distance between production and reception is implicit in the temporal gaps between the capture (normally across two consecutive performances), its post-production mix to edit out potential disruptions by pigeons, helicopters and party boats on the Thames, and the release of Globe on Screen cinema broadcasts and DVDs the following year. This strategy privileges on-demand access over the eventness of a live broadcast; however, it was only arrived at after an initial attempt at temporal liveness. The South Bank Shakespeare presented by Sue Judd's broadcast of Tim Carroll's production of *Richard II* on 7 September 2003 on BBC4 put a heavy emphasis on the production team's research into 'Original Practices'. Interview material with practitioners introduced viewers to presentational performance and the use of an all-male cast. 'If the Globe has a mission,' Head of Theatre Music Claire van Kampen affirmed, 'it's reconnecting the audience with the play . . . *everybody* can come and experience a play here.' '*Here*', though, was neither the broadcast nor viewers at home but Shakespeare's Globe. The use of the Globe's stage, galleries and tiring house as backdrops to the interviews introduced viewers to every nook and cranny of the building, with the camera lingering on specific features. The paratexts thus literally *presented* the Globe as a unique and separate place filled with arcane performance practices that were not just geographically, but also 'culturally remote' (Carson 2008: 121). Meanwhile, the overdetermination of the spatial orientation betrayed an anxiety regarding the ability of the broadcast to act as a surrogate for bodily experience. Although in his introduction, presenter Andrew Marr belaboured the risk inherent in this live broadcast and tried to portray its liveness as a guarantor of a shared experience (Purcell 2013: 213), his warning to the television audience that 'if it rains, then you, along with the actors, may have to struggle a little bit' backfired in stressing the potential sensory disconnection between television viewers dealing with sound disruption and theatre audiences struggling with dripping ponchos.

The documentary framing of the production effectively overwhelmed the broadcast of the production itself, which ended up as little more than an illustration of the research and performance methods described in the frame. Through its extraordinary visual closeness to the fetishized building, costumes and make-up, the *Richard II* broadcast adopted the medium's equivalent of a presentational performance style by *presenting* the building and the 'Original Practices' approach to its viewers without giving them *presence* within it. When, to start the performance, an actor asked the theatre audience to refrain from recording the production, he raised a laugh from the Globe audience which he acknowledged by admitting that they 'may have noticed that there is a great deal of audio and video recording equipment in the theatre tonight'. Since that equipment was carefully located outside the image frame, the comment cemented the broadcast audience's separation from the Globe experience: they would be watching the 'groundlings' watching the play and its recording but would be neither able to see nor to laugh in the same way. Unlike the community-building laugh in Corden's 'corpsing' that reached out to the broadcast viewer, the laugh here acted as a reminder of the boundary between theatre and broadcast audiences.

Following a more low-key BBC4 broadcast of *Measure for Measure* in 2004, when HD video recording of Globe productions resumed under Dominic Dromgoole in 2007, all pretence at temporal liveness vanished, as did the paratextual apparatus setting Shakespeare in his historical South Bank context. Instead, most Globe cinema broadcasts, recorded theatre DVDs and online streams start with an establishing shot of the theatre's exterior timber frame with audiences entering before promptly cutting to the inside of the wooden 'O', thus briskly setting up the geographical location of the Globe as a place. This is followed, within the broadcasts themselves, by camerawork that typically affords viewers an 'open and theatrical perspective' onto the stage (Sullivan 2017: 640).

Kriss Russman's camerawork for *As You Like It*, filmed in 2009 and released as a DVD the following year, is typical in its constant inclusion of the Globe audience either visually or through sound. Thea Sharrock's production, like many at the Globe, repeatedly spilled from the stage into the pit, with Jack Laskey's Orlando throwing Charles the wrestler off the stage or carrying old Adam through a throng of schoolchildren. Remediated as a DVD, the effect is spatially and affectively distancing, in that the groundlings' fright and delight when performers encroach on their space cannot produce the same reaction in the broadcast audience, for whom the space is *not* transactional. Instead, the moment emphasizes the remote viewers' exclusion from the Globe. The fact that individual audience members are an integral, recognisable, part of the broadcast is also alienating if viewers, who for example enjoy the facial expressions of a group of schoolchildren in the yard, suddenly see them replaced by grown-ups because audiences from two performances are edited together. A different type of disengagement is occasioned when Tim McMullan's Jaques insults the Globe audience by pointing at them in a slow circular motion as the 'fools' he is invoking 'into a circle' (2.5.56–57). Even if a viewer of the DVD laughs along with the Globe audience, the cause and even the mood of the laughter in the two audiences are fundamentally different. The groundlings' laughter signals the 'affective affirmation' typical of laughter as a social practice in the Globe (Caldwell 2013: 397), tying them into an experiential community in an indicative mood in the here-and-now of the performance. By contrast, the broadcast audience's laughter is appreciative and in a conditional mood, demonstrating affective understanding of how the situation would be funny had they been part of the there-and-then of the performance.

The bulk of recordings of productions at Shakespeare's Globe are thus 'live' only in the sense that they are 'captured "live" in high definition' in the presence of an audience – a digital surrogate for an analogue surrogate of an always remote authentic Shakespeare (Shakespeare's Globe 2014).[4] To return to the definitions set up in our introduction, these are simply 'theatre broadcasts' which may, as Margaret Jane Kidnie explains in Chapter 8, benefit from the liveness effects generated by NTLive's dominance in cinema programming, but which do not themselves aspire to generate the illusion of simultaneity and distributed presence. Because, as Chui-Yee Cheng explains, 'the building and the audience themselves perform, they are part of the show, and it's what gives it its live quality' (personal interview, 11 March 2017), remote audiences are, by definition, separate from this experience. The emphasis of Globe recordings is on an understanding of 'access' as (to return to Carson's formulation) 'physical, cultural and intellectual' rather than spatial and affective. Globe-style South Bank Shakespeare, while deriving authenticity from its building and the Globe performativity it presents to its viewers, incorporates the ruptures characteristic of surrogation in its temporal and geographical separation of theatre and broadcast audiences, each in their proper place with affects appropriate to their respective experiences. The Globe experience hinges on considering the building itself as a performer, which creates a unique atmosphere within which Shakespearean subjectivity emerges as the result of architecture, performer and audiences coming together in a single place and time. As a result, broadcast audiences experience the building as a distinct place in which the broadcast is anchored but from which they are geographically and affectively separate.

Coda: South Bank Shakespeares converge

The opposition between the NTLive's illusionist South Bank Shakespeare proclaiming its modern relevance and the presentational recordings of Globe productions that harken back to an always remote Shakespearean authenticity has been challenged by broadcasts from the two theatres in 2016 and 2017 in which those approaches showed signs of convergence. As theatre directors decided to work against the affordances of the buildings and broadcast directors followed suit, the resulting hybrid South Bank Shakespeare meshed the illusionist and the presentational into a hybrid of both. In response, viewers of the Globe broadcast changed their engagement in a manner that reflects the current trends in audience engagement through social media Sullivan and Nicholas explore in greater detail (Chapters 3 and 4).

When Emma Rice took over the artistic direction of Shakespeare's Globe, she promptly had big holes drilled into its oak beams to accommodate a modern sound system and stage lights. In collaboration with the BBC and with experienced Globe broadcast director Ian Russell at the helm, Rice then used the BBC's 2016 'Shakespeare Lives' online platform for a live stream of her inaugural production of *A Midsummer Night's Dream* on 11 September 2016. The broadcast opened with presenter Meera Syal standing in the yard and situating the present-day playhouse in relation to its Shakespearean ancestors just 'a few hundred yards away'. Syal's interval interview with Rice, who declared herself 'hugged by the space', was joyously celebratory. Gesturing at the crowd of spectators milling around her, Syal's enthusiasm for the building and its historical associations with Shakespeare could not be disentangled from her love of the 'exciting and fresh' interpretation of the play that spoke to the preoccupations of the present. As Rice pointed out, each night, a character walked on 'reading the *Metro*, and it's today's paper, today's news!' Through their celebration of the theatre's past and the sensory warmth of its architecture, Syal and Rice were also acclaiming its qualities as a physically, financially and culturally accessible, profoundly transactional space which interacts with the wider cultural context of present-day London. As Rice exclaimed: 'I love the space so much: you can wander along the river and come in for five pounds and see the most amazing plays performed so fresh and live!'

The emphasis on an atmosphere of free-flowing, chatty, joyful 'liveness' in the broadcast frame spilled into the performance, which insistently brought the past into the present in a transgression of 'the law of the "proper"' and affirmation of the theatre's transhistoricity that affected every aspect of this production. Liveness was also evident in Russell's camerawork, which responded to the production in the moment, without prior rehearsal. The positioning of six cameras around the 'wooden O' of the building's two galleries allowed Russell to show every part of the performance space, which extended through the yard where actors performed on table-tops, at some point in the fading daylight. When Katy Owen's Puck force-fed a banana she had previously licked to an audience member, the disgusting hilarity of the situation was increased by the shocked and delighted facial expressions of the bystanders included in the frame, with laughter and disgust combining to work against the Globe's separateness as a 'place'. And as night fell and the stage lights increasingly plunged the groundlings into darkness, creating something akin to the erasure of the theatre audience and potential for a more immersive broadcast experience familiar from NTLive, broadcast audiences, like their counterparts in the theatre, could 'feel the darker themes falling and the cost of the troubles us mortals get into' (Rice).

The laughter that was so prominent a feature of both paratext and production reached out to the online audience in an invitation to 'enter into the play frame' even as the format of live-streaming made the distributed presence fostered by NTLive hard to achieve. What this production's broadcast modelled instead was a mode of engaging with the Globe as a space that can have its cake and eat it, that can accommodate multiple technologies and subjectivities that span the four hundred years separating us from Shakespeare. The production's set was Shakespeare's Globe itself, in the heart of present-day multicultural, metrosexual London in which the inconstancy of Ncuti Gatwa's Demetrius could be explained by his repression of homosexual desire for Ankur Bahl's camp 'Helenus'. 'Rita' Quince (Lucy Thackeray), a Globe usher, in her burlesque of a health-and-safety address, acknowledged the building's recent history through her reference to having received her tambourine as a gift from Mark Rylance. And even while Rice's use of amplified sound and light flew in the face of the building's reputation as 'stripped of technological intervention' (Carson 2008: 121), Quince's prohibition of mobile phones was a nod to the aversion to modern technology associated with previous artistic directors. What reconciled these contradictions were the fairies, who bridged the gap between the early modern and the present, since their dissolute state and mash-up of Elizabethan and modern dress could be explained by the fact that they had, as Rice put it, 'been around for four hundred years. They've done every drug, every party, they're absolutely wrecked'.

Against the background of the fairies' exhausted continuity, Syal presented the production as engaging in a series of surrogations that charted a narrative of progression towards the joyous here-and-now of this live stream event: the original Globe burnt down, was rebuilt, destroyed, and is now rebuilt as Shakespeare's Globe; Shakespeare's company was replaced by male artistic directors who are now replaced by Rice; Shakespeare's Athens made way for 'Bankside' and 'Hoxton'; Helena was replaced by Helenus, and so on. Syal's direct address to the broadcast audience meanwhile not only reminded them of *when* they were ('live'), but also *where* they were: in front of a computer 'already steeped in heavy interactivity' (Harries 2002: 176), part of a digital 'participatory culture' that acted as a surrogate for Globe performativity (Jenkins et al. 2009: 5–10). As Sullivan demonstrates in Chapter 3, locked out of the 'proper' place of the Globe, online audiences responded to the broadcast's joyfully free-flowing chattiness 'tactically' by creating a surrogate yard (de Certeau [1984] 1988: 36–7), sharing their laughter and partaking in quick-fire discussions on social media beyond the control of Shakespeare's Globe. If the dominant mode of engagement with an NTLive Shakespeare broadcast is attention in a presence distributed across theatre and cinema, in this broadcast it was multi-tasking in a presence distributed across the broadcast space and social media. Viewers organized themselves spontaneously into a community of fans in exchanges that were 'dynamic, collective and reciprocal' (Jenkins 2002: 160). Rice's reinterpretation of the affordances of the Globe as including present-day performance technologies had a tangible impact on how online viewers experienced the broadcast's atmosphere as offering the tactical opportunity to generate a surrogate yard.

As the Globe rebranded its South Bank Shakespeare as relevant, digitally interactive, communal, potentially immersive, and affectively 'live', under Rufus Norris' artistic direction and with Emma Keith as Head of Broadcast, NTLive evolved in the opposite direction. In September 2015, it launched 'National Theatre: On Demand. In Schools', a selection of broadcasts linked to the National Curriculum that are free at the point of access for all UK primary and secondary schools. With this initiative, NTLive began to move away from the brand's previous emphasis on liveness and ephemerality (Buckeridge 2017). The broadcast of Simon Godwin's *Twelfth Night* directed for screen by Robin Lough on 6 April 2017 also marks a shift in approach. Responding to this production's mix of naturalistic and presentational performance styles in which characters repeatedly broke through the 'fourth wall' to talk to the audience, Lough's camerawork switched between illusionist immersion in the stage space and acknowledgement of the theatre audience. Disturbingly, his most marked use of the theatre audience as a proxy for the cinema viewers occurred during the letter scene and the direct address to the audience of Feste – that is, at the moments when Tamsin Greig's Malvolia was cruelly mocked for expressing her previously repressed sexual desire for Phoebe Fox's Olivia (re-gendered homosexual characters were all the rage on the South Bank in 2016–17). Throughout the broadcast, the soundtrack regularly offered broadcast viewers an affective sound bridge of laughter to connect them with their counterparts in the theatre. But at those moments when laughter became politically charged, Lough's cameras provided broadcast viewers with a visual anchor for that shared laughter by including the front row of the stalls in the frame. Laughing at the humiliation of a scapegoated lesbian was facilitated for broadcast audiences by camerawork that included a proxy theatre audience showing no particular restraint in siding with the production's straight characters, whose 'homophobia [was] largely played for laughs' (Duncan 2017). My own experience of this broadcast, as a result, was conflicted and contradictory: when immersion in the illusion switched to presentation of direct interaction with the theatre audience at Malvolia's expense, I felt a disjunction between my own response and that modelled by the theatre audience. Resistance to laughter translated into my experience of separation from the Olivier auditorium as a discrete place even as both the production and the broadcast worked against the affordances of the Olivier to create an approximation of Globe performativity.

Just forty-four days after the live stream of Rice's inaugural *Dream*, Neil Constable (CEO, Shakespeare's Globe) announced her departure. He explained how Rice's introduction of artificial sound and light had broken the mould of the theatre and concluded that in 2018, programming would once more be 'structured around "shared light" productions without designed sound and light rigging' (Constable and Rice 2016). How the appointment of Michelle Terry as the theatre's fourth artistic director will affect broadcasts from Shakespeare's Globe is unclear at the time of writing, though the CinemaLive live theatre broadcast of *King Lear* to cinemas in the UK on 21 September 2017 – another innovation under Emma Rice's leadership – is yet more evidence of the emergence of a hybrid South Bank Shakespeare. What is clear, however, is the extent to which broadcasts from Shakespeare's Globe and the neighbouring National Theatre hinge on a complex combination of narratives regarding the buildings' histories, their Shakespearean connections, and their technological affordances. These factors shape the distinctive brands of South Bank Shakespeares they produce through their paratexts and the camerawork of the broadcasts themselves. Even when they work against the affordances of their respective buildings to create a more hybrid broadcast experience, these broadcasts produce complex engagements with the companies' histories and performance styles, using the buildings and their locations as a means of anchoring their global Shakespeares firmly in London's South Bank to generate complex and evolving modes of participation in South Bank Shakespeare for their remote audiences.

Acknowledgements

Thanks to Flo Buckeridge (General Manager, NTLive) and Chui-Yee Cheung (Film and Digital Distribution Manager, Shakespeare's Globe) for their insights; to Jennie Borzykh (National Theatre archives) for her assistance, to Stephen Purcell for a productive conversation about *One Man, Two Guvnors* and to Susanne Greenhalgh and Laurie Osborne for sharing their counts of audience shots of NTLive's *Twelfth Night*.

Notes

1 The history and process of NTLive has been documented by Barker (2013), Buckeridge (2017), Rosenthal (2013), Bakhshi and Whitby (2014), Stone (2016) and Way (2017). For the funding of NTLive, see Groves (2012) and Rosenthal (2013). In this volume, see especially Bennett and Kidnie.
2 The speed of the mix was made possible by the camera scripts' unusually high number of cues: 1,322 overall compared to Lough's 852 for *Othello* (camera scripts for *As You Like It* and *Othello*, National Theatre Archive, London).
3 *A Timon for Our Times* was directed for NTLive by Adam Low, edited by Joanna Crickmay and researched by Emily Thomas.
4 The thirty-two online live streams on The Space broadcast as part of the 2012 'Globe to Globe' Festival are the exception (see Appendix).

References

Aebischer, P. (2013), *Screening Early Modern Drama: Beyond Shakespeare*, Cambridge: Cambridge University Press.
Bakhshi, H. and D. Throsby (2010), *Beyond Live: Digital Innovation in the Performing Arts*, NESTA Research Briefing, February. Available online: https://www.nesta.org.uk/sites/default/files/beyond_live.pdf (accessed 12 July 2017)
Bakhshi, H. and A. Whitby (2014), *Estimating the Impact of Live Simulcast on Theatre Attendance: an Application to London's National Theatre*, NESTA

Working Paper 14/04. Available online: https://www.nesta.org.uk/sites/default/files/1404_estimating_the_impact_of_live_simulcast_on_theatre_attendance.pdf (accessed 12 July 2017)

Barker, M. (2013), *Live to Your Local Cinema: The Remarkable Rise of Livecasting*, Kindle Book, Basingstoke: Palgrave Macmillan.

Böhme, G. (1993), 'Atmosphere as the Fundamental Concept of a New Aesthetics', *Thesis Eleven* 36 (1): 113–26.

Bolter, J.D. and R. Grusin (2000), *Remediation: Understanding New Media*, Boston: MIT Press.

Buckeridge, F. (2017), 'National Theatre Live: From Stage to Screen', *FuturePlay Festival*, 11 May. Available online: https://www.youtube.com/watch?v=jbIcNuEpEyU (accessed 12 July 2017).

Caldwell, W.C. (2013), 'The Comic Structure of the Globe: History, Direct Address, and the Representation of Laughter in a Reconstructed Playhouse', *Shakespeare Bulletin* 31 (3): 375–403.

Carson, C. (2008), 'Democratising the Audience?' in C. Carson and F. Karim-Cooper (eds), *Shakespeare's Globe: A Theatrical Experiment*, Cambridge: Cambridge University Press, 115–26.

de Certeau, M. ([1984] 1988), *The Practice of Everyday Life*, Berkeley: University of California Press.

Constable, N. and E. Rice (2016), 'Press Release: Statement Regarding the Artistic Direction of Shakespeare's Globe', Shakespeare's Globe, 25 October. Available online: http://www.shakespearesglobe.com/uploads/files/2016/10/statement_regarding_the_artistic_direction_of_shakespeare_s_globe_final.pdf (accessed 12 July 2017).

Duncan, S. (2017), '[Review] *Twelfth Night*, dir. Simon Godwin, National Theatre', *Clamorousvoice*, 28 February. Available online: http://clamorousvoice.com/tag/tamara-lawrence/ (accessed 22 June 2017).

Escolme, B. (2005), *Talking to the Audience: Shakespeare, Performance, Self*, Abingdon: Routledge.

Gilbert, R. and A. Forney (2013), 'The Distributed Self: Virtual Worlds and the Future of Human Identity', in R. Teigland and D. Power (eds), *The Immersive Internet: Reflections on the Entangling of the Virtual with Society, Politics and the Economy*, Basingstoke: Palgrave Macmillan, 23–36.

Ghose, I. (2008), *Shakespeare and Laughter: A Cultural History*, Manchester: Manchester University Press.

Greenhalgh, S. (2014), 'Guest Editor's Introduction', *Shakespeare Bulletin*, 32 (2): 255–61.

Groves, N. (2012), 'Arts Head: David Sabel, Head of Digital, National Theatre', *The Guardian*, 10 April.

Harries, D. (2002), 'Watching the Internet', in D. Harris (ed.), *The New Media Book*, London: British Film Institute, 171–82.

Jenkins, H. (2002), 'Interactive Audiences?' in D. Harris (ed.), *The New Media Book*, London: British Film Institute, 157–70.

Jenkins, H. with R. Purushotma, M. Weigel, K. Clinton and A.J. Robinson (2009), *Confronting the Challenges of Participatory Culture: Media Education for the 21st Century*, Cambridge, MA: MIT Press.

Marr, A. (2003), Broadcast Introduction, *Richard II* [TV broadcast] BBC4, 7 September.

National Theatre (2017), 'About the National Theatre'. Available online: https://www.nationaltheatre.org.uk/about-the-national-theatre/ (accessed 19 March 2017).

Purcell, S. (2009), *Popular Shakespeare: Simulation and Subversion on the Modern Stage*, Basingstoke: Palgrave Macmillan.

Purcell, S. (2013), 'The Impact of New Forms of Public Performance', in Christie Carson and Peter Kirwan (eds), *Shakespeare and the Digital World*, Cambridge: Cambridge University Press, 212–25.

Roach, J. (1996), *Cities of the Dead: Circum-Atlantic Performance*, New York: Columbia University Press.

Rosenthal, D. (2013), *The National Theatre Story*, E-book, London: Oberon Books.

Shakespeare's Globe (2014), 'Press Release: Shakespeare's Globe launches Globe Player', 4 November. Available online: http://www.shakespearesglobe.com/uploads/files/2014/11/2014_11_03_globe_player_release_final2.pdf (accessed 12 July 2017).

Shakespeare's Globe (2017), 'About Us'. Available online: http://www.shakespearesglobe.com/about-us (accessed 13 June 2017).

Stone, A. (2016), 'Not Making a Movie: the Livecasting of Shakespeare Stage Productions by the Royal National Theatre and the Royal Shakespeare Company', *Shakespeare Bulletin* 34 (4): 627–43.

Sullivan, E. (2017), '"The forms of things unknown": Shakespeare and the Rise of the Live Broadcast', *Shakespeare Bulletin* 35 (4): 627–62.

Wardle, J. (2014), '"Outside Broadcast": Looking Backwards and Forwards, Live Theatre in the Cinema – NT Live and RSC Live', *Adaptation* 7 (2): 134–53.

Wark, K. (2017), 'Eliza Carthy and Nicholas Hytner: Art for All', *Start the Week*, BBC Radio 4, 24 April.

Way, G. (2017), 'Together, Apart: Liveness, Eventness, and Streaming Shakespearean Performance', *Shakespeare Bulletin* 35 (3): 389–406.

Worthen, W.B. (2003), *Shakespeare and the Force of Modern Performance*, Cambridge: Cambridge University Press.

Wyver, J. (2017), '"Make Choice and See": Towards a Poetics of Multims', *Shakespeare, Media, Technology and Performance*, University of Exeter, 24 June.

8

The Stratford Festival of Canada:

Mental Tricks and Archival Documents in the Age of NTLive

Margaret Jane Kidnie

The view that performance needs an audience is given comically dark tones of existential dread in Tom Stoppard's *Rosencrantz and Guildenstern Are Dead*. The belief 'that somebody is *watching*,' the Player explains to the eponymous protagonists who in a previous scene slipped out of a show performed solely for their benefit, is 'the single assumption which makes [actors'] existence viable' ([1967] 1992: 63). Years ago Marco de Marinis made the extreme case that live performance 'is, at bottom, no more than the accumulation of the results and resonances of the emotional, intellectual, and pragmatic effects which it provokes in the audience and society' in order to argue, almost from an anthropological perspective, that the sociocultural context within which a theatrical event finds meaning is 'absolutely indispensable' (1985: 384).

For Stoppard and de Marinis, the reciprocity between actors and audience gives purpose and meaning to the live theatrical event, a moment of contact that Peter Brook savours precisely because it is fleeting and transitory. Performance 'is an event for that moment in time, for that [audience] in that place – and it's gone. Gone without a trace ... [T]he only witnesses were the people present; the only record is what they retained' (Brook qtd. in Melzer 1995: 148). Here, Brook returns to a sentiment very like that of Shakespeare's Third Gentleman in *The Winter's Tale*, a character lucky enough to have witnessed 'the meeting of the two kings'. If you were not there, he explains,

'Then have you lost a sight which was to be seen, cannot be spoken of' (5.2.43–4). The issue is not just presence, but a perception of *privileged* access. Being at live theatre is defined by one's own proximity to the event and is further marked by the absence of (at least some) others. To paraphrase Brook, performance in an important sense is for *me*, the present spectator; once it is gone, there remains just me and the memories I take away from it. Theatrical presence, by these lights, always implies a kind of exclusivity.

Familiar conceptions of access have come under strain, however, since the UK's National Theatre, now joined by others including the RSC, has extended the conditions of live performance as a participatory event into spaces beyond the theatre. A spectator's technology-enabled body reaches out to engage in the moment with the actors' reciprocally-enabled bodies, troubling a seemingly self-evident boundary between presence and absence premised on the conjunction of body, place, and time. Nicholas Hytner, former Director of the National Theatre, frequently draws the analogy with broadcast live sports matches (see, for example, Rosenthal 2009), and the form of 'liveness' in which NTLive trades – a live transmission – is perhaps still most familiar through television. The difference between sports and theatre, however, to return to Stoppard and Brook, is that theatre is typically driven by the desire to establish some kind of feedback loop between stage and audience. A sporting match can be played without spectators present to witness the outcome. A stage play, by contrast, depends on the participants' knowledge, both onstage and off, that 'somebody is watching'.

Mark Shenton's insistence that this 'circuit of communication between stage and audience' depends on spectators 'sharing the same air as the performers' (2011) is not as obvious as it might have seemed once. As early as 2004, Nick Couldry identified the pressure that mobile phones and the internet are placing on conceptions of co-presence. Where liveness as a media category has traditionally 'naturalize[d] the general idea that, through the media, we achieve a shared attention to the 'realities' that matter for us as a society', internet and communications infrastructures have enabled emergent, more fragmented 'ways of coordinating communications and bodies across time and space' (356). Chat rooms, live-streaming, breaking news on websites, expanded smart phone functionality along with mobile, and so potentially continuous, connectivity all involve, as Couldry puts it, 'simultaneous co-presence of an audience ... [but lack] a plausible connection to a center of transmission' (357). NTLive taps into this contextualizing communications framework. One makes sense of this opportunity to experience theatre live alongside assumptions about accessibility and co-presence in the twenty-first century that have been learned through the use of networked personal devices.

Although there may be no potential for disruptive or any other kind of bodily contact between actors and audience during an NTLive screening such as happened the evening Laura Looner walked onstage to protest the Public Theater's production of *Julius Caesar* in New York's Central Park in June, 2017, yet there is a type of enhanced communication (communication where previously none existed at all) that the technology-enabled body is invited to accept as live. While some spectators draw strong distinctions between live transmission onto a cinema screen and performance live in the theatre, statistical evidence into patterns of reception accumulating on both sides of the Atlantic suggests that this attitude is not shared by all. The UK-based arts research group, NESTA, found in 2010 that 84 per cent of NTLive audiences agreed they 'felt real excitement' because they knew that 'the performance was live' (Bakhshi et al. 2010: 9). Three years later, a study commissioned by the Canadian Arts Presenting Association found 'some softening' among Canadians around the definition of attendance at live performance: '29% equated watching a show live on TV with attending live and another 16% equated live streaming on the Internet with live attendance' (Petri 2013: 24). For some spectators, simultaneity – whether or not they share the actors' air – seems to have become defining of the live theatrical experience.

Philip Auslander has proposed that this variably felt effect of liveness is intrinsic neither to the technology nor to the spectator. Technology hasn't completely changed the human experience of the world, nor is technology live simply because a spectator says it is. Modifying Gadamer's argument about the claim to contemporaneity a work of art makes on its audience – a demand that is fulfilled only if accepted as such by the audience – Auslander argues that there is a tension between the technology and those who embrace it that depends on 'a willed and fragile act of consciousness' (2012: 8):

> [S]ome technological artifact – a computer, Website, network, or virtual entity – makes a claim on us, its audience, to be considered as live, a claim that is concretized as a demand in some aspect of the way it presents itself to us (by providing real-time response and interaction or an ongoing connection to others, for example). In order for liveness to occur, we, the audience, must accept the claim as binding upon us, take it seriously, and hold onto the object in our consciousness of it in such a way that it becomes live for us ... The experience of liveness results from our conscious act of grasping virtual entities as live in response to the claims they make on us.
>
> (9–10)

The claim digital satellite transmission makes on geographically and/or economically constrained spectators to provide real-time connectivity, marketed as an opportunity to occupy 'the best seat in the house', is one that NTLive patrons might be especially apt to accept as binding. Mary Bernadette Cochrane and Frances Bonner, somewhat disparagingly, describe the 'compliant' spectator who, seated in a cinema, can imagine she is in the theatre (2014: 123), while Hytner intuits that 'mysteriously ... the cinema turns into a theatre. [Although] you're sitting in a cinema, you do not for some reason bring with you cinematic preconceptions' (Holland 2016a). Not only does the technology permit liveness in traditional media senses of that word, allowing a 'representative social group,' as Couldry puts it, to gain access to 'something of broader, "central" significance, which is worth accessing now, not later' (2004: 356), but the form that access takes mimics the live theatrical experience in its exclusivity. One can watch the performance live only in the theatre and the cinema, and when it ends, it disappears.

This perception of disappearance is, of course, governed by production and marketing choices. The digital satellite technology records as it transmits, which is what allows for screenings of the 'same' performance an hour or more later in different time zones and weeks later at Encore presentations; the recording is also eventually made available for viewing in person at the National Theatre archive. This recording will bear further discussion in the context of the HD initiatives recently launched by the Stratford Festival of Canada. The NTLive first-night experience, however, simultaneously cuts in two directions to powerful effect. It summons up now familiar habits of communication grounded in presumptions of accessibility, while *limiting* that access in spatial-temporal ways, so generating a form of disruption that replicates for the technology-enabled spectator a peculiarly theatrical relationship of privileged access to the live event. All that remains after the show ends, forcefully attesting to that audience's participation in the performance as event, are the memories they retain of it.

How then is one to make sense of the reception dynamic that structures both Encore performances and viewings outside of the Greenwich Mean Time zone where there is no live transmission, only stored content replay? The projected images in these cases are the same as those that flickered across the screen in what Peter Holland has described as 'the originating moment' (2016a), but one responds, for example, to broadcast presenter Emma Freud's enthusiasm for an event that is supposedly just about to happen in the knowledge that really, in another part of the world, that moment is already gone. The NESTA report remarks that it has come as 'a surprise' to NTLive to find that the 'benefits of the live experience' seem to be available to audiences at delayed screenings (Bakhshi and Throsby 2010: 14). Although he considers a stored content broadcast not quite as exciting as the live transmission, Hytner likewise notes that 'it seems to work,' perhaps because the audience 'performs the mental trick' (Holland 2016a).

The same 'fuzziness' that media scholars have identified at play in audience perceptions of televisual liveness (Couldry 2004: 355) probably contributes to the delayed screening's participatory effect. The novelty and industry impact of NTLive's transmission of *Phèdre* in 2009, however, was spurred specifically by actors' and audiences' awareness of simultaneity. NTLive makes a greater claim on spectators than, for example, the 1964 Burton *Hamlet* or a television documentary that invites one to share, as though in the moment, a family's experiences as immigrants travelling from South Africa to Britain (Corner 2004: 339–41), precisely because it promises audiences 'the best seat' in a house that is filled *at the time of your viewing* with other spectators. Delayed screenings – not the thing itself but a copy of that unique theatrical event – raise the question of how one might know the fake artwork, and perhaps even what constitutes the fake artwork, in this mediated theatrical environment. Typically in art, the copy or forgery is known through the appraiser's identification of irregularities, through the perception of inconsistencies between the original and its other. Here, however, one can guarantee originality – can know that reception happens in the same moment as production – only by verifying the experience against points of reference, such as clocks, published theatre schedules, and a knowledge of time zones, that are external to the work of art. There is nothing in the screening itself that could expose it as being, as it were, 'in' or 'out' of time.

This makes the experience (usefully) vulnerable to the kind of mental trick that Hytner describes. Spectators in many parts of the world see the same performance at the same time, on the same day – but that day and time sometimes falls in different time zones from that of the actors. 'It seems to work,' Hytner comments, but probably only so long as spectators beyond the domestic UK market prioritize digital satellite technology as the organizing technology behind the 'live' experience; in effect, they lay the claim it makes on them on top of filmed live theatre in order to mimic an absent experience. The spectator of live theatre at a delayed screening *should* be looking at an empty stage. That situation is avoided by substituting a document of performance – a recording – in place of the theatricality of the empty stage as live performance.

At some point an illusion of simultaneity in the context of delay becomes impossible to sustain. Cochrane and Bonner note, for example, that NTLive's on-screen mentions of liveness prompt 'wry laughter' among cinema audiences in Australia, where the first viewing of the recording can be weeks after the originating performance (2014: 122). To the extent, though, that delayed screenings work, it seems that the performance recording sometimes has *enough* temporal proximity to the event to 'enliven' the experience of watching filmed live theatre. In situations of delay, in other words, some spectators seem able to distinguish between a performance that is 'nearly now' as opposed to 'already gone'. This is perhaps the context in which the cinematic community – the spectators in the same cinema with whom one watches a theatrical performance – becomes a defining factor in the experience. Whereas the cinema audience in a situation of simultaneity is one part of a performance reception experience that extends to include both cinema and theatre, the cinema audience at a delayed screening is all there is – it constitutes its own (now closed-off) space of reception.

Stratford Festival HD

The Stratford Festival of Canada has been conducting their own experiments with HD technology and the broadcast of live theatre into cinemas alongside NTLive. Their goal, the achievement of which would be a North American first, is to transfer all of Shakespeare's plays into the cinema from Stratford stages. The first three broadcasts were *King Lear*, *King John* and *Antony and Cleopatra*. These shows played in the 2014 summer repertory and were released in cinemas in 2015.

This project has been realized during the tenure of the Festival's current artistic director, Antoni Cimolino, who wants to share the Festival's work with a larger national and international audience than typically gets to Stratford during the summer season. 'Getting the word out ... was paramount' for Cimolino (Holland 2016a), and, as his phrasing suggests, viewer entertainment was tangled up from the outset with other related objectives. The choice to document performance is often strategic, affording cultural and intellectual prestige to companies that might otherwise be overlooked within the canon of theatre history (Reason 2006: 65–7; see also Rogers, Chapter 9). By asserting a presence on cinematic stages with high-quality digital recordings of past productions, the geographically marginal Stratford Festival is writing itself into international theatrical and academic discourses, establishing the Festival as a world-class Canadian company and potential destination site. While the possible financial benefits of this venture are obvious in terms of growing ticket sales and supporting funding applications, J. Kelly Nestruck's 2013 comment in the Canadian press that the National Theatre and RSC are '*colonizing* Canadian cinemas with their productions of the works of Shakespeare and other playwrights' (my emphasis) suggests that the initiative is not without its cultural politics. Stratford Festival HD ensures that event cinema programming of Shakespeare stagings, both within Canada and abroad, is available in Canadian accents, not just the British accents of the major UK theatre companies.

While superficially similar in terms of venue and marketing, the Stratford Festival cinema experience is modelled quite differently from NTLive. Premiere and Encore screenings are followed up with a television broadcast ('CBC Presents the Stratford Festival'), DVD sales and on-demand streaming. For some of the plays, there is also the 'Performance Plus' website, a free online 'film and text tool kit' targeted at teachers and students, which offers a script and 'director's cut' alongside glossarial notes, interviews with the artists, lesson plans and the recorded live performance video (www.stratfordfestival.ca/Learn). Having successfully negotiated with Equity ownership rights to their recordings, the Festival will be able to market the entertainment and educational value of Stratford Festival HD in a variety of formats for years to come. The contractual situation at the National Theatre is quite different. After the premiere and Encore screenings, there are a few, very selective broadcasts to schools for educational purposes. The recordings are thereafter only available for viewing at the National Theatre archive.

An even more fundamental difference between the two initiatives is that Stratford Festival HD screenings never coincide temporally with the actors' performance. The performances are filmed during the season in front of a live theatre audience, but edited before release. There is an opportunity to reshoot anything that went wrong on the night and to film additional material. The storm scene in *King Lear*, for example, performed on the thrust Festival stage and starring Colm Feore with Stephen Ouimette as the Fool, includes shots of the actors captured by an onstage camera looking out towards the centre block of spectators. The sequence of shots in this scene is visually rich; Joan Tosoni, the director of film, uses the camera work to pull a cinema audience into the onstage storm and emotionally into the storm in Lear's mind. A DVD playback, however, shows that those 'out from back of stage' shots in which the audience forms a backdrop to Lear and the Fool were filmed with extras in the audience; only the first few rows of the stalls are filled, with the seats behind covered with a tan fabric to fool the eye.

The Festival thus prioritizes quality control over the simultaneity, and concurrent risk, of live transmission. The atmosphere at a performance at which the show is filmed is comparable to the National Theatre and RSC experience (see Raby, Chapter 6) – banks of seats are removed to accommodate cameras, Cimolino welcomes the theatre audience to the filming experience before the show begins, and he builds up the performance as a special event – but these spectators are also invited to join the cast for follow-up filming. The Festival is on somewhat familiar ground here, as they broadcast a few of their stagings on CBC television in the twentieth century, mostly in the 1980s, subsequently making the recordings available on VHS, and latterly DVD. They made the shift from television to cinema in the twenty-first century with G.B. Shaw's *Caesar and Cleopatra*, filmed in association with Bravo!, and starring Christopher Plummer.[1] Recorded over three days in front of live audiences in the summer of 2008, the production was screened in eighty Canadian Cineplex cinemas on 31 January 2009. This Gemini-nominated film was followed up in 2010 with a production of *The Tempest*, again starring Plummer and presented by Bravo!, which was recorded over two days in July and screened on 6 November.

Between *The Tempest* in 2010 and the launch of 'Stratford Festival HD' in 2015, just two things changed at Stratford, both in response to the success of NTLive. The screenings became structured not as one-offs, but as an annual season of shows, which, as Nestruck (2013) notes, was a North American first, and the Festival took over control of its own film production. The Festival has reinvented itself, in effect, as a multimedia production company, an opportunity made possible by the falling costs of distribution associated with digital film.

The other substantial shift since 2009, looking beyond Stratford, are the circumstances of reception within which one comes to these screenings. When Stratford 'went to the movies' early in 2009, NTLive had yet to launch. Six years later, Stratford's *King Lear* was part of an inaugural season of three HD films that competed in 2015 with ten productions screened under the NTLive banner, including Ivo van Hove's acclaimed *View from the Bridge*, and Lyndsey Turner's *Hamlet*, starring Benedict Cumberbatch, with its record-breaking domestic and international box office. One's experience of a Stratford Festival broadcast 'filmed live in spectacular HD' is informed by the NTLive production one might have seen, or at least seen promoted, in the same cinema a year, a month, a week earlier. Stratford, of course, is explicit that these films are edited before distribution and that they blend together more than one performance. But the distinction between NTLive and Stratford Festival HD for a North American audience is not as obvious as it might at first seem – both are HD, both are constructed as seasons of programming, both offer an Encore screening, and in both cases the premiere screening of live theatre is recorded film. Without positing that spectators fail to recognize the differences between the two initiatives, the Stratford Festival HD season borrows something from an altered reception culture formatively shaped by its UK cousin. The 'mental trick' that makes NTLive 'work' in North America has the potential to make Stratford cinematic broadcasts, post-NTLive, likewise seem more live – more immediate, more driven by the energies of live performance – than would have been possible prior to the landmark screening of *Phèdre* in 2009.

Live transmission and archival records

That liveness effect, however, is by no means inevitable. I saw *The Adventures of Pericles* (dir. Scott Wentworth) at Stratford's Patterson stage in June 2015 and also went to the HD premiere screening (dir. Barry Avrich) the following May; I have since returned to this production in the Festival archives. The broadcast film is highly watchable and provides a good sense of the staged production – the film script maps onto the promptbook in uncontroversial ways, and the balance of shots allows the viewer to absorb the theatrical space while registering the detail of actors' performances. Avrich's choices are broadly in line with the policy of RSCLive, as described by John Wyver, to 'construct with clarity the narrative of the performance for an attentive audience assumed to be viewing with others in a darkened auditorium' (2015: 290). When the Lords enter to demand that Helicanus rule the country, for instance, the film briefly captures the striking chiaroscuro play of their shadows on the back wall, thereafter occasionally reminding the viewer of this detail of the *mise en scène*. Those theatre spectators whose seats in the thrust space permitted them a view of the back wall had the option, of course, to focus exclusively on this shadow play if they so chose, but the film provides enough screen information for viewers to infer that stage effect even when the shadows are out of shot. Scene changes are typically condensed, at times leading to a slight sense of spatial disorientation as the action moves unexpectedly quickly from one stage set-up to another, but otherwise the pacing of each scene maps nearly precisely onto the fixed-camera recording. The camera work only feels somewhat intrusive in a couple of sequences that are clearly directed to enhance a cinema audience's perception of atmosphere and emotional urgency. During the scene of Thaisa's death at sea, for example, the camera mimics the ship's movement, while tight close-ups sharply angled from below suggest embedded reportage and exigencies occasioned by the storm. A subtle dolly zoom in an earlier scene creates for the viewer a kind of vertigo effect as Pericles reveals to Helicanus his discovery of incest at Antioch.

The Adventures of Pericles was deservedly nominated for two Canadian Screen Association awards (Best Performing Arts Program and Best Performance by an Actor in a Leading Role in a Dramatic Program or Limited series), and yet watching it in the cinema felt, for me, a bit like a trip to the archives with a hundred strangers to watch a recording of a show without access to the playback function. I felt the absence of live performance, perhaps because my memories of seeing it at the Stratford Festival the previous summer were still so vivid. Not only was the understudy, Sean Arbuckle, playing the lead the night I saw it, but I was conscious of watching the show alongside dozens of other Shakespeare scholars, many of whom had never previously been to Stratford. The disappointment I felt reading the programme insertion announcing the casting change shifted at the start of show into the alert intensity that comes from being in an extreme thrust space with a group of actors working at full concentration, spectators and actors alike aware that there is the very real potential for something to go wrong. Spotting both the director and the Festival's artistic director sitting together in the audience only heightened my awareness of the risks of live performance. As it happened, the show unfolded without any perceptible glitches.

Eleven months later at my local Cineplex, with Evan Buliung as Pericles and the film, to use a dated metaphor, in the can, nothing could go wrong. And that, quite probably, is what went wrong. Nothing could go wrong with that performance precisely because it was not live. The 'now' of my cinematic experience of *Pericles* mapped onto a stage in Stratford, Ontario that at that moment was either empty, or in rehearsal with a different show. My active participation in the creation of live theatre – so intense months earlier – turned instead to an archival curiosity about a now historical production, and technical interest in Avrich's choice of shots. Cochrane and Bonner describe a similar disengagement with NTLive premieres in Australia, citing the example of one of them, recently returned from a research trip abroad, spotting the back of her own head in the London audience (2014: 126).

The achievement of liveness – when and if it is achieved – is fleeting, and live transmission will inevitably, eventually, transform into recorded live theatre. While mental tricks might delay that process, at some point the live performance becomes a thing of the past. You were there to see it, technology-enabled or otherwise, or you weren't. I am curious how some spectators' experience of reception liveness might thereafter shape scholarly attitudes to the HD recording. John Wyver, drawing in part on Sarah Bay-Cheng's excellent formalist analysis of 'the inherent distortions of the recording apparatus' behind mediated theatre (2007: 41), has rightly insisted that the creative and technical process behind today's transmissions of live theatre into cinemas 'is in no sense neutral':

Translation to the screen involves a visual language of framings, movement and montage that effects emphases and exclusions, contrasts and connections in a complex play of new meanings. This visual language is clearly closely related to that of film, but at the same time, because it is employed in real time and within a coherent space with its own fixed geometries it is a specifically *televisual* language. I would suggest that we are only right at the beginning of a poetics for this language.

(2016: 10–11)

Erin Sullivan, taking steps to fill this interpretive gap, has recently studied more than a dozen Shakespeare transmissions in order to detail their 'film grammar' (2017: 629). While I welcome ongoing innovation of the methodologies with which we analyse live broadcasts, I am also reluctant to lose sight of some cinema spectators' inclusive experience of the performance specifically as live theatre. To apply Brook's words, quoted earlier, to theatrical *and* technology-enabled audiences participating in a live performance, this was 'an event for that moment in time, for that [audience] in that place', an event, moreover, which is now gone 'without a trace'. Of course performances left traces in Brook's time; his aesthetic and political point is that the 'real' performance lives beyond the ephemeral event only in memory. Eugenio Barba argues, along similar lines, that theatrical performance 'resists time' by continuing to transform in the individual spectator's memory, where it takes on new life (qtd. in Varney and Fensham 2000: 91).

How then is one to approach the HD recording that survives that event, a recording that from the perspective of technology-enabled spectators is a precisely accurate document of *something* to do with the performance in which they participated, but not the performance event itself, nor their experience of it? To analyse this recording as an 'adaptation' of the live performance (Wyver 2014: 104) seems to miss something important about the context of reception that was at one time defining of the experience, and not only because the experience was always in the process of disappearing. These recordings document the technology-enabled spectator's view of the performance as designed by the broadcast director for live transmission. Every seat in a theatre will have its own distinctive features as experienced by the peculiarly-enabled spectator. These recordings document the particularities of the so-called 'best seat' afforded the geographically and/or economically impaired spectator. This is not to imply that they are interpretively neutral, but to insist that the less-than-transparent HD recording survives as a trans-medial archival record of a lost reception moment; not an 'adaptation' of the thing itself, but a *trace* of it. Approached from the perspective of the theatre archives, which is indeed the only way scholars can physically get hold of NTLive recordings once the transmission is gone, these recordings provide substantial evidence of a now-gone production in a manner comparable with – and with many of the same limitations of – the tradition of the fixed-camera recording.

To return to the *Lear* production, for example, the quality of the fixed-camera recording in the Stratford Festival archives is too poor to allow a viewer to see facial expressions with any clarity. Although one gets a broad sense of the stage action during the Fool's banter with Kent upon the Fool's first entrance, Lear (seated just right of centre stage) attracts the viewer's interest only when he jerks his head away as though stung by the Fool's comment that he 'did the third [daughter] a blessing against his will'. The exchange between the Fool and Kent as recorded on HD, mostly handled as a shot-reverse-shot sequence, allows the spectator to watch the face of the speaking actor. But immediately after the Fool invites Kent to 'take my coxcomb', the camera turns to look at Lear, who is staring vacantly ahead, slightly slumped in his chair and angled away from the other two. His brief, albeit sustained, disengagement, unrecorded in the promptbook, is underscored by a knight standing nearby, animatedly listening to the Fool and Kent.

Moments of distraction and blankness such as this accumulated in Cimolino's production to become a keynote of Feore's interpretation of the King. Nestruck, for example, praises Feore's performance as one 'that will ring absolutely real to anyone who has watched an ageing relative losing his mind to dementia' (2014). A slightly different example is found in the play's opening moments, the fixed-camera recording failing to preserve a silent visual exchange between Gloucester (Scott Wentworth) and Edmund (Nigel Bennett), even though both actors are clearly visible on-screen. In the HD recording, the spectator is positioned to register, just as Lear enters, both Edmund's surprise and dismay at hearing that he is to be again sent away, and Gloucester's silencing of that protest with a sharp look. These are surely the kinds of details Karen Fricker has in mind when she claims that these broadcasts are a 'gift' that years from now will tell us 'what early 21st-century Canadian Shakespeare looked and sounded like' (2017).

Without question, as many have noted, there are gaps and distortions in this particular kind of performance record (see, for example, Bay-Cheng 2007; Cochrane and Bonner 2014; Wyver 2015; Holland 2016b), but frustrations associated with what fails to survive the years comes as standard with archival research. My goal here, moreover, is precisely not to privilege one type of recording over the other (or over any other document of performance) in terms of its archival merit. The close-ups and mid-range shots of the HD recording of Edmund's introduction to Kent, for example, discussed earlier, themselves obscure the craft and confidence with which Wentworth works the Festival's thrust stage during his speech about the 'good sport' had at Edmund's conception. Standing with his back to the stage-right audience, he keeps his head turned sharply to the right so that the audience behind, who sees him in profile, feels included in his locker-room joke. Neither of these Stratford Festival recordings captures the performance itself – although the HD version might have approximated it once, despite its pick-ups and trimmed change-over time between scenes, due to the 'mental trick' associated with mediated liveness. Each of them mediates and documents the theatrical event in particular ways according to the company's defined priorities. Regardless of their relative entertainment value, for the purposes of theatre historians, they have a shared authority as partial witnesses to now-lost performances in a production run.

Both Cimolino and Hytner have recognized the post-cinematic commercial value of these digitally-captured performances. Although the National does not make these recordings available on DVD or on demand as Stratford does, Hytner speculates that in twenty years NT's rich and growing catalogue of recordings might well become available to the public. Should that day come, his implicit (and probably accurate) expectation is that they will find a market among curious, or perhaps nostalgic, aficionados of British theatre. Stratford's marketing rhetoric is grounded at heart in a similar appeal to theatrical tradition – potential ticket-buying audiences watching Stratford Festival HD today and in years to come are assured, through this witness to past productions, that this is the kind of theatre the Festival delivers. These HD recordings, whether or not they are available for sale, streamed or on DVD, are inherently archival artifacts, with the potential to alter the way performance scholars and theatre historians piece together analyses of the twenty-first century stage. They are a 'gift', to return to Karen Fricker's word, but they are gifts haunted by loss. An HD recording is a trace that tells us something about a live, for some spectators technology-enabled, performance that now has disappeared, a performance that, by means of twenty-first century communications infrastructures and the habits of use associated with them, rather more spectators were enabled to participate in than would have been the case in previous centuries. You may have seen it after all.

Notes

1 *Oedipus Rex*, which premiered at the Edinburgh Festival in 1956 three years after the Stratford Festival's founding, was filmed for cinema. It was Stratford's first staging recorded for public viewing and the first full-length feature film to be made in Canada. *Peer Gynt* (1957) was filmed for CBC television, followed in 1960–3 by four productions of Gilbert and Sullivan musicals. Prior to 2009, the Stratford Festival had filmed twenty-four of their productions (nine by Shakespeare), all but the first for television. The last three were *Romeo and Juliet* (1993), *Long Day's Journey into Night* (1996) and Timothy Findlay's *Elizabeth Rex* (2000).

References

Auslander, P. (2012), 'Digital-Liveness: A Historico-Philosophical Perspective', *Performing Arts Journal* 102: 3–11.

Bakhshi, H. and D. Throsby (2010), *Beyond Live: Digital Innovation in the Performing Arts*, NESTA Research Briefing, February. Available online:

https://www.nesta.org.uk/sites/default/files/beyond_live.pdf (accessed 12 July 2017)

Bay-Cheng, S. (2007), 'Theatre Squared: Theatre History in the Age of Media', *Theatre Topics* 17 (1): 37–50.

Cochrane, M.B. and F. Bonner (2014), 'Screening from the Met, the NT, or the House: What Changes with the Live Relay', *Adaptation* 7 (2): 121–33.

Corner, J. (2004), 'Television's "Event Worlds" and the Immediacies of Seeing: Notes from the Documentary Archive', *The Communication Review* 7: 337–43.

Couldry, N. (2004), 'Liveness, "Reality," and the Mediated Habitus from Television to the Mobile Phone', *The Communication Review* 7: 353–61.

Fricker, K. (2017), 'Cinematic Version of Stratford's Macbeth Adds Exciting Perspectives: Review', *Toronto Star*, 19 March.

Holland, P. (2016a), 'Peter Holland in conversation with Antoni Cimolino and Nicholas Hytner' (my own transcription), Shakespeare Theatre Association (STA), University of Notre Dame, 30 January.

Holland, P. (2016b), '*Richard II* on Screens', in Joseph Candido (ed.), *The Text, the Play, and the Globe*, Lanham: Fairleigh Dickinson University Press, 155–72.

de Marinis, M. (1985), '"A Faithful Betrayal of Performance": Notes on the Use of Video in Theatre', *New Theatre Quarterly* 1 (4): 383–9.

Melzer, A. (1995), '"Best Betrayal": The Documentation of Performance on Film and Video, Part 1', *New Theatre Quarterly* 11 (42): 147–57.

Nestruck, J. K. (2013), 'Stratford Festival to Film Productions for Worldwide Theatre Distribution', *Globe and Mail*, 7 November. Available online: https://www.theglobeandmail.com/arts/theatre-and-performance/stratford-festival-to-film-four-productions-each-season-for-worldwide-theatre-distribution/article15309859/ (accessed 23 August 2017).

Nestruck, J.K. (2014), 'Stratford's King Lear: Feore's Fallible, Fleshly Lear Is Unforgettable', *Globe and Mail*, 27 May. Available online: https://www.theglobeandmail.com/arts/theatre-and-performance/theatre-reviews/sratfords-king-lear-feores-fallible-fleshy-lear-is-unforgettable/article18864293/ (accessed 23 August 2017).

Petri, I. (2013), *The Value of Presenting: A Study of Performing Arts Presentation in Canada*, Canadian Arts Presenting Association. Available online: http://www.capacoa.ca/valueofpresentingdoc/ValueofPresenting_Final.pdf (accessed 23 August 2017).

Reason, M. (2006), *Documentation, Disappearance and the Representation of Live Performance*, Basingstoke: Palgrave Macmillan.

Rosenthal, D. (2009), 'Dame Helen Is Live and in HD as National Theatre's *Phèdre* Is Beamed into Cinemas Worldwide', *The Independent*, 24 June. Available online: http://www.independent.co.uk/arts-entertainment/theatre-dance/features/dame-helen-is-live-and-in-hd-as-national-theatres-phegravedre-is-beamed-into-cinemas-worldwide–1717792.html (accessed 23 August 2017).

Shenton, M. and H. Hoby (2011), 'Can a Filmed Stage Show Be as Good as the Real Thing?', *The Guardian*, 6 March. Available online: https://www.theguardian.com/theobserver/2011/mar/06/national-theatre-live-frankenstein (accessed 23 August 2017).

Stoppard, T. ([1967] 1992), *Rosencrantz and Guildenstern Are Dead*, New York: Grove.

Sullivan, E. (2017), '"The forms of things unknown": Shakespeare and the Rise of the Live Broadcast', *Shakespeare Bulletin* 35 (4): 627–62.

Varney, D. and R. Fensham (2000), 'More-and-Less-Than: Liveness, Video Recording, and the Future of Performance', *New Theatre Quarterly* 16 (1): 88–96.

Wyver, J. (2014), '"All the Trimmings?": The Transfer of Theatre to Television in Adaptations of Shakespeare Stagings', *Adaptation* 7 (2): 104–20.

Wyver, J. (2015), 'Screening the RSC Stage: The 2014 Live from Stratford-upon-Avon Cinema Broadcasts', *Shakespeare* 11 (3): 286–302.

Wyver, J. (2016), '"Straight from the Theatre" Stuff: Television, Cinema and Live Outside Broadcasts of Shakespeare', Seminar Essay, World Shakespeare Congress, Stratford-upon-Avon, England.

9

Talawa and Black Theatre Live:

'Creating the Ira Aldridges That Are Remembered' – Live Theatre Broadcast and the Historical Record

Jami Rogers

As David Olusoga observes in *Black and British: A Forgotten History*, 'black history and black people [have been] largely expunged from the mainstream narrative of British history, [therefore] we have been left with a distorted and diminished version of our national past' (2016: 25). That diminished version of Britain's history has included the erasure of black and Asian artists from many accounts of Shakespearean performance history. One prime example of this process of erasure – and subsequent reclamation – of British black theatrical history lies in the story of the African American actor Ira Aldridge. Having emigrated from America to Europe, Aldridge became the first black actor to play Othello in London in 1826. Through his theatrical work – including performances as Lear and Shylock – Aldridge was thought to have been 'the most famous black man in Europe' (Chambers 2011: 38), yet he remained little known even after the publication, in 1958, of the 'pioneering biography' of Aldridge by Herbert Marshall and Mildred Stock (Chambers 2011: 2). The reclamation of Aldridge's story since the 1980s has been gradual, comprising disparate scholarly and creative activities that have combined to build a picture of Aldridge's life and career, gradually situating the actor within mainstream British theatrical history.

The myriad difficulties inherent in documenting black theatre history include 'a predisposition toward London, mainstream venues, and their stars' (Chambers 2011: 6). The invention of recording technology has featured in the reclamation of later aspects of black theatrical history, notably in the preservation of the BBC's 1955 *Othello* featuring Gordon Heath. Heath – another African American actor working in Britain – had played the Moor for Kenneth Tynan in an Arts Council tour in 1950. In the absence of archival records of Tynan's theatrical production, the BBC recording preserves this important piece of history in the first televised *Othello* with a black actor in the lead. Today, it is live theatre broadcast that enables the systematic capture of Shakespeare productions and consequently is recording the work of ethnic minority performers for posterity.

In the BBC's influential Shakespeare series Anthony Hopkins' presence as Othello epitomizes the problem of lack of representation that the broadcasts I examine in this chapter seek to address. Hopkins had not been the BBC's first choice to play the lead because, as Peter Plouviez (General Secretary, Equity) recalled, 'The BBC had said that it was obliged to cast a black actor, for without it one could not sell the programme to America' (1990). The BBC's original choice for the part had been the African American actor James Earl Jones. At the heart of the dispute between Equity and the BBC was the casting of an American over his black British peers: whereas, the BBC claimed that 'there were no black actors in Britain capable of playing the part', Equity rejected this claim (Plouviez 1990). The BBC's assertion illuminates contemporary attitudes that contributed to the exclusion of black actors in Britain from roles in classical theatre, even as late as 1979.

The subtext of the BBC's assertion that 'no black actors' were '*capable* [my italics]' of playing the part speaks to the near-wholesale exclusion of black actors from the classical canon. Compared to their African American peers like Jones, black actors in Britain were simply not getting the opportunities to play Shakespearean roles. As the actor Norman Beaton noted in response to the BBC–Equity dispute, black actors had 'sat back patiently, or fumed impatiently, while directors and producers overtly ignored their existence' while classical theatre remained 'virtually a closed shop', supposedly because of the lack of experience of black British performers in the classical repertoire (1979). This 'closed shop' is demonstrable in the data held in the British Black and Asian Shakespeare Performance Database, which depicts how inclusivity in classical theatre did not begin in earnest until the early 1980s. Without the proposed black Othello, the BBC Shakespeare series' ethnic minority representation throughout its thirty-seven plays amounted to Hugh Quarshie as Aaron in *Titus Andronicus*, Ben Kingsley as Ford in *Merry Wives* and a handful of minor roles played by Darien Angadi, Cassie McFarlane and Jay Ruparelia.

Since the BBC Shakespeare series finished airing in 1985, the presence of black and Asian performers in televised Shakespeare has undoubtedly increased. This is not, however, without its problems in terms of representation and ethnic minority performers have often been confined to what has cemented into a 'black canon' of roles, which acts as a glass ceiling for classical actors of colour (Rogers 2013: 22–3). Educational productions such as Tim Supple's 2003 *Twelfth Night* have tended to be more diverse than their counterparts, but the television Shakespeare sector has been dominated by productions of Shakespeare's plays derived from theatrical performance, either as adaptations or filmed in the theatre. Few of these, however, have regularly included the work of more ethnically diverse companies; instead, the choices have created a record of productions with well-known (white) leads and/or directors. For example, Richard Eyre's *King Lear* (NT 1997) featured Ian Holm in the title role with the only two BME performers playing France and Burgundy (Nicholas Bailey and Adrian Irvine). Susanne Greenhalgh and Robert Shaughnessy note the nuance involved in a similar casting for a television adaptation of another National Theatre production: in Deborah Warner's *Richard II* (1995), the titular king had a Court that was 'multiracial, cosmopolitan and sexually liberated' in contrast with 'Bolingbroke's aggressively masculine, exclusively Caucasian entourage' (2006: 96). This does not disguise the fact that the production cast two black actors in a succession of minor roles: Scroop, Fitzwater, Welsh Captain and Bagot. Many of these castings have conformed to what Ayanna Thompson has identified as 'another permutation' of colour-blind casting, one in which performers of colour are cast in ways that 'make a socio-political statement about the character's subjugation, outsider status, untraditional knowledge, and so on' (2006: 7). This on-screen representation embeds discriminatory stereotypes that also send a message that ethnic minority performers are not prevalent in Shakespeare's plays because they are confined to smaller roles.

As well as the glass ceiling, the numeric ratio of white to ethnic minority representation is problematic in many of these recordings of Shakespeare's plays for television. According to the data held in the British Universities Film and Video Council online database, seven stage-to-screen productions of Shakespeare that originated in the theatre in Britain between 1999 and 2007 and were broadcast on British television between 2002 and 2010 (four were also broadcast in America).[1] Of those, two had no ethnic minority presence (Rupert Goold's *Macbeth* and Trevor Nunn's *King Lear* for the RSC, both 2007), while two live broadcasts from Shakespeare's Globe (*Richard II* and *Measure for Measure*) each featured one black actor. The exceptions were the *Hamlet*s of Peter Brook and Gregory Doran, the former employing Adrian Lester in the title role along with a multicultural cast, while the latter assembled a total of eight BME performers for a three-play repertory season, five of whom had roles in *Hamlet* (starring David Tennant) and Trevor Nunn's *Merchant of Venice*, which included six BME performers. These recordings that act as an archive of classical performance are nevertheless often disproportionately white.

More recently, the twenty-first-century resurgence of voices decrying the lack of diversity in the contemporary entertainment industry (from Equity and Act for Change to high-profile performers such as Idris Elba and David Oyelowo) has resulted in a demonstrable increase in diversity on Britain's national stages. Now that both the National Theatre and the Royal Shakespeare Company regularly offer live cinema screenings of productions, coupled with this increased awareness of diversity, live theatre broadcast has become a place where ethnic minority performers are regularly featured. Since NTLive launched in 2009, audiences of their broadcasts have seen black actors play leads in *Othello* (Adrian Lester), *Comedy of Errors* (Lenny Henry) and *Twelfth Night* (Tamara Lawrance), and many other BME performers in significant roles including Macduff (Ray Fearon), Laertes (Kobna Holdbrook-Smith; Giles Terera) and Cordelia (Pippa Bennett-Warner). A worldwide audience encountered a black actor as Othello (Hugh Quarshie) opposite a black Iago (Lucian Msamati) when the RSC broadcast its 2015 *Othello*. In 2016, the RSC's live broadcasts included *Hamlet* set in Africa with a majority ethnic minority cast, including the first black actor to play the Dane on the RSC's main stage, Paapa Essiedu, and in 2017, RSCLive from Stratford-upon-Avon broadcast Josette Simon's Cleopatra as well as Sope Disiru playing the title role in *Coriolanus*. These are also history-making castings, as Simon was the first black British actress to play Cleopatra at the RSC and Disiru the first ethnic minority actor to play Coriolanus at a major venue in the UK.[2]

The RSC has also been systematically releasing each of its RSCLive from Stratford-upon-Avon broadcasts in DVD format for purchase that, in time, will provide an important record of the work of BME artists at the highest level of the profession. This poses questions about the importance of theatre broadcasts in forming a high-quality archive that will rival the BBC's Shakespeare series in a complete box set DVD format. Whereas the RSC and the National Theatre have the resources to have their productions recorded for posterity, however, smaller theatre companies are at a disadvantage in their ability to archive their productions. Much of the ground-breaking work by regional and minority-led theatre companies has therefore been erased simply by virtue of not being recorded. Digital theatre broadcasting provides new opportunities for these organizations to ensure their work can claim a space in the historical narrative.

The remainder of this chapter considers how theatre broadcasts create a potential archive through the prism of two companies: Talawa Theatre Company and Black Theatre Live. The work of the two companies is largely undertaken by practitioners of ethnic minority heritage, most visibly as performers. The discrimination to which performers of colour have historically been subjected underpins my research. I begin by placing the companies within their historical contexts before briefly looking at the productions themselves and considering how live theatre broadcast is important to Talawa's and Black Theatre Live's audience development and archival goals. Live theatre broadcasts, I argue, have become a major means of integrating ethnic minority work in classical theatre's historical narrative.

Talawa Theatre Company and Black Theatre Live

Talawa Theatre Company was founded in 1986 to counteract, as the company's website notes, 'the lack of creative opportunities for Black actors and the marginalisation of Black peoples from cultural processes'. Thirty years later, with the industry now demonstrably more diverse, the work of companies such as Talawa is being integrated into the mainstream subsidized sector, ending years of marginalization. Under artistic director Michael Buffong, Talawa has forged relationships with the National Theatre and Manchester's Royal Exchange, which has enabled the company to stage modern classics by Errol John (*Moon on a Rainbow Shawl*) and Arthur Miller (*All My Sons*) at major venues.

Black Theatre Live, by contrast, is a fledgling consortium of eight small- to mid-scale venues, rather than a stand-alone theatre company. Spearheaded at Tara Arts in 2014, it emerged as an antidote to what Jatinder Verma and Jonathan Kennedy, Tara's Artistic Director and Executive Director respectively, viewed as a sustained crisis in small- to mid-scale touring of black and minority ethnic work. Its structure allows venues to pool resources, effectively co-producing touring theatre and thus spreading the financial risk as well as providing a platform for a sustained national touring programme of new and classical work.

Shakespeare has been embedded in the repertory of Talawa and Black Theatre Live from early in their respective histories. For the former, staging classical theatre was an opportunity 'to show that black-British actors can be judged by the same professional standards as their white counterparts' (Igweonu 2014: 237). Talawa's first production of a Shakespeare play – Yvonne Brewster's *Antony and Cleopatra*, staged in 1991 – was a political act aimed at defying the 'closed shop' in classical theatre Beaton had identified. As Brewster noted recently, '[Talawa's] policy was to give black actors work they weren't being offered – and nobody was offering them the chance to do Shakespeare' (Jays 2016). *Antony and Cleopatra* was a groundbreaking production featuring an all-black cast which also made history by being the first professional production in Britain to cast a black woman as Cleopatra: Doña Croll. *Antony and Cleopatra* was followed by *King Lear* (1994) and *Othello* (1997) in rapid succession, before Shakespeare dropped out of Talawa's repertory for two decades. With Black Theatre Live, Tara Arts' 2014 production of *Macbeth* was its pilot programme. Kennedy recalls that it was 'tied into the application [to the Arts Council] so that we had something solid to start the consortium off with'. As with Talawa's early productions, staging classical theatre ensured that ethnic minority performers were 'playing all those major roles' (Kennedy, personal interview, 15 February 2017).

Kennedy's comment highlights the state of contemporary casting in classical theatre for BME performers. Although Shakespeare is no longer a 'closed shop', there remains a fundamental lack of opportunity for performers of colour to play the first-tier roles of the canon. By 2016, the issue was no longer *access* to work in the classics but instead the question of which roles black and Asian performers were cast to play (Rogers 2013, 2016). The much-heralded 2016 RSC production of *Hamlet* with Paapa Essiedu *signalled* that parity had been achieved. But lurking beneath Essiedu's success is the fact that he was only the seventh BME actor to be cast as Hamlet *on any UK professional stage since 1930*; Raphael Sowole became the eighth in Black Theatre Live's production. Don Warrington was, likewise, only the seventh performer of colour to play King Lear since 1930 (British Black and Asian Shakespeare Performance Database 2015). Along with their own artistic merits, the importance of Jeffery Kissoon's production of *Hamlet* and Buffong's *Lear* lies in the rarity of having a black actor play a Shakespearean lead.

Talawa's *King Lear* and Black Theatre Live's *Hamlet*

Talawa's re-entry into Shakespearean production after nearly two decades was the result of the relationship Buffong had built with Manchester's Royal Exchange. Buffong was encouraged by the Exchange's artistic director, Sarah Frankcom, to consider staging *King Lear* with Don Warrington – who had played Joe Keller in *All My Sons* – a challenge both Buffong and Warrington readily took up (Buffong, personal interview, 16 February 2017). While three years would pass between *All My Sons* and *King Lear*, the genesis of Black Theatre Live's *Hamlet* was closer to five years. Kissoon recalls that he and his collaborator-adaptor, Mark Norfolk, first had the idea after seeing a production of *Othello*. 'After the show,' he said, 'I opened my mouth and I said [to the actor playing Othello], "I want to direct you as Hamlet in Peter Brook's [version of] *Hamlet*"' (personal interview, 11 February 2017). The concept crystallized when both Kissoon and Norfolk found themselves simultaneously in Columbus, Ohio, as Kissoon toured the RSC's 2012 *Julius Caesar* and Norfolk attended a festival screening of a film he had scripted. As Norfolk notes, 'We were [originally] going to do this [*Hamlet*] in Ohio' (personal interview, 11 February 2017), but the production was scrapped at a late stage and Black Theatre Live thus became its producer for a UK tour. In our interview, Kennedy explained:

> What we don't expect is that you have to be a company to make a show...With Jeffery and Mark it was very clear, this was a show they wanted to do. So we found ways of making it work across the consortium

by working in co-production with Watford Palace to build the set and rehearsing at Stratford Circus and for Tara to effectively fund all the contracting and all the pragmatic side and the budget to make the show happen, all under the brand of Black Theatre Live.

The timing for the two productions of *Lear* and *Hamlet* converged in 2016, the year in which the quatercentenary of Shakespeare's death was commemorated.

Both directors built their productions in part around giving voice to the histories that have largely been ignored by the dominant historical narrative. With his concept for *Hamlet*, Kissoon devised a production that signalled an unbroken timeline between ancient Egypt and contemporary Britain, depicted in the design's amalgamation of the two cultures. Immediately upon entering the auditorium for *Hamlet*, the theatre audience was immersed in the sound of a low, vibrating chant of 'ohm', which gradually grew into what Norfolk's stage directions describe as the 'chanting prayers in a mourning ceremony' (2016: 30). The aural landscape changed quickly from the Egyptian motif to a female voice singing a distorted version of *Jerusalem*, which catapulted the audience from Africa to contemporary England through the sound design. The live broadcast emphasized this link with the camera in close-up focusing on an oval metal disk that had Egyptian hieroglyphs carved into it, thus stressing the production's melding of the ancient world with contemporary Britain. Projected onto this set piece, Claudius addressed his new court as the production began with a truncated version of 'Though yet of Hamlet our dear brother's death . . .' (1.2.1–39). As Claudius concluded, a crescendo of drumbeats, fireworks and cries began. With the court transfixed, a thunderbolt struck and the ankh hanging just below the hieroglyph disk split in two; in the blackout the sound faded to church bells ringing in celebration. Kissoon's production thus meshed ancient Africa with twenty-first-century Britain to produce a vision of *Hamlet* that reflected the black British experience.

In his staging of *King Lear*, Buffong also interlaced the ancient and the modern. The director set the production in ancient Britain and Warrington's Lear, wearing a tunic that featured a golden lion's head – symbol both of the English nation and of African nobility – protruding from his chest, entered to the ceremonial sound of a solitary, repeated drumbeat. The dark cloak with large fur collar he wore over the tunic (a staple of productions from Paul Scofield to Laurence Olivier to Antony Sher's 2017 RSC performance) emphasized Lear's Britishness. An image of Britishness was important to Buffong, who explained in his interview that he wanted to depict 'a black King in England in ancient time' because 'the black presence in this country goes back thousands of years' yet it is 'visually something that is never shown'. Seeing a black or Asian English king on stage is a rarity, despite performers of colour having been included in the casts of Shakespeare as a matter of course since the early 1980s.

Creating a record with live broadcast

For Black Theatre Live, the live stream of its production of *Hamlet* was part of the consortium's long-term audience development strategy. As Kennedy recalled, the inclusion of a live broadcast component for the tours grew out of research on 'combinations of venues' as he was putting together the funding bid in 2015. At the time, there were also 'reports coming out about mid-scale touring struggling because it was being taken up by a cheaper version of touring of the classics: NTLive' (see also Freestone 2014 for further context). At the time, venues were suspected of programming screenings of live broadcasts of theatre, rather than touring productions, because of the cost. For Kennedy, it was a choice of 'either fight it and resist it or you can go with it'. In picking the latter course, Black Theatre Live's series of online broadcasts became integral to its brand.

Black Theatre Live approached Pilot Theatre to be its partner for digital recording for the first three years of the project. Founded in 1981, Pilot has emerged not only as a company touring innovative stage work, but also as one of the leaders in integrating digital technologies into arts production. With their provision of HD digital technology and high quality live streaming through a three camera set-up (one camera fixed, two with operators) and the ability to record on disk for posterity, Pilot was the ideal collaborator for Black Theatre Live. The costs of live streaming were budgeted in from the outset and funding was acquired from the Arts Council and various foundations (Kennedy, personal interview). The first live stream to result from this collaboration was the consortium's pilot tour of Tara Arts's *Macbeth*. Directed by Pilot's Ben Pugh and recorded live in March 2015 at Stratford Circus Arts Centre (in east London) with a simple three-camera set-up, the stream was available only on Black Theatre Live's website. Since then, Kennedy has been continually improving the event experience. By the time *Hamlet* was produced, the Web stream had developed 'using a bit of the NTLive model' into including a social media component that consisted of pre-show introductory remarks, live audience reaction at the interval and a post-show Q&A session with director Kissoon and adaptor Mark Norfolk (Kennedy, personal interview; for NTLive's paratexts, see Aebischer, Chapter 7).

With the company more established than the emergent Black Theatre Live consortium, Talawa was able to draw on greater resources for its filming of *Lear*. The company's partnership with the Royal Exchange Theatre in Manchester provided one catalyst for Buffong, who had 'been aware that [live theatre] capture had been done before' at this major regional producing house. Sarah Frankcom's 2014 production of *Hamlet* with Maxine Peake leading a gender-blind cast was arguably the precursor of the broadcast of Talawa/Royal Exchange co-production of *Lear*. Frankcom's production of *Hamlet* had been recorded by MJW Associates and Genesius Productions and directed for screen by Margaret Williams and was subsequently distributed to cinemas for a March 2015 screening, followed by a premiere on Sky Arts and a DVD release.

After initial approaches by Talawa and the Royal Exchange to Sky and other broadcasters failed, interest in filming *King Lear* was expressed by the BBC and Arts Council England, as part of The Space, their initiative to expand audiences using digital technology. When the BBC came to see the 'dress run, then [again] on press night, they were absolutely convinced that this was something that should definitely be captured and also be part of the BBC Shakespeare festival' in 2016 (Buffong, personal interview). Commissioned by The Space, *King Lear* was live-captured in collaboration with Saffron Cherry TV and in association with Lion Eyes TV. It was filmed in the round in front of a live audience at the Royal Exchange with Bridget Caldwell directing. The broadcast was initially streamed on the BBC 'Shakespeare Lives' website and on the BBC's iPlayer in July 2016, two months after it completed its theatrical run at the Birmingham Repertory Theatre.

While the filming of Talawa's *King Lear* and Black Theatre Live's *Hamlet* are undoubtedly impressive achievements for the two mid-scale companies, for both Kennedy and Buffong it was the archival potential that the films provide that was fundamental to their pursuit of the recordings. The lack of an archive of ethnically diverse performances of Shakespeare was one of the catalysts for Buffong, who recalled noticing 'how few images there were of black performers in Shakespeare, almost none in terms of *King Lear*'. The director was determined to create an accessible archive of his production as an antidote to the absence of a record of black performers. As he put it, 'My main thought was it would be great in five or ten years' time if someone got online and was searching "black productions of *King Lear*"', there would be a record of Don Warrington's performance. Kennedy is similarly aware of the dearth of images of ethnic minority performances in the United Kingdom. In looking at the possibilities of an afterlife for *Hamlet*, Kennedy has been 'talking to Digital Theatre who would like the rights to the recordings', which would provide educational access to *Hamlet* and Tara Arts' *Macbeth*, among other productions. This exploration is, as he put it, about 'ensuring that the shows become part of the DNA, as opposed to a one hit, you missed it' event lingering in the memory of the audience. Both Buffong and Kennedy are using live broadcast and captures of their productions to create a space from which ethnic minority performers will no longer be excluded, marginalized and subsequently forgotten. As Kennedy explained, 'What we aren't doing is creating the Ira Aldridges who are forgotten, we're going to create the ones that are remembered'.

The scale of the challenge that ethnic minority companies face in a culture where their voices are persistently marginalized should not be underestimated. The lack of attention to minority ethnic work in the mainstream press contributes to the problem. Despite opening in outer London at Watford and touring to venues in greater London boroughs such as Stratford Circus, east London, and Tara Arts in Earlsfield, Black Theatre Live's *Hamlet* garnered only two mainstream reviews: from *The Times* and the industry newspaper, *The Stage*. Nobody on the Black Theatre Live production team has a clear understanding of why *Hamlet* was under-reviewed. Kennedy recalls there had been 'several reviewers lined up' but 'when they knew the running time of the show and they had to get to Watford and then back to London, they pulled out'. This type of response makes the creation of a lasting archive through live theatre broadcast the only viable strategy for Black Theatre Live in ensuring the Ira Aldridges of today are indeed remembered by future generations.

However, without access to resources equivalent to those of the RSC or National Theatre or a similarly high profile, Black Theatre Live's venture cannot compete on even terms with these companies' broadcast schemes. There is a correlation between the amount of money invested and the ability to create a business model, which sustained NTLive in its launch season with grants totalling just over £110,000 from NESTA and the Arts Council (Rosenthal 2013: 796). According to the NTLive website, over 5.5 million people have watched the broadcasts in over 2,000 venues around the world. For comparison, Kennedy provided the viewing figures across the two-week window during which *Hamlet* was available via the website: 'In terms of the numbers who watched *Hamlet* live, it was 475. Not huge numbers. Then, on the catch-up that ran for about ten days following the live [stream], it was a further 470, so roughly 1,000 people [saw *Hamlet* online].' Like NTLive, the audience was international, with viewers 'watching it in America, in Australia, in Zagreb' as well as Europe and the UK. The small numbers correlate to a lack of awareness of the production, which could make it vulnerable to being erased from history, despite its importance as the first all-black production of *Hamlet* in the UK. Without reviews to document Kissoon's *Hamlet*, the production's digital footprint could prove far more important in creating an enduring record.

Audience growth – and, by correlation, greater post-production awareness – is a key strategy for Kennedy in battling the lack of attention paid to this *Hamlet* in particular and minority-led theatre in general. One cornerstone of this effort is in ensuring that BME work is available to as wide a demographic as possible. In achieving this goal, it was important to Kennedy that the Black Theatre Live consortium included venues such as the Queen's Hall in Hexham, which has a population of 11,000 in a county where the BME community is less than two per cent of its population. Rather than solely serving the minority theatre audience, Kennedy wanted to 'take all of this work across the country to an eclectic mix of venues where the audience is as diverse as our country is'. As well as widening the audience base to be as inclusive as possible, Kennedy is also aware of the need to expand the Web streams to sites with a higher profile. Citing Complicité's live streaming partnerships with organisations such as *The Guardian* and *Financial Times* as a model, Kennedy is also investigating links with similar organizations. As he observed, 'the numbers go up when you've got the media backing in terms of the profile'. Co-opting media websites for live streams would exponentially increase both viewer figures and profiles for the Shakespeare work in which BME artists are engaged.

In its partnership with the BBC, the experience of Talawa in recording *King Lear* for posterity illustrates precisely how a major media partner can drive exposure and profile. With viewing figures that come closer to rivalling NTLive's individual broadcasts, *King Lear* received 160,000 page views when the film was available on BBC iPlayer and on the 'Shakespeare Lives' website. The film is also archived on the resource that enables the recording of UK broadcast television for educational use, Box of Broadcasts, which continues to expand the film's reach to students and staff of participating UK universities. A further 120,000 people tuned in to watch the film on BBC4 when it was broadcast on Christmas Day (Sanjit Chudha [Marketing and Communications Manager, Talawa], private correspondence, 16 February 2017). In early 2018, the film of Talawa's *King Lear* was also released for purchase on DVD, further extending the recording's reach by making it available outside of educational and television archives. In achieving a DVD release, the company has been able to provide it in a format arguably more stable for preservation purposes than a solely online presence. As Buffong noted, the BBC film 'elevates our company' and has 'given us enormous reach' nationally and internationally. The higher profile now enables a person searching the Web for 'black productions of *King Lear*' to immediately find the links to both the production's reviews *and* see that a recording was made of it, potentially fulfilling Buffong's ambition to create a lasting record for future audiences. Given their lack of a level playing field in terms of audience size compared NTLive and RSCLive, the ability to create an archive may be the most important aspect of live broadcasts for minority-led companies.

Notes

1 These seven productions were: *King Lear*, Trevor Nunn (dir.), with Ian McKellen (King Lear), RSC, 2007, broadcast on More4, 2008; *Hamlet*, Gregory Doran (dir.), with David Tennant (Hamlet), RSC, 2008, broadcast on BBC2, 2009; *Macbeth*, Rupert Goold (dir.), with Patrick Stewart (Macbeth), Chichester Festival Theatre, 2007, broadcast on BBC4, 2010; *Hamlet*, Peter Brook (dir.), with Adrian Lester (Hamlet), Bouffes du Nord Theatre, Paris, 2000, broadcast on BBC 4, 2002; *The Merchant of Venice*, Trevor Nunn (dir.), with Henry Goodman (Shylock), National Theatre, 1999, broadcast on BBC2, 2001; *Richard II*, Tim Carroll (dir.), with Mark Rylance (Richard II), Shakespeare's Globe Theatre, 2003, broadcast live on BBC4, 2003; and *Measure for Measure*, John Dove (dir.), with Mark Rylance (Duke), Shakespeare's Globe Theatre, 2004, broadcast live on BBC4, 2004. The four that also had an American broadcast (all on the public broadcast network, PBS) were *Merchant* shown on WGBH/Boston's *Masterpiece Theatre* in 2001 and three on WNET's *Great Performances*: *King Lear* (2009), *Macbeth* (2010) and *Hamlet* (2010).

2 Josette Simon was the first black British woman to play Cleopatra for the Royal Shakespeare Company, which is an important distinction for black British theatre history. In 2013 the RSC's International Playwright in Residence, the African American Tarrell Alvin McCraney, created what the publicity called 'a stripped down, radical new version' of *Antony and Cleopatra*. As a co-production between The Public Theater, New York and Gable Stage, Miami, the casting was half-British and half-American with an African American actress, Joaquina Kalukango, playing Cleopatra. In writing about opportunities for black and Asian British performers in classical theatre, it has sometimes been more useful to exclude actors not based in the UK in order to focus on inherent inequalities within British live and recorded arts. While they are documented in the British Black and Asian Shakespeare Performance Database, they are omitted when discussing British performers working in the UK despite a track record of Americans performing Shakespeare in Britain, often at what was felt to be at the expense of British born performers. This was a particularly acute issue with *Othello* until the 1980s, as James Earl Jones' near-casting as the BBC's Othello illustrates, but it applies to Kalukango's appearance in an American-led production that had most of its performances in the United Stages. In 2014, Lazarus Theatre Company staged *Coriolanus* with the Mountview Academy of Theatre Arts-trained Prince Plockey taking the title role; Plockey thus became the first BME performer to play Coriolanus on a UK stage, according to the information in the British Black and Asian Shakespeare Performance Database at the time this volume goes to press.

References

Beaton, N. (1979), 'A Taste of Nothing Much', *The Guardian*, 9 February.
Chambers, C. (2011), *Black and Asian Theatre in Britain: A History*, London and New York: Routledge.
Freestone, E. (2014), 'What Live Theatre Screenings Mean for Small Companies', *The Guardian*, Theatre Blog, 20 January. Available online: https://www.theguardian.com/stage/theatreblog/2014/jan/20/live-theatre-screenings-elizabeth-freeman (accessed 20 July 2017).
Greenhalgh, S. and R. Shaughnessy (2006), 'Our Shakespeares: British Television and the Strains of Multiculturalism', in M.T. Burnett and R. Wray (eds), *Screening Shakespeare in the Twenty-First Century*, Edinburgh: Edinburgh University Press, 90–112.
Igweonu, K. (2014), 'Talawa', in G. Saunders (ed.), *British Theatre Companies 1980–1994*, London: Methuen Drama, 237–55.
Jays, D. (2016), 'Yvonne Brewster: Nobody Was Offering Black Actors Shakespeare So We Staged Our *King Lear*', *The Guardian*, 1 February. Available online: https://www.theguardian.com/stage/2016/feb/01/yvonne-brewster-king-lear-william-shakespeare-how-we-staged (accessed 20 July 2017).
Norfolk, M. (2016), *Hamlet*, Twickenham: Aurora Metro Publications.
NTLive (2017), 'About Us'. Available online: http://ntlive.nationaltheatre.org.uk/about-us (accessed 20 July 2017).
Olusoga, D. (2016), *Black and British: A Forgotten History*, London: Macmillan.
Plouviez, P. (1990), Letter to the editor, *The Independent*, 27 August.

Rogers, J. (2013), 'The Shakespearean Glass Ceiling: The State of Colorblind Casting in Contemporary British Theatre', *Shakespeare Bulletin*, 31 (3): 405–30.

Rogers, J., ed. (2015), British Black and Asian Shakespeare Performance Database. Available online: https://bbashakespeare.warwick.ac.uk/

Rogers, J. (2016), 'Is the door really open for black actors to star in Shakespeare?', *The Stage*, 6 October. Available online: https://www.thestage.co.uk/features/2016/door-really-open-black-actors-star-shakespeare/ (accessed 21 November 2017)

Rosenthal, D. (2013), *The National Theatre Story*, London: Oberon Books.

Thompson, A. (2006), 'Practicing a Theory/Theorizing a Practice: An Introduction to Shakespearean Colorblind Casting', in A. Thompson (ed.), *Colorblind Shakespeare: New Perspectives on Race and Performance*, London: Routledge, 1–26.

10

Cheek by Jowl:

Reframing Complicity in Web-Streams of *Measure for Measure*

Peter Kirwan

Renegotiating liveness

As I write this paragraph on 13 March 2017, the landing page of Cheek by Jowl's website features a bright orange countdown timer, temporarily overwhelming the rest of this theatre company's web presence (Cheek by Jowl 2017). The countdown stands at thirty-seven days, two hours, thirty-three minutes and fifty-five seconds; at 7.30pm on 19 April, the Event – a live online stream of a performance of the company's current production of *The Winter's Tale*, broadcast from the Barbican – will begin.

The countdown timer is the quintessential marker of online liveness in an age of e-commerce, and one that visualizes real time in order to create anticipation and even tension. The slow countdown of the online timer creates a pressured, delimited temporal environment that positions the viewer in relation to their future rather than their past, establishing an end-point that retroactively casts the present as a period of hiatus, or limbo. When the countdown reaches zero, the viewer shifts from being in a queue to purchasing a ticket, or from waiting to see a production to being a member of an online audience. Potential becomes actuality. The timer invites its audience to envision themselves as part of a future community of participation, and to begin generating that community.

Many cinematic livestreams, including NTLive and RSCLive, use onscreen countdown timers as the audience arrive to take their seats, and again during the interval. These timers are, however, designed for the logistical convenience of a pre-formed audience, helping customers plan their toilet breaks and bar trips, not to help form a community; at my local cinema, the tickets for live broadcasts of theatre productions have usually sold out days in advance, and this pre-configured audience only coheres as a shared presence in the physical environment of the cinema. A theatre production livestreamed over the internet, however, does not have the luxury of advance monetary buy-in. It can hope for an audience many times that of a cinema with finite capacity, but it cannot assume that that audience will show up, nor that they will stay. The 'social opprobrium' that accompanies walking out of a theatre, in Pascale Aebischer's words, is entirely absent when the person is sitting alone at home in front of their computer (Aebischer forthcoming).

Cheek by Jowl's countdown timer stands in for the advance purchase of a ticket, generating an online community with a social investment in the live event. The extended build-up allows the company to utilize its social networks and stakeholders to inculcate a collective sense of participation long in advance of the livestream itself, with the ticking clock rendering the moment of the event newly urgent each time it is viewed. The company sends out repeated reminders on its social media channels, and depends on its supporters to broadcast them further. The invitation is not to buy, but to come together as part of a virtual viewing community. In this way, the company's approach to community generation validates Philip Auslander's observation that the experience of communality in a mediatized environment may be more 'genuinely communal' than that experienced by the physically live audience (2008: 65), the engaged, sociable dialogue on social media contrasting with the communally silent conventions of mainstream British theatre. In generating the collective sense of buy-in, Cheek by Jowl builds the groundwork by which a disparate online audience can take shared ownership of, and shared responsibility for, a live virtual event.

Cheek by Jowl's mission statement has always privileged the sense of immediacy and collaborative frisson that inheres in the quotation from *A Midsummer Night's Dream* that forms the company's name (Reade 1991: 11). Founded in 1981 by Declan Donnellan and Nick Ormerod, the company has grown to be one of the most critically acclaimed of European touring companies, bringing celebrated fresh takes on perennial favourites and neglected gems to six continents, and expanding to produce work in Russian and French in addition to English. Despite the company's prestige, however, it has consistently preferred to tour to mid-size venues (including the Silk Street Theatre at its UK base, the Barbican, rather than the much larger main house), insisting on the importance of 'intimacy and communication' between audience and company and prioritizing the quality of the work (Matthews 1995). Further, as the company's international reach has grown, the number of performances it is able to offer in any one country has diminished, limited by the costs of touring. The result can be that watching a Cheek by Jowl production live is a privilege, aligning the company and audience as fellow travellers who have often come some way to share the experience of being guests at a host venue.

Although Donnellan and Ormerod directed their first feature film, *Bel Ami*, in 2012, it was watching a cinematic screening of a recording of their 1991–5 *As You Like It* in 2014 that convinced them that the appetite and technology for properly remediating their theatrical productions was there. Choosing a free livestream rather than a commercial model is a logical decision for a company which wishes to broaden and diversify its audiences, particularly in younger age brackets, while acknowledging the prohibitive costs of both touring and attending a production. The free livestream also mitigates the company's longstanding policy of limiting the number of school tickets available for each production by offering an alternative mode of viewing, and the liveness of social media and online events can be used to generate excitement among a much broader and internet-savvy crowd.[1] By beginning with two productions in languages other than English, the Russian-language *Measure for Measure* and the French-language *Ubu Roi*, the company opened up its work for potential audience members to try for free, in the hope that those who discovered the company's work through this medium would be more encouraged to make the journey for the in-person experience on future tours. However, the choice of an internet livestream – however much the countdown timer emphasized the importance of the live event – decentres the shared experience of the physical space hitherto at the heart of the Cheek by Jowl ethos. Not only is the viewer of the stream invited to watch the production alone, but the choice of the small(est) screen – the computer, tablet or phone, as opposed to the cinema – risks jeopardizing the scale and effect of a company style that is rooted in a distinctively *theatrical* use of the whole ensemble. Cheek by Jowl's work foregrounds the body of the actor and the spatial relationships between actors; Ormerod's design ('expressive minimalism ... a visual poetry of suggestion', Rutter 2005: 347) emerges in response to, rather than precedes, the rehearsal process, and Donnellan's direction treats space as abstract and fluid, the empty space between actors as significant as that which is occupied.

This chapter focuses on the first of the company's live-streamed productions, *Measure for Measure*, to consider how the livestream affects the company's aesthetic. This production offers a unique opportunity for comparative analysis as two different versions of the livestream survive: the production as originally broadcast, directed and live-mixed by Thomas Bowles, and a second version re-edited by Donnellan and Ormerod for later use, including as part of an interactive education pack.[2] This remixed version – importantly, of the *same performance* – prioritizes different elements of the production, allowing for two similar but importantly different screen versions.[3] For a production with such political bite, particularly in its acknowledgement of the potential complicity of its audience in witnessing scenes of staged aggression, the two versions also invite consideration of Martin Barker's response to Catherine Belsey's concerns about the 'forced perspective' of screen viewing, which Barker argues livecasting can resist (Barker 2013: 50). By reading selected scenes closely, this chapter will unpack the ways in which the two different versions capture empty space, prioritize different characters' subjectivity and ultimately reflect on the live audience's complicity, indicating some of the ways in which the editors of the live camera footage utilize the active potential of liveness.

Framing empty space

Cheek by Jowl's *Measure for Measure* was first staged at Moscow's Pushkin theatre in 2013, and was the first Russian-language production directly produced by Cheek by Jowl, following previous successful collaborations with the Maly Theatre and the Chekhov International Theatre Festival. It had toured to Spain, France and Estonia before arriving at the Barbican, where the live broadcast was filmed in partnership with the Roundhouse on 22 April 2015, for the relatively low cost of *c*. £15,000, and broadcast via the company's own website and *The Telegraph*, a distribution partnership in which no money changed hands. The company's decision to begin its live-streaming experiments with a Russian-language production already electronically remediated in its live setting via surtitle screens offered a bold statement about Cheek by Jowl's identity as a multilingual company. *Measure for Measure* was celebrated long before its arrival in London, with reviewers across Europe repeatedly turning to the resonances with Putin's Russia, 'anatomised' in the show (Cheek by Jowl 2015). Performed in contemporary dress, the production explored the severity of a state clamping down on deviant sexuality, the moral complexity of a ruler who watches everything and manipulates his own homecoming, and the compromized choices of Isabella, captured in the poignant final scene as brother Claudio gave her the cold shoulder, cradling his wife and child while Anna Khalilulina's Isabella looked on tearfully.

This emotional and political impact was dependent on a visual structure that enabled watching and reacting. A central pillar of Cheek by Jowl's style is the presence and participation of the whole ensemble; indeed, in productions as recent as *Macbeth* (2009–11) and *'Tis Pity She's a Whore* (2011–14), the majority of the company remained visible onstage for the duration of the performance. Members of the Cheek by Jowl ensemble move fluidly between named characters, unmarked bodies and a liminal state in which actors present their characters while keeping them spatially detached from the scene in question, often responding visibly to scenes in which they are not active. In these productions, characters are constantly watching, a state particularly apt for *Measure for Measure*, a play constructed around the Duke's surreptitious surveillance of his people. Especially at the production's start, a tightly knit body of characters silently watched the action, leading to the stage's construction around a tripartite structure of gazing: the characters within a given scene at one another; the onstage chorus at the primary scene; the audience watching both scene and chorus.

For much of the production, the disguised Duke (Alexander Arsentyev) joined the Chorus in order to watch events (often in horror) regardless of his literal presence in a scene. When I first saw the production in Moscow, the Duke's constant presence as both participant and observer rendered him quite clearly (to me, at least) the central character of the production.[4]

In the Silk Street Theatre at the Barbican, the company utilized the full width and depth of the stage, providing a cavernous environment for the different groups onstage to watch one another, often over large distances; as Christopher Innes and Maria Shevtsova put it, 'all the better to see and be seen, the eyes leading to what is at stake between them' (2013: 213). The wordless opening sequence, which established the Duke's spatial relationship to the chorus within Ormerod's 'expressive minimalism', offered a particular challenge to the cameras in its use of a great deal of empty space, and the extreme differences in the two versions of the stream are instructive. The production was filmed using four cameras, as explained in Table 10.1.

The four cameras evoked a range of the potential perspectives from which audience members in the theatre could view the production, as well as showing part of the theatre audience, doing some virtual community-building for the viewer at home. None of the cameras appears to have had the ability to move, though C and D could pan and zoom. The proximity of stage and audience in this studio theatre, where front-row audience members have their feet on the stage, meant that cameras C and D were often shooting at an almost perpendicular angle to the actor-audience axis when following actors downstage.

Measure for Measure opened to a set comprised of five red cubes, three in a horizontal line bisecting the stage at roughly halfway along the upstage-downstage axis, and two at extreme stage left and right, a little downstage of the others. The five cubes formed a downstage playing space, about half the area of the whole stage, brightly lit by hanging vertical lamps whose

TABLE 10.1 *Camera positions, Cheek by Jowl's* **Measure for Measure** *broadcast (2015); the designations of letters to cameras are my own.*

Camera A	Situated at the very top and back of the raked audience seating, capturing a wide angle overview in which audience members were visible.
Camera B	Dead centre of downstage, within the audience and almost at stage level.
Camera C	At stage level in front of the live audience, at extreme stage left.
Camera D	At stage level in front of the live audience, at extreme stage right.

beams could be seen against the surrounding blackness. During this opening sequence, a group of individuals, closely packed, appeared between two of the cubes. The group moved around the stage in a sequence of choreographed positions until Arsentyev's Duke was produced from within the ensemble and separated from them. He then moved independently while the group responded to him; he seemed at some times to flee the group and at others to be coaxed into sitting on a chair. The sequence used the whole width and much of the depth of the stage.

On the livestream, the dominant viewpoint in this extract is that of Camera A, used for two minutes and fourteen seconds of the whole sequence (about half of the total five minutes and seven seconds from lights rising to the first line of dialogue). This wide angle captures the shape of the entire stage space, doing the work identified by Susanne Greenhalgh for 'cinema audiences [who] need the theatrical space and what it symbolizes to be clearly delineated ... [with the] juxtaposition of wide or high angle establishing shots' (2014: 259) and here emphasizing the distinctive Cheek by Jowl interplay of bodies and space. Actors' faces are not distinguishable for large portions of the sequence, and the overall effect is of a body splitting away from a mass. This individual body is positioned constantly in relation to the mass, making visible the gulf of space between them at certain moments. The 'strange formality' of the wide shot, and the palpable anxiety of the Duke, allow for an emblematic reading of the figure isolated from the pack, produced by but newly separate to the people (Barker 2013: 15).

By contrast, Camera A is entirely absent from the remixed feed, which prioritizes the off-centre angles of Cameras C and D that give medium and close shots of the actors' faces, with regular reference to Camera B to indicate the broad shape of the stage. The whole stage space is never visible: Camera B only shows the three central red cubes, which makes the angles from C and D disorienting at times, as they regularly frame actors at almost exact right angles to B against the otherwise unseen cubes at the far sides of the stage, resulting in what Erin Sullivan refers to as 'a series of visually disconnected zones that can be difficult for remote audiences to imagine back together' (Sullivan 2017: 641). The cameras instead work to fill the frame with bodies and colour, as opposed to the black empty space that fills Camera A. The difference between the two versions is most apparent as the Duke and Chorus react to one another across the width of the stage. The Duke is at extreme stage left, the Chorus at stage right. They move upstage and then downstage together, mirroring one another's movements. The Chorus then begins crawling across the floor towards him; he paces and keeps his distance. In the live version, Camera A's view emphasizes the gulf between the two groups and the symmetry of their movements. The remixed version, however, cuts between Cameras C and D in a standard angle/reverse-angle pattern, alternating the views of the Duke and Chorus as they react to one another, privileging their emotional reactions (confusion and fear for the Duke, hopeful expectation for the Chorus). The remixed version of this opening sequence is far more in keeping with screen conventions, with its privileging of facial performance, relative close-up and emotional reaction. The livestream retains something more of the theatrical experience with its constant reminders of the entire *mise en scène*, its insistence on establishing the actors within delimited space, and the emphasis on blocking and symmetry over individual performance. The remix reflects the transition of this product from theatre to live broadcast to edited theatrical film, remediating liveness for the Web viewer and education pack user, and in doing so the production conceptually shifts; the 'gain' is the access to expression and internal conflict from multiple potential perspectives; the 'loss' is the stage environ that makes formal sense of the blocking.

In the first few minutes of Cheek by Jowl's first live broadcast, then, a tension arises between the company's hallmark use of empty space and the ability of the screen to capture that space. In a Cheek by Jowl production, abstracted space disrupts realistic conceptions of human interaction; for instance, when placing characters having an intimate conversation at opposite ends of the stage, talking to each other as if in direct proximity, the empty space speaks to the psychic and emotional distance between the two. Space is always active in a Cheek by Jowl production, representing the conflicts and barriers between people. The early spatial separation of the Duke and Chorus is significant given the close bond with which they began; yet in the remixed version, with its preference for 'more insistent mediations of multiple camera shots framed tightly on individuals and small groups and the editing between these' (Wyver 2014: 106), epitomized in the cross-cutting between Duke and Chorus, the active space disappears. They are still clearly separate, but the precision and fluidity of that separation disappears in editing.

Framing the subject

While the livestream may have captured more of the spatial dynamics of this opening sequence, it makes for poor screen entertainment, especially for an audience unused to fixed-camera archive recordings. The relatively static screen and depersonalized character movements of the livestream are replaced by close attention to expression and reaction in Donnellan and Ormerod's re-edit, providing direct access to the emotional stakes of the scene: a decision that both takes advantage of the opportunities provided by close-ups, and makes the remixed version more useful to the education pack with which it is paired, which includes several activities and interviews focused on character.[5] Yet the choices of which cameras capture the action have the potential to subtly but significantly change the meaning of the production, as for example in the case of the introduction of Andrei Kuzichev's Angelo.

The opening wordless sequence ends with the Duke standing with Escalus, and the two of them engage in an edited version of the opening dialogue of 1.1, at which point both filmed versions align more closely, prioritizing a close shot from Camera C that frames the two characters entirely. The livestream, however, includes a cutaway to Camera A, which reveals the position of the Chorus at stage right (where they have presumably been standing throughout the conversation) watching the two; the remixed version remains focused on the diegetic scene between the Duke and Escalus. When the production reaches Escalus's lines 'If any in Vienna be of worth / To undergo such ample grace and honour, / It is Lord Angelo' (1.1.22–4), the Chorus jogs across to stage left, sweeping Escalus with them and leaving the Duke alone centre-stage, holding out his hand to the newly-absent Escalus. The Duke then removes his glasses to wipe them. In the livestream, Camera B captures the whole sideways movement, including Escalus being caught up as if in a tide by the jogging ensemble. A cut to Camera D shows the reverse angle, with the Chorus now at stage left looking back at the Duke; then, a dramatic cut to Camera A reveals that another lone figure has been left at stage right: Angelo, dressed identically to the Duke, who has been revealed from within the Chorus exactly as the Duke was earlier. The Duke starts when he notices him.

In the remixed stream, this whole sequence shifts to privilege the Duke's perspective. On 'It is Lord Angelo', the sound of the jogging is heard, but the shot stays with Camera C. The Chorus suddenly enter the frame from nowhere and move through it; while the sweeping away of Escalus remains visible, it is the Duke's reaction that is central. The shot then shifts to Camera D (as with the livestream), but stays with Camera D until he turns and jumps. Only *then* does a cut to Camera C reveal Angelo in a medium shot, framed against the red background of one of the cubes. For viewers of the remixed version, Angelo's location on the stage is unclear.

The differences here offer a fundamental recategorization of theatrical space, to extraordinary effect. The livestream offers a reading of the scene as an emblematic transfer of power in the stage space. In the play, Escalus and the Duke talk and Angelo enters to them. In Cheek by Jowl's stage version, the entire spatial organization of the stage switches to indicate a change of focus, or 'target', to borrow Donnellan's preferred term for an actor/character's objective (Donnellan 2005: 16–29). The Chorus sweeps across the stage space like a pendulum, replacing the actor playing Escalus with the isolated figure of Angelo, to whom the Duke now turns. Further, Angelo is present and distinguishable long before the Duke reacts to his presence, creating a visual dramatic irony that contributes to the ongoing nervousness of the Duke. In the remixed version, Cameras C and D focalize the scene through the Duke's perspective. Camera C is predominant while the Duke and Escalus talk, showing the Duke's full face but the back and side of Escalus's head. The movement of the Chorus across the stage is effectively non-diegetic, the camera ignoring it to stay on the Duke. Only once the Duke is aware of Angelo's presence does the camera show him.

As with the earlier elision of active empty space, Donnellan and Ormerod's *filmic* choice in the remixed version to conceal Angelo until the Duke sees him operates against another recurring feature of their *theatrical* practice. Cheek by Jowl's dramaturgy highlights characters when they are spoken about as well as when they are literally present in a scene, what Innes and Shevtsova refer to as 'tableau-freeze . . . signifying that they belong to the whole story of the play', although in recent years the company has shown a preference for a mobile rather than frozen visible ensemble (2013: 215). The remixed version nixes this, substituting the (differently effective) jump cut between two very similarly dressed men, now aligned within screen space (their position within the frame) rather than theatrical space (their symmetrical revelations and blocking). The remixed version re-reads the scene from the Duke's perspective, isolating him within a flurry of movement and disconnecting him from his spatial surroundings. The loss is the symbolic resonance of Angelo's own spatial isolation; while both edits frame him as being alone, the distinction is much less clear and the distance of his physical separation is, again, elided in the remix. The gain is the emotional alignment of audience with protagonist, with the viewer invited to share the Duke's surprise at Angelo's unexpected presence.

Something subtler, and perhaps unintentional, is at work in the move from theatrical production to livestream to remixed digital video. Across the three versions, the ensemble and the empty space become progressively less visible, while individual facial expression and subjective experience come to the fore. In the livestream (and, I would argue, the production in the theatre), the dominant visual motif is of subjects *being watched*; in the remixed version, it is the subjects *themselves looking*. This is also a movement from the structured politics that position an individual in relation to the state, to the experience of an individual discovering their own subjectivity, as is perhaps most apparent in the first encounter between Angelo and Isabella in 2.2. Pascale Aebischer has written about the ways in which the live broadcast repeatedly 'refused to focus on Isabella at key moments or showed her from the point-of-view of a character in whose eyes she embodied repressed sexual desire rather than chastity', and the partial rehabilitation of this by Donnellan and Ormerod in the remixed version (Aebischer forthcoming). This is, inevitably, not neat enough for an absolute distinction between versions – in 2.2, for instance, the livestream focuses on Khalilulina's Isabella almost without interruption, while the edited version's shot/reverse-shot mode repeatedly turns from her to Angelo – but most of the shifts between livestream and remix contribute to Isabella's experience, including framing her as she waits to be admitted to Angelo, where the livestream lingers on him in close-up. The most important effect of this comes as she sits down. In the remixed version, Camera C frames her as she sits and responds to the unseen Angelo; in the live version, Camera B shows her sitting down *in front of him*. The live feed gives an overview of the scene of conflict, structured by the theatrical space between the actors; the remixed version prefers her experience of the scene, capturing her subjectivity.

Framing complicity

These close readings can only be indicative, but cumulatively they offer a version of the performance that, I suggest, lends itself to a readjustment of the production's politics. In these scenes, Bowles's original live edit privileges the Duke, the ensemble and the space of the state, while Donnellan and Ormerod's remixed version privileges Isabella, individual reaction and the personal space. Both versions are partial, each version focusing on aspects deprioritized by the other while offering a coherence relative to its own priorities. In allowing such different readings of the production's interests, I would like to conclude by arguing that the existence of these two edits draws attention to the relative complicity of the audience in the events of the play, particularly within a 'live' – if virtual – environment.

While the remixed version gives much more space and time to Isabella, the Chorus is rendered largely invisible. In the theatre, the constant presence of the Chorus was a defining aspect of the production, stressing the surveillance state and always showing the reactions of those affected by the main action. 'The space is not neutral', to borrow one of Donnellan's adages, and a character 'cannot do whatever she likes in the space' (Donnellan 2005: 125); in this production, the Chorus of onlookers loads the space with meaning. The dynamic of on-stage watching particularly served the character of the Duke, who was usually at the front of the Chorus when not directly involved in a scene. The shot/reverse-shot structure of the remixed version understandably focuses on the participants in the scene, and thus inadvertently reads the work of the Chorus as reactive, passive, and thus excludable, so deprioritizing the role of the Duke.

At the end of 2.2, Angelo delivers his soliloquy revealing his reaction to Isabella. The remixed version shows this by alternating between Cameras B and D, framing Angelo as by himself – as indeed the scene calls for him to be. Yet the live version includes an establishing shot from Camera A that reveals the Chorus are standing at upstage right, watching – and implicitly judging – Angelo as he speaks. When Angelo crosses to stage right during his soliloquy, the remixed version continues to frame him with Camera D, which keeps him in his isolated psychic space, rather than switching to Camera C, which would have framed him against the Chorus. By including or excluding the Chorus, the editors of the screen versions invite very different readings of the speech. However, the remixed version's decision to exclude the Chorus is thwarted by a moment in which Angelo starts fondling and smelling the chair on which Isabella had been sitting, at which point the Chorus cross to him. The live version, which had already shown the Chorus at the side of the stage, reads this as a moment in which the Chorus are prompted into motion by the extremity of Angelo's action. In the remixed version, which remains in close-up on Angelo, he is suddenly and inexplicably joined in the frame by a selection of unannounced feet.

This moment is revealing of the difficulties inherent in translating Cheek by Jowl's use of theatrical space and non-diegetic activity to the screen. The shots of the remixed version read the scene literally, preserving the integrity of the scene's imagined location and Angelo's isolation, but treating the scene in this way does not account for the intervention of the non-diegetic Chorus, unseen by Angelo but intruding in his theatrical space. Cheek by Jowl's visual aesthetic is fluid in the theatre: not only do characters appear and move among scenes that they are not supposed to be participating in, but their scene transitions deliberately overlap dialogue and blocking, so that scenes blur into and comment on one another rather than being demarcated. While the remixed version better captures the emotional arcs of individual characters and scenes, this comes at the expense of a frame that shows a confused image when confronted with the non-diegetic, fluidly theatrical aspects of the production.

Even more importantly, the two versions frame complicity differently, as is most apparent in 2.4. As with 2.2, the livestream makes greater use of Cameras A and B to keep both actors in shot at the same time, framed as sitting together at the same table, whereas the remixed version uses a shot/reverse shot format to juxtapose Angelo and Isabella as they speak (and, as Aebischer [forthcoming] points out, to better privilege Isabella's experience of the scene). More significant, however, is the divergence in the treatment of direct address. When Angelo asks Isabella 'Who will believe you?' (2.4.153),[6] he gestures downstage. The remixed version stays focused close on the two actors, but in the livestream the shot cuts quickly to Camera A, showing and thus implicating the theatre audience as the 'Who', and making clear their silence. Subsequent to this, Angelo moves to centre stage, sits in a chair and unbuckles his belt. The remixed version continues capturing this using Camera B, showing the space between the two actors and framing this as a private moment; the livestream uses Camera A, not only continuing to implicate the audience as silent bystanders, but more pointedly bringing the Chorus back into the shot. The attempted rape that follows is a private scene of trauma in the remixed version, but the livestream invites the viewer to note the silent observation of this by two separate groups of onlookers. Following the assault, as Isabella begins her soliloquy 'To whom should I complain?' (2.4.171), the livestream again cuts out to Camera A, which not only puts pressure on the theatrical and, implicitly, the Web audience to identify themselves as the 'whom', but also shows Angelo sat back at his desk, nonchalantly going through his papers as if nothing has happened. The remixed version, shown almost entirely from Camera C, isolates Khalilulina's Isabella against blackness, removing her from both the subject of her monologue and from her audience, suggesting that she is indeed alone in her complaint. The remixed version, I suggest, better captures the pathos of Isabella's cry; the livestream better holds to account the abusers and those rendered complicit in the abuse by their silence.

It is on this last point that I wish to close by returning to the value of liveness, which in the context of these two versions of the same production allows for the challenge to Belsey's 'forced perspective' that Barker believes the livecast can offer (Barker 2013: 50). The remixed version of this production was designed for use after the event, primarily as part of the company's education package. While a real-time document of a live performance, therefore, it was never watched live; its presence is a construct of the past, its actors locked into a mechanically reproduced moment. Its focus on emotional truth as captured in the faces of actors is better suited to the recorded medium it occupies. The live webcast, by contrast, carries with it – as do all live broadcasts – the spectre of the unknown, the possibility of the unexpected. The unexpected is usually imagined as the potential for failure, the frisson of knowledge that something may go wrong. But the evocation of complicity and the implicit judgement of a silent audience speaks to something that only resonates as part of the live event, in which it remains possible (if highly unlikely) that an intervention could happen and the assault could be stopped, that something could go *right*, from the perspective of social responsibility if not theatre etiquette. The livestream acknowledges the choice I have made to participate in a virtual, real-time community by foregrounding, at these moments, the presence and silence of the physical audience, an audience that is dispersed in the version released for post-event viewing, but with whom I share complicity in the live moment. The choice to be part of a live event is also the choice to be accountable.

Notes

1. The company's policy to limit school groups to twenty-five per cent of the total audience, and to split large parties into groups of four or five around the auditorium, was designed to limit distraction and help younger audience members 'gain a fully adult experience of what going to the theatre is all about' (Cheek by Jowl 1990).
2. This chapter is possible only thanks to the generous support and access provided by Cheek by Jowl, especially Dominic Kennedy and Sarah Fortescue, to both versions. The Cheek by Jowl website includes a 'screenplay' prepared by Emma Davis (2015), assistant producer for the broadcast, which the reader may wish to consult for visual reference. The 'screenplay' is a shorthand camera script for the camera operators, but captures a detailed picture of the production's main blocking.
3. Camera rehearsals take place about five days before the broadcast, without Ormerod and Donnellan in the room. The directors then re-watch the recording of the camera rehearsal and provide notes to the director for the livestream. The decision to re-edit the live broadcast for later use, including the education pack, was not repeated for the next broadcast production, *Ubu Roi*, filmed in New York on 26 July 2015. I am grateful to the company's Executive Director, Eleanor Lang, for her insight and information about the project and process.
4. The Duke was played by Valery Pankov at this performance, 24 November 2014 at the Pushkin Theatre. It is worth noting that I do not speak Russian, and

performances in Moscow were obviously not surtitled; this interpretation, therefore, may speak as much to my unusual dependence on the visual dynamics of the production rather than the oral/aural qualities.

5 The Education Pack is not publicly available, but is provided on request by Cheek by Jowl to schools and academic institutions.
6 Here and elsewhere I use the wording of the on-screen subtitles; the Arden edition records the line as 'Who will believe thee, Isabel?' (2.4.153).

References

Aebischer, P. (forthcoming), *Shakespeare, Spectatorship and Technologies of Performance*, Cambridge: Cambridge University Press.

Auslander, P. (2008), *Liveness: Performance in a Mediatized Culture*, 2nd ed., London: Routledge.

Barker, M. (2013), *Live to Your Local Cinema: The Remarkable Rise of Livecasting*, Basingstoke: Palgrave Macmillan.

Cheek by Jowl (1990), poster for Box Office staff promoting *Hamlet*, V&A archives THM 24/2/12.

Cheek by Jowl (2015), '*Measure for Measure*: Reviews', *Cheek by Jowl*. Available online: http://cheekbyjowl.com/measure_for_measure.php#reviews (accessed 21 April 2017).

Cheek by Jowl (2017), 'Home', *Cheek by Jowl*. Available online: http://www.cheekbyjowl.com (accessed 21 April 2017).

Davis, E. (2015), '*Measure for Measure* Screenplay', *Cheek by Jowl*. Available online: http://archive.cheekbyjowl.com/wp-content/uploads/2015/04/Screenplay.pdf (accessed 21 April 2017).

Donnellan, D. (2005), *The Actor and the Target*, rev. ed., London: Nick Hern Books.

Greenhalgh, S. (2014), 'Guest Editor's Introduction', *Shakespeare Bulletin*, 32 (2): 255–61.

Innes, C. and M. Shevtsova (2013), *The Cambridge Introduction to Theatre Directing*, Cambridge: Cambridge University Press.

Matthews, B. (1995), Fax Correspondence, 28 April, V & A archives THM 24/2/17.

Reade, S. (1991), *Cheek by Jowl: Ten Years of Celebration*, Bath: Absolute Classics.

Rutter, C.C. (2005), 'Maverick Shakespeare', in B. Hodgdon and W.B. Worthen (eds), *A Companion to Shakespeare and Performance*, Malden, MA: Blackwell, 335–58.

Sullivan, E. (2017), '"The forms of things unknown": Shakespeare and the Rise of the Live Broadcast', *Shakespeare Bulletin* 35 (4): 627–62.

Wyver, J. (2014), '"All the Trimmings?": The Transfer of Theatre to Television in Adaptations of Shakespeare Stagings', *Adaptation* 7 (2): 104–20.

PART FOUR

Reaction Shots

11

The Curious Incident of Shakespeare Fans in NTLive:

Public Screenings and Fan Culture in Japan

Kitamura Sae

In 2006, Henry Jenkins defined convergence as 'the flow of content across multiple media platforms, the cooperation between multiple media industries, and the migratory behavior of media audiences who will go almost anywhere in search of the kinds of entertainment experiences they want' (2006: 2). In a convergence culture, users, creators and distributors participate in transmedia activities. Users access a universe in which franchises are created in various media simultaneously, and companies present each work across different media platforms. Theatre broadcasts enable viewers within geographical reach of the originating theatres to experience the media landscape of convergence, as they can enjoy the same production through stage performances and, additionally or alternatively, through public screenings.

This framework of convergence, however, cannot be readily applied to the recent public screenings of Shakespearean plays by NTLive in Japan. These screenings bring into sharp relief the crucial role of the cultural context of reception. Because Japan is geographically and linguistically distant from London and has rarely undertaken tours of London-based productions, playgoers in Japan have long been denied access to those popular theatrical performances. However, the introduction of public screenings has allowed Japanese audiences to enjoy high-profile Shakespearean productions; the audience attends cinemas in Japan because they cannot visit theatres in London.

This chapter defines this type of transmedia behaviour as 'negative convergence', a phenomenon that occurs when a fan cannot obtain a certain type of media experience for geographic, social, economic or cultural reasons and settles for a replacement. 'Negative' has multiple meanings, two of which matter here: 'expressing the absence rather than the presence of distinguishing features' (*OED* 4a) and 'unhappy, unpleasant . . . uncomfortable' (*OED* 4d). Sometimes fans must choose an unsatisfying media product due to a lack of access to the product that they would have preferred. These situations highlight the willingness of fans to search for an experience that will please them despite the barriers between media, as well as negative feelings, such as frustration with cultural environments that offer only limited platforms and poorer-quality products. For these fans in Japan, public screenings are opportunities for negative convergence and provide sometimes frustrating experiences. This essay discusses how these fans in Japan have responded actively to the changing cultural situation in the global world: using social media, they have appealed directly to distributors to improve their audience experience.

NTLive in Japan

NTLive launched its Japanese project (hereafter NTLive Japan) in 2014 with *Frankenstein*, starring Benedict Cumberbatch and Jonny Lee Miller. The film distributor, Culture-ville, distributed the shows in collaboration with TOHO Cinemas, a Japanese cinema chain. Marketing is under the strict control of NTLive in the UK (hereafter NTLive UK; 'Interview' 2014). As of February 2018, NTLive Japan had screened twenty-four productions, five of which were Shakespeare plays: the 2013 production of *Coriolanus*, directed for the stage by Josie Rourke, for the screen by Tim van Someren and starring Tom Hiddleston; the 2014 production of *King Lear*, directed for the stage by Sam Mendes and for the screen by Robin Lough; the 2010 production of *Hamlet* and the 2013 production of *Othello*, both directed for the stage by Nicholas Hytner and for the screen by Robin Lough; and the 2015 *Hamlet*, directed for the Barbican stage by Lyndsey Turner, for the screen by Lough and starring Benedict Cumberbatch. Some productions, such as *Frankenstein* and the 2015 *Hamlet*, had 'encore' screenings.

As evident from the attention these showings received from gossip websites, the stars constitute the principal appeal of NTLive Japan. Shakespeare's name did not have much pull in Japan, unlike the reception of early NTLive productions in the UK (Barker 2013: 34–35; for Hong Kong, see Ingham, Chapter 12). According to Culture-ville and TOHO Cinemas, however, Cumberbatch and Miller's popularity, owing to their appearances in the TV series *Sherlock* and *Elementary*, *was* an incentive to strike a deal to make the broadcasts available in Japan ('Interview' 2014). In response to the arrival of *Frankenstein*, *Joshi-Spa!*, a women's gossip website, enthusiastically welcomed the broadcast, lamenting that 'you can get as much information about such theatrical performances as you like on the Internet, but you can never watch them ... This is practically torture for fans' (Biwako 2014).[1] The article states that Japanese female fans had tried to visit the National Theatre Archive in London to watch the recording of *Frankenstein*, demonstrating their longing to see these international stars on stage. There is more evidence to suggest that NTLive Japan specifically attracts women: according to Kano Yoshiki, a Japanese Shakespeare scholar, the number of 'young female viewers changed the atmosphere of the cinema' when *Frankenstein* was screened (2015: 10). If the *Asahi Shimbun*, a Japanese newspaper, is to be believed, these fans are now morphing into a recurring audience for these showings because of their quality ('British and American Masterpiece' 2015). The earliest screenings of NTLive UK also had more female supporters than male but they mainly attracted senior citizens (Bakhshi and Throsby 2010: 32–33). NTLive Japan's marketing target from the outset consisted of younger women.

In Japan, public screenings necessarily function as substitutes for live theatre experiences that remain out of reach. Most viewers watch these screenings because it is impossible to attend theatres abroad; in fact, NTLive events represent some fans' first encounter with theatre. Japan has a less prominent theatre culture than does England; in 2014, 2.2 million people attended stage performances in Japan (Pia Soken 2016), compared to 2.8 million in England – although the latter has less than half Japan's population (Arts Council England 2016: 25). Lynette Porter, who attended NTLive's screening of *Frankenstein* with her students in Florida and reviewed it in *Studies in Popular Culture*, notes that the 'students who attended the local screening had never seen a professional theatrical performance and were thrilled at the quality of acting and stagecraft' (2013: 11); many members of NTLive's Japanese audience would agree with this assessment.

When Cumberbatch's *Hamlet* was screened in Japan, the public screening's role in negative convergence became visible. On *Filmarks*, a Japanese website for sharing film reviews, many users commented that they wanted to attend a live performance or hoped to experience theatre in London someday, even though they were not familiar with theatre or were seeing Shakespeare for the first time ('Reviews of *National Theatre Live: Hamlet* (2016)' n.d.). Some viewers, possibly more experienced playgoers, criticized the camerawork or the subtitles; some felt that public screenings lack the excitement of live performances; and others even argued that public screenings looked reactionary or unauthentic – to use Peggy Phelan's phrase, they seem to believe that '[P]erformance in a strict ontological sense is nonreproductive' (1993: 148). These responses to the broadcasts revealed both fans' excitement and dissatisfaction, hinting that public screenings are a frustrating substitute for the audience's desire to see live performances.

From negative convergence to fan protest

In the landscape of negative convergence, linguistic barriers cause additional discomfort. Since few Japanese-speaking fans understand English, subtitles are essential, but those offered by NTLive are often of poor quality. Dissatisfaction with the subtitles leads to another convergent activity: fans exchange complaints on Twitter, which develops into a type of fan protest. Although the fans' complaints originate in the linguistic barrier surrounding negative convergence, when they begin discussing a broadcast on Twitter and contacting distributors, their activities move closer to the type of convergence that Jenkins details, 'where the power of the media producer and the power of the media consumer interact in unpredictable ways' (2006: 2).

Every time fans complain about NTLive screenings online, users create 'Togetter matomes'. Togetter is a Japanese Web service analogous to Storify, through which a Twitter user can make a 'matome', or collection, of tweets and give it a title and an introductory section.[2] Some matomes collect general comments on NTLive, while others focus on the subtitles. Although it is common for playgoers in Japan to create a matome about a theatrical production, what distinguishes the matomes about NTLive is the vast amount of criticism of the subtitles. Matomes attacking the policies of distributors are more typical among film fans than playgoers.[3] The critical nature of these matomes can be ascribed to the fan base for these productions overlapping with that of films.

Few shows have escaped subtitle complaints, and Shakespeare's plays, especially *Coriolanus*, have suffered many slings and arrows, partly because the speeches are more complex and voluminous than those in other plays and because the subtitle quality is poor despite the availability of translations. A Togetter matome entitled 'Responses to the Subtitles of NTLive *Coriolanus*' created by @The4thDiamond in April 2014 included over 100 complaints, more than *Frankenstein* and Turner's *Hamlet*, the subtitles of which were also criticized, but to a lesser extent.[4] Many mentioned omissions or distorted text, and some suspected that the subtitles contained borrowings from Matsuoka Kazuko's translation, without giving proper credit or having the subtitles checked by a native Japanese speaker. Typographical errors in kanji characters were heavily criticized; in one scene, because of a kanji error, the phrase 'common fools' (3.1.100) [愚昧な民衆] was translated as 'a crowd of stupid younger sisters' [愚妹な民衆], provoking particular derision.[5] The introduction to the matome recommended that fans make their concerns known to NTLive's Twitter accounts, @ntlive and @ntlivejapan, bringing fans together into a pressure group.

These complaints imply that Japanese viewers are used to fairly high-quality print translations of Shakespeare. Devoted fans of Hiddleston had already read translations of *Coriolanus* by Matsuoka or Odajima Yushi. They found these translations easy to understand, and sometimes beautiful, and expected a similar quality from the subtitles. One user pointed out that the omission of Coriolanus' speeches on Aufidius' virtue (1.1.227–31) made the characters' relationship difficult to understand, although in the translation this was clear.[6] Some said that they had read a translation before the screening because of rumours about the subtitles. These comments reveal the viewers' trust in the print translations and their conception of how Shakespeare's speeches should sound in Japanese. They had created an ideal image of 'true' Shakespeare through the translations in a more traditional version of convergence. They wanted their own Shakespeare in Japanese.

The power of this theatre fandom was realized when a non-Shakespearean play, *The Curious Incident of the Dog in the Night-Time,* was screened in February 2016. Fans complained so much that @hawk_v created a matome on the subtitles, 'NTLive *The Curious Incident of the Dog in the Night-Time* Subtitle Problems'. Some fans, including @hawk_v, wrote directly to NTLive's Twitter account in English, adopting the tactics proposed in the previous matome on *Coriolanus*. It turned out that NTLive UK was responsible for the errors in the subtitles, and the matome's introduction said that it would support NTLive Japan's negotiation with NTLive UK.

The distributors could not disregard the fans' chorus of disapproval. On 3 March 2016, NTLive Japan posted a notification of the subtitle changes on Facebook in English and Japanese, promising that they would be checked in Japan (NTLive Japan 2016). The posts in both languages were similar, but the comment that the distributor had sent the fans' feedback to NTLive UK appeared only in Japanese. This move acknowledged and acted on the fans' desire to make their feedback known to NTLive UK. Culture-ville had already hinted in 2014 that NTLive UK had not understood the issues arising from the language barrier, citing their reluctance to translate the official English website into Japanese ('Interview' 2014). NTLive Japan had good reason to welcome the fans' protest.

On 4 March, @hawk_v added a word of thanks to the matome. The number of complaints about the subtitles to NTLive screenings in Japan has subsequently declined. BranaghTheatreLive, distributed by Culture-ville in Japan later in 2016, was not criticized for its subtitles ('Read after Watching *The Winter's Tale!*'). Cooperation between the fans and the Japanese distributor led to improved screenings. Although modest, the fans' protest bore similarities to the more conventional convergent activities by other fan communities, such as online activism within Harry Potter fandom to defend against the restrictions on the use of Harry Potter materials imposed by Warner Bros., as explained by Jenkins (2006: 169–205). Both groups successfully improved audience satisfaction by reaching out to the distributors.

Conclusion

In Japan, the introduction of public screenings of English theatrical productions initiated and subsequently strengthened a desire to see productions staged outside Japan, and generated online protest by Japanese-speaking fans, highlighting their high expectations of theatre experiences in general, and concerning Shakespeare in particular. In a form of negative convergence, they accept – with reservations – theatre broadcasts as a substitute for live performances, due to the impossibility of attending London productions and frustration when the productions cannot be understood properly because of poor subtitles. The exchange of complaints about the subtitles on Twitter and Togetter shed light on their reception of Shakespeare and vibrant convergent activities, displaced onto the platforms of social media in the absence of access to London performances. Rather than directing their protest towards NTLive Japan, fans targeted NTLive UK, which had not recognized the importance of effective localization of cultural products. Communicating directly with NTLive UK, they showed that in spite of the hegemony of English-language culture in a global context, there exist many non-English-speaking audiences. Therefore, good translation is essential to marketing to various cultures: because the fans' dissatisfaction with the subtitles began with the translation of Shakespeare, a cultural symbol of the dominance of English language, Japanese fans' protest could be regarded as an attempt to adapt English culture to the pleasures of their own cultural experiences. Japanese-speaking fans gained a small but meaningful victory in the arena of global culture.

Notes

The research presented in this chapter is partly funded by JSPS KAKENHI Grant Number 26884055 and the Fukuhara Memorial Fund for the Studies of English and American Literature.

1 Quotations from Japanese articles, including article titles, are my translations.
2 I do not cite each tweet from the matomes when multiple users mention similar issues.
3 I discussed the use of Togetter among film fans in 'The Unpopular Bard' (Kitamura 2017).
4 '*Frankenstein*', a matome of general comments, contains tweets about the subtitles. Benedict Cumberbatch Japan, a website dedicated to Cumberbatch, also criticized *Frankenstein*'s subtitles in 2014, encouraging fans to buy an English digital programme if they can read English, for it was not available in Japanese, although Japanese programmes of several productions became available later in paper format. The 2015 *Hamlet* was first shown with no subtitles in November 2015 and with subtitles in January 2016; some complained about typographical errors. See @izmrk, in Japanese, 4.05, 27 January 2016, https://twitter.com/izmrk/status/692181483532976128 (accessed 15 March 2016).
5 Quotations from Shakespeare refer to the Arden editions.
6 @muginchi, in Japanese, 12.44, 26 April 2014, https://twitter.com/muginchi/status/460006586530811904 (accessed 15 March 2016).

References

Arts Council England (2016), 'Analysis of Theatre in England'. Available online: http://www.artscouncil.org.uk/sites/default/files/download-file/Analysis%20of%20Theatre%20in%20England%20-%20Final%20Report.pdf (accessed 15 July 2017).

Bakhshi, H. and D. Throsby (2010), *Culture of Innovation: An Economic Analysis of Innovation in Arts and Cultural Organisations*. London: National Endowment for Science, Technology and the Arts. Available online: http://www.nesta.org.uk/sites/default/files/culture_of_innovation.pdf (accessed 7 July 2017).

Barker, M. (2013), *Live to Your Local Cinema: The Remarkable Rise of Livecasting*, London: Palgrave Macmillan.

Benedict Cumberbatch Japan (2014), 'NT Official *Frankenstein* Digital Program for Sale, with Makeup Photos, Interviews, etc.' [Meiku-chu suchiru, interview hoka no haitta *Frankenstein* koshiki-denshi-program ga NT yori hatsubai ni], in Japanese, 28 October. Available online: https://www.benedictcumberbatch.jp/news/2014/10/frankensteinnt-d8ce.html (accessed 7 May 2017).

Biwako (2014), 'The Legendary Stage Where You Watch Cumberbatch's Ultimate Performance Arrives in Japan' [Cumberbatch no kyukyoku no engi ga mirareru 'maboroshi no butai' ga nihon joriku], in Japanese, *Joshi-Spa!*, 28 January. Available online: http://joshi-spa.jp/65608 (accessed 15 March 2017).

'British and American Masterpiece Theatre in Japanese Cinemas, Recorded with Subtitles' [Eibei no kessaku butai, nihon no eigakan de jimaku-tsuki joei] (2015), in Japanese, *The Asahi Shimbun*, Evening Edition, 14 May: 3.

'*Frankenstein*', in Japanese, Togetter. Available online: http://togetter.com/li/634056 (accessed 15 March 2017).

'Interview: Hoping to Allow the Audience to Enjoy the Show in S-Class Seats – "Behind-the-Scenes" of the Screening of *Frankenstein*, Featuring Benedict and Jonny' ['Subete no okyakusama ni S-seki de miru kikai o tsukuritai' Benedict × Johnny shuen *Frankenstein* screen joei no 'butaiura' interview] (2014), in Japanese, *Kaigai-Drama-Navi*, 8 February. Available online: http://dramanavi.net/staff/2014/02/022783.php (accessed 14 March 2017).

Jenkins, H. (2006), *Convergence Culture: Where Old and New Media Collide*, New York: New York University Press.

Kano, Y. (1996), 'London Theatre on Screen' [Screen de London no engeki o], in Japanese, *Artlet: Keio University Art Center Newsletter*, 44 (2015): 10–11.

Kitamura, S. (2017), 'The Unpopular Bard: The Reception of Recent Shakespeare Films in Japan', *Shakespeare Film East West*, 22 January, Waseda University, Tokyo.

National Theatre Live (Japan). http://www.ntlive.jp/ (accessed 15 March 2017).

NTLive Japan (2016), 'NTLive's Notification on *The Curious Incident of the Dog in the Night-Time*' [National Theatre Live yori, 'Yonaka ni inu ni okotta kimyo na jiken' ni kansuru oshirase desu], *Facebook*, 21.04, 3 March. Available online: https://www.facebook.com/ntlivejp/posts/1709387272639640 (accessed 15 March 2017).

'NTLive *The Curious Incident of the Dog in the Night-Time* Subtitle Problems' [NTLive 'Yonaka ni inu ni okotta kimyo na jiken' jimaku no mondai-ten] (n.d.), in Japanese, *Togetter*. Available online: http://togetter.com/li/942912 (accessed 13 March 2017).

Phelan, P. (1993), *Unmarked: The Politics of Performance*, London: Routledge.
Pia Soken (2016), 'Summary', in Japanese. Available online: http://live-entertainment-whitepaper.jp/pdf/sammary2016.pdf (accessed 15 July 2017).
Porter, L. (2013), 'It's Alive! But What Kind of Creature Is National Theatre Live's *Frankenstein*?', *Studies in Popular Culture*, 35 (2): 1–21.
'Read after Watching *The Winter's Tale*!' [Fuyumonogatari o mitara yomu!] (n.d.), in Japanese, Togetter. Available online: https://togetter.com/li/1045319 (accessed 17 March 2017).
'Responses to the Subtitles of NTLive's *Coriolanus*' [NTlive *Coriolanus* jimaku hanno matome] (n.d.), in Japanese, Togetter. Available online: http://togetter.com/li/659748 (accessed 15 March 2017).
'Reviews of *National Theatre Live: Hamlet* (2016)' [National Theatre Live 2016 *Hamlet* no Kanso Review] (n.d.), in Japanese, *Filmarks*. Available online: https://filmarks.com/detail/64559 (accessed 15 March 2017).
Shakespeare, W. (1983), *Coriolanus*, in Japanese, trans. Odajima Yushi, Tokyo: Hakusuisha.
Shakespeare, W. (2007), *Coriolanus*, in Japanese, trans. Matsuoka Kazuko, Tokyo: Chikuma-Shobo.

12

Shakespeare and the Theatre Broadcast Experience:

A View from Hong Kong

Michael Ingham

For nearly a decade, cinema-theatre hybridity in the form of theatre broadcast performances has captured the imagination of audiences worldwide, not least in the former British colony (latterly British Dependent Territory until its 1997 retrocession) of Hong Kong. Shakespeare, thanks to broadcasts by NTLive, RSCLive, Shakespeare's Globe and KBTCLive, has in recent years increasingly become part of Hong Kong screen culture. In this 'reaction shot', I will discuss the extent to which aesthetic/artistic criteria for audiences and knowledge of texts in a second or other language are necessarily subordinate to those of actor star-status – which is naturally prominent in the publicity – and a sense of cultural elitism/superiority among Anglophone audiences. The chapter will also interrogate the absence of Chinese language subtitling, as mandated by the city's trilingual, biliterate public policy, as well as the significance of Shakespeare in the currently charged political atmosphere in Hong Kong.

Given Hong Kong's demographic of an approximately 98 per cent ethnically Chinese population and 2 per cent non-Chinese, my investigation of the extent to which screened Shakespearean drama is being accessed in the city provides an initial sense of the response to Shakespeare theatre broadcast. Although outside the US and the UK such putatively 'live' performances are in reality recorded for the global market, in Hong Kong, as in cities across the world, screenings of live performances appear to retain their 'virtual liveness' for audiences (see also Kidnie, Chapter 8 and Elam, Chapter 13). This raises some fascinating ontological and phenomenological questions about the quality of 'liveness' and the interpretation of attendance and presence in relation to both livestreamed and delayed live broadcasts, as Auslander (1999) and Barker (2013) have expounded. Their influential studies inform this exploratory investigation of Hong Kong theatre broadcast of Shakespeare.

Shakespeare in Hong Kong

Theatre broadcasts in Hong Kong have acquired a distinct cultural presence, even if there remains scope for higher-profile promotion and publicity. The branding is of particular relevance in this exceptionally brand-conscious, cosmopolitan city, and, in a culture far more oriented toward star vehicles than toward prestigious directors or theatre companies, international actor celebrities have been a major factor in such recognition (see also Kitamura, Chapter 11). However, no celebrity performer names have had quite as much resonance – whether in stage drama, opera or ballet – as that of Shakespeare. Undoubtedly the longstanding tradition for Shakespeare amateur performances in Hong Kong, established during its experience under British colonial rule between 1841 and 1997, has ensured greater familiarity with his name and work than in most East Asian cities. This has been strengthened by visiting professional companies, mainly from the UK and Australia, as well as by a wide range of Asian Shakespeare productions, including local performances in Cantonese translation, notably those by translation scholar Jane Lai. In addition, child performers such as the Shakespeare4All project and university students at the Chinese University of Hong Kong's Shakespeare Festival have promoted greater appreciation and knowledge of Shakespeare's work. Latterly Hong Kong has achieved worldwide recognition for its Cantonese-language productions by the Tang Shu Wing Theatre Studio, the first of which, *Titus Andronicus* (captured live in 2012 at the 'Globe to Globe' Shakespeare Festival in London), was screened in Hong Kong cinemas in 2013. The second major production, *Macbeth*, has yet to be filmed and broadcast in cinemas.

Broadcasting of stage dramas has established a firm foothold in Hong Kong's cultural landscape, aided by a strong tradition of touring stage productions, preceding digital theatre broadcasts. One obvious difference between theatre broadcasts and touring productions, such as Gregory Doran's 2016 'King and Country' *Henriad*, is that the former have relied more heavily on famous actors with international appeal, including the likes of Tom Hiddleston, Helen Mirren, David Tennant, Benedict Cumberbatch and Lily James, whereas the live stage productions that come to Hong Kong rarely include high-recognition celebrity actors. Significantly, though, the touring 2016 Globe Theatre Company's production of *The Merchant of Venice* featured Jonathan Pryce as Shylock, implicitly acknowledging the need for a name actor in response to stiff competition from Shakespeare stage and screen rivals, the RSC and National Theatre.

Reviewing the Shakespeare captured live productions of the last few years, one can detect a marked upswing in Hong Kong audience interest in screened Shakespeare, perhaps enhanced by the relative popularity among audiences of mainstream film adaptations, including Justin Kurzel's *Macbeth* and Ralph Fiennes' *Coriolanus* (2010). Sold-out NTLive screenings of Josie Rourke's 2014 *Coriolanus* and Lyndsey Turner's *Hamlet* in the Autumn–Winter season of 2015 also helped to consolidate the audience for theatre broadcast cultivated by the screening of Peter Morgan's immensely popular vehicle for Helen Mirren, *The Audience*, earlier in the year. A likely ripple effect of this regularly encored production could be observed in the enthusiastic uptake for Encore screenings of Gregory Doran's *Richard II* (RSCLive 2016) and *The Tempest* (RSCLive 2017), and Ashford and Branagh's *Romeo and Juliet* and *The Winter's Tale* (both KBTCLive 2016) respectively.

These have been among the most successful 'live' theatre screenings, although non-Shakespeare plays with international stars have also performed well at the box-office. Somewhat less in demand were the RSCLive *The Merchant of Venice* (2016) and *King Lear* (2017), seemingly lacking in celebrity appeal, despite Antony Sher's impressive interpretation of Lear in the latter. In the circumstances it is predictable, given Hong Kong's younger demographic for screened theatre than for the live-on-stage variety, that the screen-star system – both small and large screens – is a key factor in enticing audiences in Hong Kong. This probably plays a bigger part, ultimately, than the choice of play or director or other variables such as the synchronicity between world events and dramatic themes or scenarios. Such contemporary allegorical readings of Shakespeare tend to have less resonance for Hong Kong or Asian audiences outside the UK or Western context, as Adele Lee's empirical research on Shakespeare in Hong Kong (2009, 2013) has shown.

Arguably more engaging for the typical composite audience of locals and expatriates – observed in roughly even distribution at screenings – is the cutting-edge technology manifested so promisingly by Doran's *The Tempest*. The motion-capture and computer-generated effects devised in collaboration with IT specialists Intel and performance-capture experts Imaginarium Studios, and deployed in the production to enhance virtual stage presence, point the way forward in terms of their flexibility of staging and their freedom of scenographic imagination. Sequences such as *The Tempest's* challenging masque conjured up by Prospero for Miranda's and Ferdinand's nuptials and the flights of fancy involving Mark Quartley's Ariel avatar and other spirits are vividly brought to life by the sensor-driven motion-capture technique, only to become 'melted into air' (4.1.150), reinforcing Prospero's metaphor of life, and indeed theatre, as an 'insubstantial pageant' (4.1.155). In this groundbreaking RSC production the 'rough magic' (5.1.50) of theatre, as an experience based on transience and illusion, is fittingly captured by the production's innovative use of virtual reality technology. The live event integrates the theatricality and embodied kinaesthetic of the stage with the phenomenologically disembodied kinaesthetic of the screen;

in the broadcast experience the stage production's state-of-the-art visuals are further refracted in what may be described as a 'meta-mediation' process, reinforced by the pre-performance and interval documentary material on the production's cutting edge technology. The evident success of *The Tempest*, co-sponsored by the Hong Kong Arts Festival in their popular Festival Plus programme, suggests that typical Hong Kong audiences' predilection for celebrity names can be rivalled by technically spectacular productions of Shakespeare plays.

Theatre broadcast in the Hong Kong context

On account of the significant time-zone differences between Hong Kong and both the UK and the US – seven or eight hours ahead of London and twelve or thirteen hours ahead of New York, depending on whether standard or daylight saving time is being observed – the livestreaming of theatre and other cultural or sporting events is impractical. This means that theatre broadcasts are always 'delayed live' or 'captured live', therefore essentially recordings, although the captured productions are screened without any editorial intervention subsequent to the original livestreamed event. Typically, each captured live performance will be screened three or four times within a month-long period, once or twice in each of a small number of state-of-the-art multiplex cinemas located in major shopping malls in the commercially busiest districts of Central and Admiralty on Hong Kong Island and Tsim Sha Tsui on Kowloon-side. Non-discounted tickets currently cost 200 Hong Kong dollars – approximately £20. Participating cinemas boast excellent sound systems and the latest digital projection facilities, and all are located in the most cosmopolitan districts of the city. These cinemas belong to the Broadway Group (Palace IFC in Central; The One in Tsim Sha Tsui, Kowloon) and the AMC group (AMC Pacific Place in Admiralty, Hong Kong), which control the franchise. Screenings are rarely scheduled for other more residential locations in Kowloon or the New Territories, many of which have their own local cinemas. A new venue for RSC Shakespeare began operating in late 2017 outside the Central and Tsim Sha Tsui orbit so familiar to Western expatriates. This is the Movie Movie cinema at Cityplaza, Tai Koo Shing, where RSC productions such as *Titus Andronicus* and *Twelfth Night* have been screened, mainly for non-Western audiences, according to observation.

Box-office figures and observational evidence point to proven success, with full or near-full houses for the vast majority of screenings of such cultural events, whether opera, ballet, or stage drama. This is partly a reflection of the strictly limited number of screenings available to the public, reinforcing the notion of cultural elitism or exclusivity. The Encore screenings referred to above are scheduled in cases where demand for tickets is high. Concomitant with the optimism that such screenings have commercial potential for niche audiences comes an ingrained sense of caution, mistrust even, of 'high culture' on the part of the city's film distributors. In short, the common preconception is that theatre broadcast is only viable in locations commonly frequented by a cosmopolitan mix of expatriates from Western countries or the Antipodes, as opposed to predominantly local Hong Kong Cantonese residents. There is, as yet, no readiness to move outside this restrictive commercial model, and test the waters among secondary and university students living in residential areas of Hong Kong Island, Kowloon and the New Territories. For the purposes of Hong Kong audience-building, particularly among the younger demographic of cinema-goers drawn to shopping malls and self-consciously part of an advanced 'mediatised culture' (Auslander 1999), the attractions of visual pyrotechnics, as used in Doran's *The Tempest*, are palpable.

Better market research on the potential for expansion might well result in proliferation, albeit gradual and tentative in keeping with the fairly conservative attitudes discernible in Hong Kong toward the role of arts in the life of the community. A key reference point for future Hong Kong audience market research is provided by the questions for further investigation with which Barker ends his study: 'Who goes to these livecasts? What do they want, expect and get out of them?' And the corollary that particularly motivates my own perspective: 'How are their producers managing the balance between the home audience ... and the much larger distributed cinema audience?' (2013: 10–11). One manifestation of Hong Kong audiences' awareness of the remoteness of distance in time and space encapsulated by 'as live' broadcasts is that there is rarely much correspondent reaction discernible in the remote audience to moments of humour or emotion which are often shared by cinema audiences at theatre broadcasts in the UK or the US (on shared affect, see Aebischer, Chapter 7). Shakespeare's Early Modern English clearly accentuates this distance, but the reluctance to exhibit affective reaction in Hong Kong probably stems from a variety of factors, including phenomenological consciousness of geographical remoteness, culturally acquired public comportment values, and excessively respectful and monumentalized preconceptions concerning Shakespeare's work.

In stark contrast to the UK and other European countries where there has been lively press debate about the extent to which the increased popularity of screened stage performances has had a detrimental effect on theatre attendance, inter-media rivalry appears negligible in Hong Kong. Local theatre in Cantonese retains its loyal core audience-base, and there is no real competition or overlap between visiting theatre companies at special events – such as the annual Hong Kong Arts Festival from mid-February to mid-March – and stage productions scheduled for cinema screenings. Tang Shu Wing points out: '[broadcast theatre] has not generated a negative impact as far as the mainstream audience is concerned. For our case, our *Macbeth* was sold out in last year's [2016] Arts Festival.'[1] Press coverage in Hong Kong has been generally well-disposed and more informative than critical; if anything, a screened professional production is more likely to generate interest in reviving a classic play by both professional and amateur Cantonese-language companies, as stage versions of not only Tang's *Macbeth* and *Titus Andronicus* but also other companies' *Hamlet* and *The Merchant of Venice* suggested. Echoing Tang's perception, and judging by the apparent popularity to date of theatre broadcasting in Hong Kong, awareness of and reservations about lack of immediacy or physical presence in digital cinema do not appear to generate as much debate as in the UK or the US.

Perhaps more of an issue for cultivating audiences, raising the number of screenings and increasing the outreach potential of Shakespeare in view of the syntactic and lexical complexities posed by the Early Modern English in which his dramatic verse is couched, is that of subtitles. At present there are English-language subtitles, but a more consistent policy of providing both Chinese and English subtitles, as mandated for mainstream cinema and television channels in the city, is needed. Despite being exposed to considerable Anglophone pedagogic and popular culture influence on a daily basis, the majority of Hong Kong audience members almost certainly rely heavily on visual performance semiotics and subtitles for comprehension. In the context of Hong Kong's official biliterate and trilingual policy covering Cantonese, Putonghua and English it is incumbent on the distributors to address this anomaly. The provision of subtitles would increase potential for mirroring the real-time audience affect in the cinema discussed above. Likewise, there is potential for expansion of the model into selected suburban areas – New Territories, both literally and metaphorically – at least on an exploratory basis and with more energetic promotion.

Conclusion: concerns, challenges, opportunities

If theatre broadcast of Shakespeare warrants such strong promotion, it appears that the cultural cachet of 'big-time' Shakespeare – to employ Michael Bristol's term (Bristol 1996) – is synonymous with British-style Anglophone education, and is thus a signifier of Hong Kong's nostalgic adherence to its quasi-British heritage. Certainly, the residue of a former predominantly English-medium education system, while emphasizing English for practical vocational purposes much more than literary-cultural aims, does provide a basis for audience development. Shakespeare continues to represent a major presence, at least notionally, in the curriculum of secondary schools and universities, but more so in international colleges and expatriate-targeted schools than in Cantonese- or Putonghua-medium institutions. Even in local high schools there is a Shakespeare option on the syllabus of today's very marginal 'Literature in English' subject. The British Council's 2016

'Shakespeare Lives' initiative, linking up with schools and universities and co-presenting with the Broadway Circuit screenings of NTLive and KBTCLive, together with related exhibitions, was timed to coincide with the quatercentenary of Shakespeare's death.

Moreover, in a period of growing tension between Hong Kong and the city's Beijing rulers over a range of issues, and exacerbated by localist rhetoric advocating independence in place of the existing 'One Country, Two Systems' formula agreed under the terms of 1984's Joint Declaration, Shakespeare may yet be seen as a potent and iconic reminder of cultural diversity. The age-old arguments over Shakespeare as a progressive cultural figure as against his depiction as political reactionary are ironically highlighted in a context where left-wing and right-wing perspectives are so confused as to be virtually irrelevant to the current sociopolitical scenario. Recent provocative rhetoric by China's ambassador to the UK to the effect that Beijing is set to renege on the provisions of the 1984 Joint Agreement between the two nations has only served to exacerbate tension between them. To what extent the embrace of Anglophone cultural products can be interpreted as a form of cultural resistance to the social and political hegemony of the new China, particularly in the current climate, as it flexes its political and economic muscle and embarks upon a new form of culturally revisionist revolution, remains to be seen.

Pro-mainland nationalist perspectives on the persistence of UK cultural identity in Hong Kong interpret any manifestations of the latter as a continuation of cultural imperialism and soft-power politics. Nevertheless, as Enid Tsui's 2016 article on the celebrations of the Shakespeare quatercentenary in China argues, Shakespeare remains an important 'brand' across the border from Hong Kong. NTLive has gained some traction in China with its productions now broadcast in major cities, including Beijing, Shanghai and Chengdu, all of which are screened with simplified-character subtitles. Whether or not this initiative can endure and thrive in the mainland, which has a strong tradition of Shakespeare translation and adaptation to traditional theatre forms, depends to some extent on the degree to which Shakespeare's work is represented as emblematic of so-called 'white liberal' ideology. The latter is becoming as much anathema to China's increasingly repressive one-party state as it was in earlier eras. Censorship of specific lines in screened Shakespeare productions or of whole productions – in the event that Shakespeare's name were to be associated with calls for genuine Hong Kong democracy – is not as remote a possibility as it might seem to those who assume that Shakespeare does not speak to audiences today. Thanks to 'brand recognition', subliminal or otherwise, judiciously selected broadcast Shakespeare productions, in spite of their linguistic challenges, will probably serve to create interest among younger audiences. So, amidst these challenges and opportunities – to appropriate the British Council's publicity – 'Shakespeare Lives' and will continue to do so in Hong Kong!

Notes

1 Oral response to a question posed by the author on 10 June 2017.

References

Auslander, P. (1999), *Liveness: Performance in a Mediatized Culture*, London: Routledge.
Barker, M. (2013), *Live To Your Local Cinema: The Remarkable Rise of Livecasting*, London: Palgrave Macmillan.
Bristol, M. (1996), *Big Time Shakespeare,* London: Routledge.
British Council (2016), 'Shakespeare Lives'. Available online: https://www.britishcouncil.hk/en/programmes/arts/shakespeare-lives (accessed 10 June 2017).
Lee, A. (2009), 'One Husband Too Many and the Problem of Postcolonial Hong Kong', in A.C.Y. Huang and C.S. Ross (eds), *Shakespeare in Hollywood, Asia, and Cyberspace*, West Lafayette: Purdue University Press, 195–204.
Lee, A. (2013), 'Shakespeare in Hong Kong', University of Greenwich. Available online: http://enterprise.gre.ac.uk/case-studies/shakespeare-in-hong-kong (accessed 17 July 2017).
Tsui, E. (2016), 'Why China's love affair with Shakespeare endures', *South China Morning Post,* 1 August. Available online: http://www.scmp.com/magazines/post-magazine/long-reads/article/1996061/why-chinas-love-affair-shakespeare-endures (accessed 19 June 2017).

13

Very Like a Film:

Hamlet Live in Bologna

Keir Elam

Hamlet bolognese

On 19 April 2016, just four days before the fourth centenary of Shakespeare's death, *Hamlet* appeared 'live' in Bologna. That evening the NTLive broadcast of the tragedy went out to cinemas worldwide, including over 180 venues throughout Italy: three in Bologna alone. This was the fourth screening of Lyndsey Turner's production, following the first UK national broadcast on 15 October 2015, the national Encore a week later, and the first international Encore of 15 November, which had not reached Italy. The April 2016 Italian distributor was Nexo Digital, which describes itself as a 'glocal network' covering live events of various kinds, including opera, ballet and exhibitions (Nexo Digital 2017). Turner's *Hamlet* (directed for screen by Robin Lough) was therefore not the first experiment in live broadcast in Italy and, more specifically, in Bologna, since Nexo had already transmitted live to Bolognese venues events such as ballet from the Bolshoi, opera from La Scala, live rock concerts, as well as London plays. It was not even the first Bolognese *Hamlet*, or indeed the first Bolognese NTLive *Hamlet*, since Nexo had previously broadcast Nicholas Hytner's National Theatre (Olivier) production in select Italian cinemas (also directed for screen by Robin Lough), including The Space Cinema in Bologna, on 28 January 2014. The centenary broadcast, however, received far greater national and local publicity and reached a much wider audience than earlier transmitted stage productions. For many Italians it was their first experience of the theatre broadcast phenomenon.

The theatre broadcast is a hybrid creature, part live performance, part cinema, part distinct genre in its own right (see also Aebischer and

Greenhalgh, Introduction, and Nicholas, Chapter 4). The perceptual framing of the event may be conditioned by its venue, since different cinemas have distinct cultural histories, and attract, at least in part, different kinds of audience. This was certainly the case with the three Bologna venues: the Lumière, an independent *cinema d'essai* belonging to the Bologna Cineteca, a well-known public institution; the Odeon, one of the oldest and most popular private cinemas in the city, part of the Bologna Cinema Circuit specializing in, among other things, English-language films and mix-genre events; and the Space, a multiplex commercial cinema, part of the national Space Cinema chain, located out of the city centre in the north of Bologna. I would argue that the reception of the same, simultaneous, event may have been different in the venues in question, due to conditioning by their respective micro-cultural contexts. In this chapter I wish to consider and contrast the reception of *Hamlet* in two of the venues in question, namely the Lumière and the Odeon.[1]

A tale of two cinemas

Bologna is in many ways a 'cinema city', due to its large number of both commercial and independent venues, its festivals celebrating film history – such as *Il cinema ritrovato*, dedicated since 1986 to rare and 'lost' movies, or the *Biografilm Festival* devoted to biopics – and especially to its specific vocation for film restoration. The Bologna Cineteca, founded in 1962, is internationally known for its experience and expertise in restoring films. Its *Immagine ritrovata* laboratory has been responsible for the restoration of the complete works of Charlie Chaplin, as well as other American classics, such as Erich von Stroheim's *Foolish Wives* and King Vidor's *Wild Oranges*, together with European masterpieces like F.W. Murnau's *Nosferatu* and Fritz Lang's *Harakiri*. Many of the restored films have received their world premières at the Cineteca's Lumière Cinema, which has thereby become the Italian site par excellence for film history, thanks above all to its archive of over 70,000 films, including rare items from the Cineteca's World Cinema Foundation, set up in 1990 by Martin Scorsese with the aim of helping third-world film conservation. As a consequence, The Lumière tends to attract a self-selected audience composed primarily of cineastes, many of them students of cinema, since it is located in the University of Bologna performing arts campus.

The *Hamlet* theatre broadcast, the first live event to be shown at the Lumière, was scheduled as part of a film series in honour of the fourth centenary of Shakespeare's death, entitled 'Shakespeare and cinema: faithfulness and betrayals' ('*Shakespeare e il cinema, fedeltà e tradimenti*'), which included film classics such as Kozintsev's *Gamlet* and Brook's *King Lear*. The projection of the NTLive *Hamlet* in the Lumière's Scorsese theatre, moreover, was offered as an alternative to the simultaneous

FIGURE 13.1 *Lumière Cinema programme note for the NTLive* Hamlet, *Bologna Cineteca.*

screening, in an adjacent theatre, of the restored version of Louis Malle's 1957 noir *Ascenseur pour l'échafaud* (see Figure 13.1).

The paratextual material surrounding the event, therefore, consigned it unambiguously to the domain of film. This is confirmed by the programme note, which told us that the performance of *Hamlet* had taken place at the Barbican the previous October (Figure 13.1). No reference is made, title apart, to the supposedly 'live' nature of the screening, still less to the fact that it may involve a new and hybrid media genre. What the audience was offered, therefore, was the film of a past stage performance, which might well have been conserved, alongside Malle and the rest, in the Cineteca's vast archive. This was, moreover, a one-off event: the Lumière has subsequently abandoned the live broadcast field in favour of its more familiar terrain of avant-garde movies and classics.

The Odeon, on the contrary, had already 'trained' its audience in mixed-genre events, thanks to its 'When theatre meets cinema' series ('*Quando il teatro encontra il cinema*'), which, since 2013, has brought live prose, dance and operatic performances to the screen through Nexo. It has thereby created a small but returning Bologna audience for the live theatre event, a micro-community that over the years has acquired experience and competence in the reception of *il teatro al cinema* as a hybrid mode of spectacle with its own characteristics and its own rules, transcending traditional genre boundaries. The Odeon correspondingly billed the National *Hamlet* as a live mixed-genre event, with emphasis on its theatrical, as opposed to cinematic, affiliations. Indeed, the transmission inaugurated a season of what the Bologna Cinema Circuit bills as 'Great English theatre at the cinema' ('*Il grande teatro inglese al cinema*'), a cycle that has subsequently come to include Ashford and Branagh's *Romeo and Juliet* (KBTCLive) and Rupert Goold's *Richard III* (Almeida Theatre Live), among other London stage performances (CCB 2017).

Camel, weasel or whale?

The distinct, and in some ways opposed, presentation of the same 'live' event at different Bologna cinemas raises more general issues regarding the theatre broadcast phenomenon. The Cineteca's underplaying of the liveness of the event may have been an expression of cool *savoir faire* by people accustomed to changing film genres, but was not altogether unjustified. The liveness of this and similar events is to some extent a constructed quality, a sort of 'simultaneity effect' analogous to Barthes's celebrated 'reality effect' ([1968] 1989). As Laurie Osborne observes, 'The idea of "liveness" ... remains theoretically crucial to performance, so important that mediatized reproductions exploit and develop codes of sound, *mise en scène* and camera work to represent the "liveness" that reproduction both celebrates and eliminates' (2006: 62–3). Visual and auditory signals arrived from the Barbican to confirm the simultaneity effect: laughter and applause from London for Cumberbatch and others (sometimes, but not always, echoed by the Bologna audience), and during the interval, images of the theatre audience moving, talking or rising, 'contemporarily' with the cinema audience (see also Aebischer, Chapter 7). Of course, such behavioural mirroring could have been, and to some extent was, illusory, since the audience, like the play, was filmed. The shared interval time, however, longer than the standard interval in Italian cinemas, encouraged identification, although at the Lumière and Odeon (unlike Ohio; see Martinez, Chapter 14), there were no interval drinks, only popcorn.

Such signals of contemporaneity were somewhat contradicted by clear signs of intermedial mediation. The use of Italian subtitles, unknown in Italian stage performances, was reminiscent of avant-garde movies, although so-called 'surtitles' are a familiar part of live opera. More important, the broadcast resorted to a standard repertory of cinematic camera work that the Lumière cineastes would have been quite able to identify: what Barker terms a 'balancing act between wide stage-shots (to maintain a sense of overall production design, and to convey blocking), two-shots (for key dialogue scenes), and semi-close-ups (close enough to make monologues and moments of focused emotion emphatic, but "semi" for the sake of theatre's larger bodily gestures) ... [and] bravura moments created by editing, dissolves, and camera movements' (2013: 19). In the case of *Hamlet*, the use of semi-close-ups for Benedict Cumberbatch's monologues powerfully contrasted with wider shots taking in Es Devlin's two-floor set and with camera movements following Hamlet's scurrying across the lower stage or up and down the stairs. Liveness translated here into technological control.

Literal simultaneity of performance and broadcast reception is in any case probably a chimera (see, especially, Kidnie, Chapter 8). Time differences between transmission and reception give rise to what Bernadette Cochrane and Frances Bonner term 'live relays' (2014: 2), a phenomenon that is equally true of other kinds of broadcasts such as sports events: what we think we are watching in real time is inevitably, for technical reasons when not for difference in time zone, faux-live rather than strictly live. Such differences are also reflected in the less than transparent NTLive rhetoric, with its unexplained distinction between the original live broadcast and so-called 'international Encores' (NTLive 2017), which in reality are not 'Encores' in the sense of additional performances, but simple re-transmissions across space and time of a recording of the first broadcast, and which therefore have little or nothing of the initial 'liveness' left in them.

There are, however, other modes of simultaneity that may make the theatre broadcast a real-time communal phenomenon for those involved. Even when technically relayed, the broadcast is nevertheless shared in time at a national network level and even more so at a local level. Perhaps more significant than the existence or otherwise of an actual time lag is the audience perception of simultaneity. The awareness of being involved in an event within a global networked community (Albert et al. 2009) – in this case, the international audience for the NT *Hamlet* on the same day in April – conditions the spectator's perception of her own participatory role. Such perceived global simultaneity becomes actual within the more circumscribed national community, for example within the Italian Nexo network, which guarantees 'real time' coincidence between broadcast and reception: not with regard to the original London performance, but with reference to the mediated Nexo transmission itself, thereby creating what we could call the Italian 'live' *Hamlet*. Contemporaneity becomes even more actual at a local level, where two or more cinemas show the same event at the same advertised time: the Bologna *Hamlet*, that brought together audiences at the various venues in a virtually shared experience within real time, even if in different theatrical spaces.

In this way, the theatre broadcast phenomenon tends to support Philip Auslander's questioning of the 'before and after' hierarchy between the live and the transmitted event, within what he calls 'the mutual dependence of the live and the mediatized ... that challenges the traditional assumption that the live precedes the mediatized' (2008: 11). Audience experience of the event makes the 'mediatized' equivalent to the 'live' for those who wish to perceive their role as part of a simultaneous communal experience, although it does not exclude the possibility for others of taking the transmitted performance as a purely mediated construct: *Così è (se vi pare)* ('*Right You Are (If You Think So)*') in Pirandello's words. The micro-community of the Odeon may wish to perceive the performance event as live – at a global, national or local level – while the cineastes at the Lumière may prefer to think of the same event as a strictly cinematic offering. One is reminded of Polonius's cloud: *Hamlet* live? 'Tis like a stage play indeed, 'tis backed like a broadcast, 'tis very like a film.

Notes

1 Regretfully, in this brief chapter, I cannot dedicate attention to the third venue, The Space Cinema. I wish to thank Andrea Morini and Isabella Malaguti, of the Bologna Cineteca, and Elena Roda, of the Circuito Cinema Bologna, for sharing information and ideas.

References

Albert, S., D. Flournoy and R. LeBrasseur (2009), *Networked Communities: Strategies for Digital Collaboration*, Hershey, PA: Information Science Reference.

Auslander, P. (2008), *Liveness: Performance in a Mediatized Culture*, 2nd edn, London: Routledge.

Barker, M. (2013), *Live to Your Local Cinema*, Basingstoke: Palgrave Macmillan.

Barthes, R. ([1968] 1989), 'The Reality Effect', in trans. R. Howard, *The Rustle of Language*, Berkeley and Los Angeles: University of California Press, 141–48.

CCB (2017), 'Il Grande teatro inglese al cinema'. Available online: https://www.circuitocinemabologna.it/p/il-grande-teatro-inglese-al-cinema--2 (accessed 30 August 2017)

Cochrane, B. and F. Bonner (2014), 'Screening from the Met, the NT, or the House: What Changes with the Live Relay', *Adaptation* 7 (2): 121–33.

Nexo Digital (2017), 'Chi siamo'. Available online: http://www.nexodigital.it/chi-siamo/ (accessed 29 April 2017).

NTLive (2017), 'The Encore Series'. Available online: http://ntlive.nationaltheatre.org.uk/media/html/ntlin2-war-horse/page-page-465 (accessed 29 April 2017).

Osborne, L.E. (2006), 'Speculations on Shakespearean Cinematic Liveness', *Shakespeare Bulletin* 24 (3): 49–65.

14

Shakespeare at a Theatre Near You:

Student Engagement in Northeast Ohio

Ann M. Martinez

Theatregoers who attend a live show expect an immersive experience – seating, lighting, and sound are some factors that can influence audience engagement. However, for a broadcast performance, despite the screening venue's potentially theatre-like spatial dynamic, the audience might expect the immersive quality to be diminished; by factors such as temporal delay because of difference in time zones, and distance, both regarding geographical location (viewers' regional proximity to live-performance venues) and physical proximity between the viewer and the events on screen. That is not always the case, though. Students from my two Shakespeare classes travelled to two different Cinemark Theatre locations in Northeast Ohio to attend NTLive's first and Encore broadcasts of Lyndsey Turner's production of *Hamlet* at the Barbican Theatre in London (2015), starring Benedict Cumberbatch.[1] Contingent on their previous familiarity with theatre and its conventions their experience was affected by spatial dynamics, their shared view of the screen, and shared pre- and post-broadcast conversations. They entered the cinema with a history of class discussion on which to base their experience but also were members of a cinema audience, able to imagine that they were collectively sharing the performance with a theatre audience whom they saw on-screen.

The theatre-like nature of the event, emphasized by the venue, prompts further discussion of what Peter Holland calls 'the theatre audience's community of perception' (1994: 52). Holland finds this experience lacking in filmed and televised Shakespeare due to the audience's isolation; however, my students spoke precisely of a communal experience. Interestingly, they even used theatre terminology to describe the screening, referring to the *stage* and never the *screen*. While belonging to a generation who frequents cinema, for them this experience was not just another day at the movies. Joe Falocco discusses his students' preference for what he terms 'Bard on Demand', accessing Shakespeare plays on their phones or computers (2017: 57). However, advertising of the broadcast, which emphasized its theatrical origins, caught and held the interest of my students in what they deemed as altogether a different experience from a typical film adaptation. Collectively, they indicated that watching the performance at a cinema rather than on a television or computer screen changed their experience for the better. Rather than a 'community of perception', I would argue my students were members of a community of *reception* as they took in various aspects of what became a multi-sensory experience where visual, auditory, and spatially-related aspects coalesced. In this chapter, I will interrogate how a broadcast performance can foment a communal experience, which in turn leads to a more complex reception than previously assumed of what many are calling a new hybrid form.

In our region of the United States big-budget, live theatre productions of Shakespeare are not readily available. Our campus is located 55 miles south of Cleveland's Great Lakes Theater district, which regularly stages Shakespeare plays. For some students, this distance is negligible, but for others it seems unsurmountable. Our campus, a regional branch of a state university, has been working hard at overcoming that distance. Students attended NTLive's *Hamlet* for classes in which viewing films and live performances of Shakespeare was required.[2] One component of the class involved travelling to live performances at the American Shakespeare Center in Staunton, Virginia, which is home to the Blackfriars Playhouse, a reconstruction of Shakespeare's indoor theatre. The intent was not only to experience live theatre, but to do so at a Renaissance-style thrust stage venue and thus enhance understanding of Early Modern performance conditions.[3] Before the class trip, some of my students had never even been inside a theatre. Other students, however, lived in a theatre, so to speak. The majority were English majors, with a focus on literature, and a handful were Theatre majors – this added to a bevy of different reactions when they attended the *Hamlet* broadcast.

A key element enhancing immersion is the venue's spatial quality. As André Bazin noted, '[t]here can be no theater without architecture' (1967: 104). The multiplexes in Northeast Ohio that hosted the broadcasts, like most indoor cinema venues, are designed in a proscenium fashion; and as some of my students noted, this helped them prepare mentally to see a theatrical performance. NTLive's current policy not to make these performances available on DVD marries the depiction on the screen to the physical space of a theatre by taking away the choice to own a copy for home viewing. In part because they attended the screening at a physical theatre, and because the venue deliberately fostered a live theatre experience by broadcasting *Hamlet* in the screen room with the most elegant double-door entrance, employing an usher with a flashlight to guide people to their seats, and opening the private concession stand adjacent to the screen room for intermission, my students joined a community of reception more readily (see Elam, Chapter 13, for a point of comparison). A more experienced theatre-going student was skeptical at first. She noted: 'It was weird to watch a movie of a play that tried to mock what going to the actual play would have been like. As someone who has seen multiple plays in a live theatre environment, seeing one in a movie theatre was very hard to adjust to at first.' But this soon changed for her because of the theatrical ambiance the broadcast provided. She added, 'I liked that the [introduction] film showed us shots of the audience in order to make us feel as if we had just sat down next to this section of seats and we were about to see this play live, too. They also included an intermission, which was when I began to really feel like I was at a live showing.' It was in fact the intermission, signalled by the lights coming on in the cinema, which transformed the spatial dynamics around her and allowed her to suspend her disbelief for the remainder of the performance. Another student explained that Cumberbatch's plea to the audience at the end of the performance to consider donating to the Syrian refugee cause made her conscious of the interconnectedness of the audience attending the live performance and those watching the broadcast because she felt equally addressed by the appeal.

Further contributing to my students' communal experience was the viewpoint of the performance that they shared, as the same shot is shown on screen for all to see. When my students visited the Blackfriars Playhouse, they were constantly aware of the proximity and distance of the actors, amongst each other and in relation to the audience. Digital broadcast ultimately eliminates the single vantage point (based on seat location) and establishes a communal view – one where the audience, seeing the exact same screen shot, can look directly into the actor's eyes one moment, and scan the whole stage the next. There is no longer a front, back, or a side to the stage because the camera can take the viewer anywhere, one aspect of what Nicholas Hytner calls the 'limitless' potential of 'a new genre' (2009: 6). Instead, there are degrees of distance. A cinema audience member can experience the feeling of floating over the stage, in the space of the stage, and through the scene itself. The camera angles offer the broadcast audience an almost omniscient view, yet one that remains located within the theatre stage. As one student noted, 'the multiple angles we were able to view [the play] from because of editing actually enhanced the experience ... The National Theatre [*sic*] had a very beautiful and elaborate stage that was meant to be seen from more than just a singular point of view.'[4] This new fluid digital stage, along with a viewer's experience of theatre conventions, creates an experience that is primarily the product of the movement of the cameras, close-ups and sweeping shots from different angles, which compartmentalizes the stage into various interconnected smaller parts.

Theatre broadcasts to cinemas blur the lines of seating arrangements – there is no such thing as a first-row or last-row seat. Therefore performances become, in a way, very 'democratic' since in the United States, undiscounted ticket prices cost the same regardless of one's seat location. As Janice Wardle explains, NTLive's 'ambition [is] to bring the remote viewers the equivalent of the "best seat in the house"' (2014: 136). The visual proximity allows an audience member to see, through a close-up of Cumberbatch's face, Hamlet's eyes tearing up as he approaches Ophelia (Sian Brooke), or to notice that bald spots appear in her scalp, as if she has pulled her hair out by the root, when Ophelia's downward spiral begins. Writing about NTLive's *Coriolanus* (2014), Erin Sullivan credits part of the 'excessively emotional' performance to the 'multi-angle close-up'. The movement of the camera, she adds, leads to feelings of empathy and identification as Virgilia's, Volumnia's and Coriolanus' tears all glisten clearly for the cinema audience (2014: 1). Through a time-delayed broadcast, my students in Northeast Ohio were able to witness Hamlet's and Ophelia's pain more closely than could some audience members at the Barbican.

However, when attending a live performance, an audience member can look around in any direction and for any length of time while taking in the stage and its surroundings. When attending a broadcast, someone else chooses for the viewer and the audience experiences a forfeiture of viewing autonomy. The audience's gaze is limited to what appears on the screen. This loss refers to the audience's 'rights of reception' – the viewer's right to 'look where and when they choose, accumulating their own personal apprehensions of the action' – a phrase first used by Bernadette Cochrane and a colleague at a conference presentation (qtd. in Cochrane and Bonner 2014: 127). In exchange for fluidity, my students lost the ability to look where they chose. This loss was more acutely felt by my Theatre majors. The less experienced theatregoers equated the broadcast more with film, likely accustomed to having their viewpoint guided by another. A Theatre major interested in stage design wanted to take in everything she could about the stage. She said: 'There were a couple of scenes when I was watching a part of the set and the camera flipped to a different angle ... I am very weird about what I look at when I am watching a play, and I would rather have the freedom to see what I want rather than a different angle from a camera [that gives me a new perspective].' By contrast, an English major fixed her attention on the actors' movement on stage. She said: 'Even though I wasn't there [at the Barbican], I felt the emotion of [Cumberbatch's] performance *in my bones*. He utilized the entire stage in every scene he was in. He moved this way and that way, carried a prop here, touched a person's shoulder there – every action he made had a purpose to further enhance his role' (emphasis original). For this student, the footage of Cumberbatch's use of the stage added to her understanding of the character. She got to see everything she wanted to see.

David Sabel, former executive director of NTLive, asserts: 'If we've done our job, you should feel you saw a piece of theatre, not a film, even though there were probably lots of close-ups where the director was choosing what you see' (2012). At certain times during the performance of *Hamlet*, my students did not much care for a close-up of the speaker because it was not the speaker who, they felt, was communicating vital narrative information. One such instance pertains to the Ghost's first appearance to Hamlet. The Ghost stands below, while Hamlet looks down from the balcony. Even though Hamlet's loud interjections are heard, there is no accompanying visual: the camera remains on the Ghost and viewers are denied the option to look at Cumberbatch's expression. Is it one of fear? Horror? Shock? Confusion? Only a live audience could respond to such a question because there is more than one point of interest on stage. Cochrane and Bonner explain that '[t]he reactions of *other* characters can be just as informative in the development of one's perceptions of the drama. Their expressions of shock, sympathy, or resignation are as integral to the action as is the current speaker' (2014: 127). The focus on the Ghost persists, and the camera provides a close-up as he describes his death, with only quick shots of Hamlet's profile. The ghostly presence captivates directorial choice and limits the audience's view of the main character's likely emotional and psychological state – a limit my students lamented. Having discussed this particular scene in class before the screening, one student said: 'I was looking forward to assessing Cumberbatch's acting ability based on that scene. I wanted to see, written on his face, that he had just seen his father's ghost, and I wanted to believe him. But I didn't have the chance to do so.' Because of the significance we had afforded this scene during class, most of my students expected a close-up of the actor; their assumption was that key moments in the protagonist's emotional arc would be captured on camera, just like one might expect in a feature film.

However, a momentary lack of clarity may work to add a touch of shared uncertainty to the experience. As the swearing scene between Hamlet, Horatio and the soldiers (1.5.149–98) transitions into the scene of Ophelia's concerned exchange with Polonius (2.1.74–120), there is a brief interlude where stagehands change props and Hamlet interacts with Ophelia. The camera pans out and a wide shot shows Hamlet kneeling next to Ophelia retrieving items from a trunk. He leans toward her – was that a caress on the cheek or was he whispering in her ear? Her expression is one of confusion, shared by the viewing audience, unsure of what just happened. A moment later, Cumberbatch's Hamlet clearly speaks to Ophelia before kissing her on the lips and promptly leaving the stage. The elevated, distant angle of the camera leaves broadcast audience members to speculate on the interaction, and this worked particularly well for one of my students. He said: 'I don't want to see *everything*' (emphasis original). For him, having some uncertainty only opened more avenues of discussion with his classmates. 'I've been to the theatre many times,' he added, 'and for me it is the unclear actions of the characters that have always led to the best conversations with others who saw the performance.' For this experienced theatregoer, uncertainty was a welcome element and acted as a marker of a 'theatrical' mode of engagement.

I strongly suspect that the class environment greatly contributed to my students' response to the broadcast performance. Our pre-broadcast class discussions, our group attendance, and our post-broadcast discussions helped foster a sense of community, a community of reception, with their classmates. In the days leading up to the broadcast many remarked on their excitement at attending – regardless of whether they had attended a live performance before, the digital broadcast was a novelty for all. While they were required to watch certain screen adaptations for class, these were films they would watch on their own time, likely on their computer screens or even on their phones while experiencing the isolation that Holland notes. However, the NTLive *Hamlet* provided them with a very different experience – different even from what they encountered at the Blackfriars Playhouse. Because they had purchased a ticket ahead of time, travelled to a theater-like building, and sat with an audience inside a proscenium-styled space, in front of a screen hundreds of times larger than their computer screens, their engagement was different from the previous Shakespeare films they had seen, but typical, I believe, of a larger constituency – that of the tech-savvy university students who have an interest, at varying degrees, in theatre performance. They were trying to take it all in, knowing that there was no pause button they could hit, and no replay option. This felt to them like a one-time performance, almost as if it were indeed live.

The broadcast has limitations, exemplified primarily through the audience's loss of viewing independence. However, the fluidity of the camera angles, alternating between close-ups and wide shots, gives the audience new views. Each of my students in Northeast Ohio had the 'best seat' to view details of a play staged in London and experienced a one-of-a-kind perspective on the performance. As one student noted: 'For those who don't live in London, or Europe for that matter, this showing was a once in a lifetime opportunity.' It is not film. It is not theatre. It is a 'hybrid form', as John Wyver has called it (2014: 105), which incorporates qualities (and failings) of both media. As such, we should start thinking of it as a new view into a performance, and as an experience that can be immersive and communal even for a distant audience.

Notes

1 The broadcasts were screened at Cinemark Tinseltown, North Canton, Ohio, 15 October 2015, and Cinemark Cuyahoga Falls, Cuyahoga Falls, Ohio, 15 November 2016.

2 Students were enrolled in 'Shakespeare on Stage' in Fall 2015, and 'The Shakespeare Experience' in Fall 2016, at Kent State University at Stark, North Canton, Ohio, USA. I wish to thank the Deans of the Stark Campus and my English Department colleagues for their support.

3 While for the first broadcast students had not yet visited the Blackfriars Playhouse, for the encore broadcast they had. Based on student comments, having recently attended a live performance did not affect appreciation of the broadcast, but previous theatre-going experience was a factor.

4 *Hamlet* was performed and filmed at the Barbican. However, the student, unfamiliar with the London stage, assumed that the venue was called the National Theatre.

References

Bazin, A. (1967), 'Theater and Cinema: Part Two', in H. Gray (ed. and trans.), *What is Cinema?* Berkeley: University of California Press, 95–124.

Cochrane, B. and F. Bonner (2014), 'Screening from the Met, the NT or the House: What Changes with the Live Relay', *Adaptation*, 7 (2): 121–33.

Falocco, J. (2017), '"Bard on Demand": Shakespeare on Screen[s] in the Twenty-First Century', in S. Homan (ed.), *Playing Offstage: The Theater as a Presence or Factor in the Real World*, Lanham: Lexington Books, 57–68.

Groves, N. (2012), 'Arts Head: David Sabel, Head of Digital, National Theatre', *The Guardian*, 10 April. Available online: https://www.theguardian.com/culture-professionals-network/culture-professionals-blog/2012/apr/10/david-sabel-digital-national-theatre (accessed 29 September 2017).

Holland, P. (1994), 'Two-dimensional Shakespeare: *King Lear* on Film', in A. Davis and S. Wells (eds), *Shakespeare and the Moving Image*, Cambridge: Cambridge University Press, 50–68.

Hytner, N. (2009), 'Nicholas Hytner: Director of the National Theatre', *The Royal National Theatre, Annual Report and Financial Statements 2008–2009*. Available online: http://d1wf8hd6ovssje.cloudfront.net/documents/NT_Annual_Report_0809_1.pdf (accessed 29 September 2017).

Sullivan, E. (2014), 'Stage, Place, and Celebrity: *Coriolanus* at the Donmar', *Digital Shakespeares*, 4 April. Available online: https://digitalshakespeares.wordpress.com/2014/04/04/stage-screen-and-celebrity-coriolanus-at-the-donmar/comment-page-1/ (accessed 10 April 2016).

Wardle, J. (2014), '"Outside Broadcast": Looking Backwards and Forwards, Live Theatre in the Cinema – NT Live and RSC Live', *Adaptation* 7 (2): 134–53.

Wyver, J. (2014), '"All the Trimmings?": The Transfer of Theatre to Television in Adaptations of Shakespeare Stagings', *Adaptation* 7 (2): 104–20.

15

Shakespeare from the House of Molière:

The Comédie-Française/Pathé Live *Roméo et Juliette* (2016)

Pascale Aebischer

While the largest UK-based theatre broadcast companies, with NTLive at the forefront, have managed to reach international audiences, France has proved a difficult market to penetrate. The policy of 'cultural exception' pursued in trade negotiations by successive French governments from 1987 onwards in an effort to resist the forces of globalization and the 'need to defend France's identity, way of life, and cultural heritage' from Anglo-American domination has created an environment that is resistant to non-francophone Shakespeares (Gordon and Meunier 2001: 24), other than in the shape of touring productions or feature films. NTLive, RSCLive and Shakespeare's Globe have all found it difficult to penetrate the French market even though, as the four other essays in this section testify, they have succeeded in gaining a foothold and local following in geographical locations and cultures that are much more distant from the UK.

Instead, an individual tradition, which incorporates and adapts classical works from other cultures alongside French literature, has emerged from the combination of cultural protectionism and state funding for key institutions. The Comédie-Française, France's leading classical theatre troupe whose history goes back, uninterrupted, to Molière's company under Louis XIV, is one of these. In 2016, the company broke new ground by entering into a three-year deal with Pathé Live to broadcast its theatre productions to over 300 cinemas in the Francophone world (France, Belgium, francophone parts of Switzerland, and Québec) and to selected cinemas in some European capital cities. Nine years after Pathé Live became a major player in Continental Europe as the distributor for Met Live in HD and, two years later, Bolshoi Ballet, this was not as belated or gigantic a step-change for the company as might be supposed: the Comédie-Française has a long track record of broadcasts on national television, with the first live broadcast of Zeffirelli's production of Musset's *Lorenzaccio* on Antenne 2 going back to 1977 (Cousteix 2017: 7).

Nevertheless, the broadcast was billed as a significant event by both Pathé Live and the Comédie-Française's artistic director Éric Ruf: both saw it as a means to widen the reach of the company's work, with Ruf excited at being able to take its shows 'to an audience that is much broader and diverse and well beyond the big cities' that form part of the company's habitual touring circuit (Ruf 2016a). As the Pathé Live programme note proclaimed, this was about making prestigious cultural institutions, and in particular now 'the house of Molière', accessible to the largest number of people through 'satellite transmission of HD images and the 5.1 sound system' ('Chères Spectatrices' 2016).

Significantly however, in view of the stress laid on Molière in the Comédie-Française's marketing, the flagship production to be broadcast to cinemas as part of this agreement on 13 October 2016 was neither his *Misanthrope* nor Edmond Rostand's *Cyrano de Bergerac*, another stalwart of the French theatrical repertoire, which were both part of the 2016–17 Comédie-Française/Pathé Live season. Instead, the choice fell on Ruf's production of Shakespeare's *Romeo and Juliet*, in François Victor Hugo's now classic translation which combines poetic diction with moments of striking directness. The production was billed as a 'Shakespeare classic' set in a 'timeless poetic universe' (Ruf 2016a), apparently chosen to confer international cultural capital on this new venture and justify – a romantic little touch – the live broadcast of the production to a cinema in Verona, one of the few receiving locations in a non-francophone country.

On the night of the live broadcast, audiences in the Comédie-Française, located in the Place Colette in the heart of Paris' Right Bank, had to negotiate armed guards at the entrance of the building and bag-searches in the lobby before being able to enter the auditorium. None of these extra security measures implemented as part of France's anti-terrorist *vigipirate* scheme in the wake of attacks on Paris (7 January and 13 November 2015) and Nice (14 July 2016), however, affected the broadcast's viewers in cinemas on the Left Bank of the Seine. For the audience at the Les Fauvettes Pathé Gaumont multiplex in Paris – a spacious and stylish wood-and-glass arts multiplex hidden behind a nondescript Parisian boulevard façade – this was a genuinely novel way of experiencing theatre without the constraints on movement and the social etiquette of smart dress or even evening dress that was on display within the stalls of the Salle Richelieu auditorium. On arrival in the cinema, what distinguished the mainly middle-aged, middle-class broadcast viewers from other visitors to the multiplex was not their attire, but the fact that a dedicated usher handed them a Pathé Live season programme and cast list for *Roméo et Juliette*.

Once in the auditorium, broadcast viewers were immediately visually integrated in the audience space of the Comédie-Française. A live feed from the theatre showing the Salle Richelieu filling up, with audience chatter on the soundtrack, linked the theatre to the cinema while broadcast viewers, too, settled into their seats. Occasional frontal wide shots showed the empty stage, while other shots took viewers inside the control box or focused close-up on actors preparing for the performance. Panning shots of the auditorium revealed the sheer size and gilded lavishness of the Salle Richelieu. Clearly, as Ruf's foreword indicated, part of the pleasures afforded by the broadcast would be access to a theatrical experience that, along with providing 'depth, beauty, poetry and laughter', would not stint on rich 'decorative ornament' (2016a). That point was also made during the interval feature, in which a documentary explained the process behind the creation of the production's costumes, designed by no less a celebrity than couturier Christian Lacroix.

As the lights were dimmed in the Salle Richelieu, the cinema went almost completely black, lit only by the brightness of the production's white-tiled and crumbling white marble set, designed by Ruf himself to convey a decaying, impoverished inter-war Italy in which heat and violence coexisted with piety and the remnants of a once 'glorious civilisation' (Ruf 2016b). But the cognitive suturing of broadcast audience and theatre audience which broadcast director Don Kent thus achieved was ruptured as soon as Bakary Sangaré's jovial Chorus stepped onto the stage, cheerfully greeting the theatre audience with repeated calls of '*bonsoir*', which he only stopped once they greeted him back. His next question – '*elle est où, la caméra?*' ('where is the camera?') – served to distinguish sharply between the theatre audience and the broadcast audience. He identified the latter with the camera at the downstage left corner of the first circle, and then went on to address the broadcast viewers directly with '*bonsoir dans l'espace de cinéma*' ('good evening in the cinema space'), giving them a local habitation within the spatial economy of the broadcast. Throughout the broadcast, this 'broadcast audience camera' would continue to function as the spatial anchor for viewers in the cinema.

While the vantage points of the remaining seven cameras dotted around the first circle (with one, central top-down camera from the rear of the second circle) read as 'neutral' in relation to the broadcast audience, Kent's selection of shots repeatedly took on an interpretative edge. Tracking shots followed characters dashing across the stage and were particularly associated with Christian Gonon's Tybalt, so that with his death, the stylistic febrility with which Verona was portrayed during the play's comic beginning morphed into a more static approach as the plot turned towards tragedy. Wide shots of the whole stage offered broadcast audiences what Erin Sullivan describes as a 'theatrical point of view' in which actors, especially in group scenes, were 'tracked and mapped by the camera rather than firmly framed within it' (Sullivan 2017: 639). Wide shots were also used to emphasize the loneliness of Suliane Brahim's Juliet as she crouched down in one corner of her vast dilapidated bedroom to sob without restraint before swallowing Friar Laurence's potion, or to stress the vertiginous height of her 'balcony', a precariously crumbling marble window ledge at the top of a high tower along which Juliet, a tiny figure, gingerly edged herself sideways in her desperate bid for freedom. Such shots were mixed with close-ups which afforded broadcast viewers a sudden proximity to the performer's face that was almost obtrusive, as each line, trace of stage make-up and bead of sweat on Brahim's face was sharply delineated. The close-ups betrayed not only the age of the performer (thirty-eight at the time of the broadcast), but, more interestingly perhaps, the classical training behind a performance which stressed the lyricism of Hugo's translation. The corresponding close-ups on 32-year-old Jérémy Lopez Romeo, by contrast, while just as unflattering in revealing the glare on his receding hairline, also drew attention to his more casual movement and verse-speaking, so that the inability of the lovers to overcome the physical boundary of the balcony was doubled by the more fundamental incompatibility of their poetic registers.

When the lovers did meet within a shot, the juxtaposition of contraries carried an extra charge because of the way in which the careful framing of their hands created its own sequence of echoes that built up to a tragic climax. At their first encounter, in the washroom at the Capulet ball, a shot framed Romeo blowing on Juliet's wet hand to dry it. In the balcony scene, Juliet's hand reached in vain for a handhold and later, just as fruitlessly, reached down to Romeo far below her. That same hand trembled alarmingly in a tightly framed panning shot that followed its motion as Juliet, already dressed for her bigamous wedding with Paris, raised the glass with Friar Laurence's potion aloft as if to toast Romeo before gulping down the drink. The motif culminated in the monument, where dying Juliet's bloodied hand dramatically reached towards Romeo's lifeless hand, with a pan across the empty space between them emphasizing the impossibility of their union even in death.

The broadcast's formal use of framing to separate the lovers or bring them together, even as it offered the broadcast audience moments of almost uncomfortable proximity, firmly upheld the fourth wall of the proscenium arch, giving an outsider's view of the lovers' relationship. But the Chorus, who had so deliberately flaunted the fourth-wall convention at the start, returned between Acts 1 and 2 and reappeared later in the guise of the second Friar in a comic double-act with Friar Laurence. The direct interaction Sangaré had set up with the audience, both within the theatre and in the cinema, therefore continued to punctuate both the production and its broadcast: repeatedly, performers spoke directly to their audience in the stalls and lower circles. At such moments, the mix would provide a side-on view of the performer on the front of the brightly lit stage that filled roughly one third of the screen, while the remaining part of the image showed the audience in the darkened stalls below, with the use of the broadcast audience camera signalling the imaginary presence of the cinema viewers among the theatre audience addressed by the performer.

The consistency with which this technique was employed to film the throwaway asides that characterized Pierre Louis-Calixte's performance of Mercutio, or indeed the apologetic gestures Romeo made to the hapless spectators in the stalls whom Mercutio singled out during his Queen Mab speech, made the two departures from this technique the more striking. For the most statically formal of all the production's direct addresses – Juliet's 'Gallop apace' soliloquy, which marks the centrepoint of the play – the mix switched to the otherwise rarely-used top-down camera on the second circle. From this high vantage point, Juliet was shown as a slender, diminutive figure standing alone at the centre front of the vast proscenium stage that was bathed in the uniformly white light. These wide shots alternated with close-ups and mid-shots that were static and emphasized the formal nature of her direct address: although within the Richelieu auditorium, Juliet during this speech was physically closer to her audience than at any other point, the broadcast treated her with a formality that closely matched the formality of her classical verse-speaking.

The opposite was true of the broadcast's approach to Romeo, whom the play itself portrays as a gate-crasher and who, in this production, went as far in his disregard for physical and social boundaries as to grab the microphone at the Capulet feast to serenade Juliet. It was therefore fitting that, for Romeo's exile in Mantua, the broadcast should follow suit by breaking through the spatial regimes of the Richelieu auditorium altogether. The theatre audience, whose movements and bags had undergone such rigorous scrutiny before they were allowed access to the inner sanctum of the Salle Richelieu, were rooted in their seats watching Juliet's funeral procession. Exhilaratingly, meanwhile, broadcast viewers were allowed to share in Romeo's exile, which was imagined as a roaming journey free from all such constraints. A hand-held camera 'found' Romeo in the theatre's control booth and followed him as he walked through backstage spaces into the gilded corridors and vast empty staircases of the Comédie-Française's lobbies. While on the broadcast soundtrack, the ponderous funeral march for Juliet's burial could be heard emerging from the auditorium, Romeo was shown finding his way through the maze of the stairs and lobbies, eventually arriving at the stalls door, through which he entered, leaving the hand-held camera behind. An edit took the broadcast viewer to the back of the stalls, where Romeo could be seen walking through the aisle past unsuspecting spectators, with whom he exchanged greetings, and lifting himself onto the stage, where he sat for a while as he told the audience about his propitious dream.

Similar devices have, in recent years, been used for example in Toneelgroep Amsterdam's *Roman Tragedies* (dir. Ivo van Hove, 2007) and the National Theatre's *Edward II* (dir. Hill-Gibbins, 2013), where Enobarbus ran out of the auditorium to die in a gutter outside the theatre or Spencer and Baldock, in a pre-recorded sequence, were shown on the roof of the National Theatre before walking through the backstage areas (including the control box) to eventually emerge in the auditorium. The difference here is that the remediation of a journey outside the boundaries of the auditorium was clearly for the sole benefit of the broadcast audience, who were afforded an imaginary freedom of movement denied to the theatre audience. While the theatre audience partook in the grief of the Capulets, broadcast audiences were able to concentrate on the ironic juxtaposition of Juliet's funeral with Romeo's journey through the building and the hopeful state of mind caused by his dream. Direct address, in this sequence, became a means of creating an experience for the broadcast viewers that transformed their 'exile' outside the privileged sphere of the Comédie-Française in the heart of Paris' 1er arrondissement into an experience in which they could imaginatively connect with the freedom of banishment experienced by Romeo. Within a city under constant terrorist threat, the broadcast thus – in its most daring sequence – cast its viewers as banished into an exile that had less terror in its looks than being in proximity of Juliet, trapped in the gilded cage of the Salle Richelieu.

Repeatedly, the broadcast thus drew attention to the differences between viewing experiences in the theatre and the cinema. As the education booklet produced alongside the broadcast puts it, this was unashamedly 'a production of a production, an operation of *mise en images* [setting into visuals] orchestrated by a viewpoint different from that of the viewer' (Cousteix 2017: 3). For Kent, the broadcast director is essentially a translator of the stage director's 'intentions', which in this instance he tried to understand through attending rehearsals and perusing Ruf's personal dramaturgical notes (Kent 2017: 8; Ruf 2017: 11). Having learned multi-camera direction in France, his approach is distinctive: as he explains, the French method, which involves the broadcast director himself 'touching the buttons, choosing the cameras', is analogous to 'playing a musical instrument' (Kent 2017: 9). Kent thus affirms the distinctive creative skills sets of the broadcast director that translate the stage director's intentions to the screen with an attention to the musicality of both the staging and of Shakespeare's play (Kent 2017: 9). Whereas, with varying degrees of individuality, most Shakespeare broadcasts emerging from Anglophone cultures work hard to render 'transparent' the artistic input of the broadcast director, this first Shakespeare broadcast emerging from France is typical of French cultural exceptionalism and the belief in a uniquely French approach, resulting in a strikingly unique style of broadcast.

References

'Chères Spectatrices, chers spectateurs' (2016), *Théâtre, Ballet et Opéra au Cinéma: 2016–17*, Les cinémas Gaumont Pathé.

Cousteix, L. (2017), 'Filmer *Roméo et Juliette* à la Comédie-Française', educational dossier, Comédie-Française and Pathé Live. Available online: https://www.comedie-francaise.fr/www/comedie/media/document/dossier-cfaucinema1617.pdf (accessed 14 July 2017)

Gordon, P.H. and S. Meunier (2001), 'Globalization and French Cultural Identity', *French Politics, Culture & Society*, 19 (1): 22–41.

Kent, D. (2017), 'Le réalisateur est un traducteur', educational dossier, Comédie-Française and Pathé Live, 8–10. Available online: https://www.comedie-francaise.fr/www/comedie/media/document/dossier-cfaucinema1617.pdf (accessed 14 July 2017)

Ruf, É. (2016a), 'Le Mot d'Éric Ruf', *Théâtre, Ballet et Opéra au Cinéma: 2016–17*, Les cinémas Gaumont Pathé.

Ruf, É. (2016b), '*Roméo et Juliette*: Shakespeare le raconteur d'histoires', *Théâtre, Ballet et Opéra au Cinéma: 2016–17*, Les cinémas Gaumont Pathé.

Ruf, É. (2017), 'La Mémoire du spectacle s'en trouve augmentée', educational dossier, Comédie-Française and Pathé Live, 11–13. Available online: https://www.comedie-francaise.fr/www/comedie/media/document/dossier-cfaucinema1617.pdf (accessed 14 July 2017)

Sullivan, E. (2017), '"The forms of things unknown": Shakespeare and the Rise of the Live Broadcast', *Shakespeare Bulletin* 35 (4): 627–62.

Epilogue:

Revisiting Liveness

Laurie E. Osborne

As it turns out, I am a target audience for NTLive, or so the 2011 Encore Season trailer would have me believe. Almost at its midpoint, this highly cinematic trailer shifts away from fast production clips to a black screen where the following sequence of 'quotations' appears:

'The magic of the NT was recreated'
Oxford

'Boggles the mind'
Reykjavik

'Feels like the world has just opened up to us'
Maine

'Fantastic'
Copenhagen

'Blown away'
Washington, DC

'Spellbinding'
Sydney

In this eight seconds around the world, not only do whole cities speak with a single voice, but the transitions from one testimonial to the next involve the current text moving into or away from different parts of the screen, invoking the geographical spread of NTLive over the 2009–10 and 2010–11 seasons. Reykjavik drifts into the screen centre from upper screen right but slides out to screen right, apparently dragging Maine into the middle of the screen from the left. Since I have only attended the live relay broadcasts in the Waterville Opera House, located in the middle of Maine, watching the sudden announcement that my entire state 'feels like the world just opened up for us' surprised me into disruptive laughter. In addition to being the only geographical encomiast that is a whole region rather than a city, Maine is the only entity that connotes not just remoteness, like Reykjavik, but non-urban isolation. Apparently Maine's iconic status as an idyllic rural site extends beyond the US, though it probably does not hurt that several different Maine theatres screen NTLive productions.

The promise of access for geographically divergent and socially varied audiences has resulted in the contagious development of these productions in different venues beyond the initial US and UK productions. The Australian government has issued a white paper, 'Don't Panic' (Australian Council for the Arts 2008), local theatre reviews appeared side by side with NTLive reviews in journals from South Africa (Smith 2010), and analyses from several countries have entered into critical dialogue (see Paterson and Stevens 2013; Fotheringham 2016). The success and resulting spread of 'Name-Your-Company' Live have produced a wealth of responses that is engendering deeper and more complex explorations of what counts as 'live' (see Barker 2013). In response to twenty-first-century film-savvy awareness of visual manipulation and our expanding participation in virtual synchronous interactions (see Kidnie, Chapter 8), theatre broadcasts deploy strategies that combine intimacy, 'eventness' and hybrid media conventions to create on-screen 'liveness', the virtual counterpart to what Tamsen Warner, executive director of the Waterville Opera house, calls 'in-person live' (personal interview, 21 June 2017).

Over a decade ago in 'Speculations on Shakespearean Cinematic Liveness', I examined the theatrical television broadcasts unearthed and digitally reproduced by the *Broadway Theatre Archive* in order to identify and analyse the cinematic strategies used to register the liveness of theatre on stage. Anticipating that subsequent filming of stage performances would incorporate rapidly evolving cinematic visual and aural coding to imply the live qualities of particular productions, I argued that using the capacities of film and televisual reproduction would ultimately both complicate and enable the producers' claims that their audiences were experiencing 'live' performance (Osborne 2006).

Early filmed stage productions, including Richard Burton's 'Electronovision' *Hamlet, Lincoln Center Live,* and the *Broadway Theater Archive* productions, explicitly used cinematic strategies to represent theatrical immediacy and ephemerality. Such strategies are now consistently characterized as 'cold and static' (NTLive 2011), in large part because digital technologies of recording and transmission have made HD playback on cinema screens viable. Because we are currently almost two decades past Philip Auslander's initial 1999 work on liveness and HD theatre broadcasts have become more cinematic rather than televisual in distribution and cultural presence, both the conventions of liveness and the commercial deployment of the term 'live' have shifted considerably, as many chapters in our collection attest. Although similar performative registers operate in current UK theatre broadcasts – aural effects, cinematic structuring of stage space, and theatrically delimited continuity editing – the changes in both technological immersion and commercial theatrical ambitions have reshaped 'liveness' in its broadcast format. The blends of film form and theatrical conventions deployed within theatre broadcasts and their paratexts test the boundaries and linkages between performance modes, with 'liveness' as a pivotal concept under pressure.

As these productions flourish and redefine liveness, the wealth of data about this new version of 'Electronovision' is provoking a comparable burgeoning of critical analysis. Our collection celebrates the fact that critical approaches to theatre broadcasts diverge into several modes of inquiry: historical review of recorded performance practices in film, music, and television as they influence current practices; analysis of their influence on national and local arts production, competition, and financing; exploration of how film techniques and media conventions participate interpretively with theatrical performance and design; and diagnosis of not only technological efforts to fashion audience response but also spontaneous as well as controlled audience participation by way of social media. Each engages liveness from its own context. Whatever ensues on the technical, social media or critical fronts, the challenges for both 'creatives' and critics will be balancing competing constituencies while sustaining – and continually updating – our understanding of theatre broadcasting's artistic, ontological, societal and financial consequences.

In revisiting 'liveness' here, I draw on three NTLive broadcasts and a single production from Kenneth Branagh Theatre Company Plays at the Garrick Live (KBTCLive): Nicholas Hytner and Robin Lough's 2010 *Hamlet* in the National Theatre; Josie Rourke and Tim van Someren's 2013 *Coriolanus* in the Donmar Warehouse; Simon Godwin and Robin Lough's 2017 *Twelfth Night*; and Rob Ashford/Kenneth Branagh and Benjamin Caron's 2016 *Romeo and Juliet* in the Garrick Theatre. All were Encore performances, largely because Waterville Opera House patrons asked for delayed screenings since late night live-relay Thursday performances interfered with their work schedules (Warner, personal interview, 21 June 2017). Hytner and Lough's *Hamlet*, shown as part of the National Theatre's 50th Anniversary celebration season, was even more 'formerly live' since it was screened three years after the original production.

Even if NTLive is right that 'benefits of the live experience have also been observed in audiences watching time-delayed NTLive broadcasts ... suggesting that the atmosphere of the screening and the brand are as important as the instant relay' (NTLive 2010: 14), meshing technological reproduction and on-site(s) performance can create an uneasy blend, especially within modernized productions. Consider the disjuncture between the ways that Hytner's 2010 *Hamlet* deployed men in doorways listening with earpieces to signify the constant spying in Claudius's court while also outfitting Ophelia with a visible, distracting body mike, attached to her back during her mad scenes. Clearly the audience was intended to notice one set of audio interventions as structurally meaningful within the production while ignoring the other as mere technological enhancement. In the National Theatre's Olivier auditorium, one suspects, the audience would recognize the earpieces and the implied hidden recording devices in Denmark's pervasive spies because of the actors' all-too-familiar hand-to-ear gestures as part of the predictable context for the spectacle of Gertrude and Claudius's television interview scene, while ignoring Ophelia's miking as thoroughly as those on stage do because of its lesser visibility in the auditorium. Screened in a cinema far away from the actors, where recording, transmitting, and miking become more obvious in close-ups, the production's engagement with contemporary surveillance acquired an even greater edge and underscored how thoroughly digitized recording, or represented liveness, has become a familiar fixture in our social and political lived reality. This kind of blending of cinematic form and theatre within theatre broadcasts extends into trailers, programmes, venue treatment and intervals and works to reconfigure 'live' performance through mixing features and redeploying their signalling.

Trailer mix

All MetLive, NTLive, most other theatre broadcasts and many stage-only productions are now promoted with cinema-style trailers. NTLive trailers involve aerial views of London, overcranking the already brisk traffic, and an impressive array of wipes, graphics and quick cuts that flaunt the representational capacities of film at the same time that they promote nation in the ways Susan Bennett analyses in Chapter 2. Semi-permanently available on YouTube, these promotional materials sometimes represent whole seasons, invariably include two or three versions for individual performances, appear subtitled for non-English speaking markets, and are often re-edited for Encore presentations.

For example, the self-conscious recording within Hytner's *Hamlet* shifts to explicitly cinematic forms in the trailer. As in the promotion for Lindsay Turner's *Hamlet*, starring Benedict Cumberbatch, Hytner's trailer embraces the rhetorical mode that Lisa Kernan identifies as foregrounding the desirable actor: the entire trailer shows only Rory Kinnear as Hamlet (2004: 68–76). However, in contrast to the actual 2010 theatre broadcast, this promotional teaser represents, to the point of parody, the active intervention of filming with insistent close-ups on Kinnear's face and apparent recording glitches – shaky and blurred images, replay hesitations in sound and image, near-montage abrupt shifts to hyper close-ups of facial features and hands. In fact the trailer offers exactly the kinds of camera manipulation that, according Bernadette Cochrane and Frances Bonner, are ruled out in filming the stage production because 'a close-up, a cut, even an aerial overhead view are possible for the human eye to replicate, but split screens and dissolves are not' (2014: 127; see Osborne 2006: 59). This trailer digitally creates a representational contingency peculiarly linked to film even as it promotes, in cinemas and online, a reprise of the now not-live event and recalls how insistently the production itself foregrounded filming.

In a seeming paradox, these trailers increasingly promote the liveness of the productions by foregrounding the filming in progress and deploying the kinds of wipes and camera effects eschewed in the broadcasts themselves. Energetic filming connotes theatrical energies. The bricolage of cinematic and theatrical features in NTLive trailers allies theatre broadcast with other mediated performance work in the technological arms race for spectator/consumer engagement in the virtually live.

Alternative programming

Because cinema-style trailers now promote numerous non-film artworks, both the likely (video games and stage plays) and the unlikely (books) (Vollans 2015), their role as hybrid paratexts for theatre broadcast is hardly surprising. However, both NTLive and the RSC have also produced new forms of the theatrical programme: digital programmes that complement the pre-performance interviews, themselves an adaptation of the pre-game interviews in live sportscasting (Paterson and Stevens 2013: 149–50). Supplementing the free printed sheets offered at destination venues, this new programme format includes more extensive scholarly discussion, photographic information about the production and actors that extend beyond the theatrical biographies in conventional programs, and – most important – video and digital content.

For example, the cover of the NTLive digital programme for *Frankenstein* displays either Benedict Cumberbatch, or a hybrid image of Cumberbatch and Jonny Lee Miller, or just Miller as Frankenstein's creature, depending on whether the device holding the digital programme is tilted to the left, held level, or tipped to the right. At the moment, you need not buy the *Frankenstein* programme in order to see its digital cover trick. It is available in the tellingly named 'Taster Programme' on the NTLive app and lets potential buyers sample an array of programmes before purchasing them.

The RSC digital programme for *The Tempest* (2017), itself a production that blends digitalization and in-person performance (see Ingham, Chapter 12), incorporates video or digital effects on almost every virtual page, including the coalescing and shattering image of Prospero (Simon Russell Beale) on its cover. This effect, like the variable cover images of the

Frankenstein programme, is both apropos and prophetic. Digital programmes, unlike the dead-tree version, are susceptible to 'updates'. In the case of the NTLive 'Taster Programme' (2017b), this means that new productions are added in (and inevitably old ones removed) over time.

These dynamically generated programmes vividly enact the 'flickering digital archive' that Lindsay Brandon Hunter argues should shift our understanding of both ephemerality and liveness (Hunter 2017). The programme, once a guide to and tangible souvenir of theatre attendance, enters the realm of performance itself and, in its internet-accessed, ephemeral playback, offers its own version of 'live'.

Ear candy

Programmes also become a site for testing out innovation. For example, the audio guide created by the Donmar Warehouse to accompany Encore screenings of the 2013 NTLive *Coriolanus* appropriates the conventions established for DVD director's commentaries for feature films – with a few noteworthy differences (see Balme 2006). This audio commentary is intended to supplement the NTLive filmed production concurrently as it is broadcast on screen, with suitable gaps in the commentary while the action and dialogue play out. While watching Tom Hiddleston play Coriolanus, spectators can hear background information and observations from director Josie Rourke, Hiddleston himself, and occasionally other cast members. By sharing details of the production as an event on stage during nonspeaking moments, the commentary underscores how theatre broadcast reshapes not only audience responses, as Rachael Nicholas points out in Chapter 4, but also reconfigures the visual and aural 'liveness' of the performance. When Rourke explains that Hiddleston's initial entrance from upstage was not working well, so they had him burst in from the audience, that effective bit of stage business obviously did not translate into remote venues. However, her comments establish her seemingly live participation with audience members as they watch the Encore broadcast.

Moreover, though Hiddleston cannot enter the playing space from within broadcast audiences, his voice can directly enter their awareness. The *Coriolanus* audiotrack in effect substitutes auditory intimacy for live presence at the theatre, particularly when Hiddleston speaks in the audience member's ear and on the screen the line 'Better it is to die, better to starve than crave the hire *which we first deserve*,' only to correct his slight error to 'better it is to die, better to starve than crave the hire *which first we do deserve*' (*Cor* 2.3.112–13; my italics). When Rourke 'hope[s] everyone who hears this commentary enjoyed as much as me the moment of Tom slightly simultaneously doing that and correcting himself with himself doing it on the screen' (National Theatre 2017a: 104.37), her observation that there is 'something sort of brilliantly weird about that' registers the ways that theatre broadcast, in this doubly reproduced experience, combines DVD-style voiceover with aurally shared spectatorship, all wrapped up in a digital version of a theatre programme. This particular 'brilliantly weird' immersion in theatrical filmmaking aligns the theatre actor watching, quoting, and correcting himself with the film audience watching, listening, and adapting to an interplay of live/not live. Breaking and remaking of the theatrical frame dynamically interweaves the actor on film and the actor beyond the film. The hesitation in 'which we first deserve' is all too apt since it creates the impression of an initial in-progress error akin to those always possible in live performance and reinforces the visual/aural insistence on an already filmed production.

This dynamic of live/not live offers multifaceted, intermediated performance and the implicit intimacy of Hiddleston and Rourke commenting in our ears rather than the sonic evocations of 'live' theatrical space in earlier filmed stage productions (Osborne 2006: 56–8). In *Live to Your Local Cinema,* Martin Barker lists intimacy second among 'the sheer diversity of kinds of liveness' that these broadcasts enable: 'Intimacy: this involves feeling close to the performers and the action ... It also involves sensing how performers are achieving their performances' (2013: 65). Barker catalogues a range of audience interactions with intimacy from 'immersive' to 'expert' (2012: 16), but these particular immersive effects are noticeably emergent, not established: so far only the Donmar *Coriolanus* programme includes parallel audio commentary. Moreover, its exploitation of audio interaction suggests that sound continues to be a powerful and undertheorized performance feature that influences liveness.

Mise en théâtre

As digital programmes adopt conventional theatrical paratexts and adapt them to promote contextual awareness and imaginative engagement as new markers of liveness, the broadcasts themselves engage spectators in experiencing the theatre as live through dynamic interaction with their environs. They rework the conventional theatregoer's 'eyes and mind ... in constant motion' (Hornby 2011: 197) by supplying large-screen high definition images and by using establishing shots to embed audiences in very different venues – the Barbican, Donmar Warehouse, Garrick Theatre, and so forth. Such venue-specific *mise en théâtre* can resonate or conflict with the screening theatres in dynamic ways that potentially shift the balance toward cinematic or theatrical experience (see Elam, Chapter 13).

Unlike the digital broadcasting on television that I once anticipated, cinematically distributed theatre broadcasts engage their destination audiences within their own venues. A multi-performance theatre like the Waterville Opera House, where 80 per cent of its programming occurs on stage rather than on screen, offers its predominantly in-person live experiences as the context for its audience members' awareness of the liveness of Metropolitan Opera House and National Theatre broadcasts (Warner, personal interview, 21 June 2017). Moreover, any given audience member brings different on-site experiences and expectations into their theatre broadcast attendance. While many Maine residents have watched governors and city officials sworn in on the Opera House stage, I have seen singer Mary Chapin Carpenter, Maine author Caroline Chute's public reading, and my neighbour performing in Gilbert and Sullivan's *Ruddigore* on that stage. Though certainly not thinking about these events while watching Shakespeare theatre broadcasts, I remained aware of the performance space as multi-modal. For some, flexibility in the destination venue, particularly the on-stage events, might contribute to an awareness of potential 'liveness', while others might respond differently, particularly if, as happened during the KBTCLive *Romeo and Juliet*, the feed freezes and Derek Jacobi as Mercutio becomes a still image rather than a moving one. The interaction between source and destination venues potentially enhances – or erodes – liveness, raising the stakes for both sites.

For example, the KBTCLive *Romeo and Juliet* opens and reiterates at several points a shot of the Garrick theatre set so high that the image includes the precipitate circular stalls and the theatre floor. The visually arresting but dizzying shot represents a perspective that broadcast audiences unfamiliar with Garrick's highest tier of seats could easily take to be an eagle's eye shot. It simultaneously invites the broadcast audience into the encompassing integrity of the theatre as whole and implies that their access is uniquely available cinematically. When the production reiterates this perspective at several key moments and uses somewhat less vertiginous overhead shots of Juliet in the tomb and the two lovers in the final tableau, it treats the Garrick as both a theatrical and cinematic space.

Perhaps because Branagh himself, like so many current actors and directors, works in both cinema and theatre, the KBTCLive *Romeo and Juliet* also displays how thoroughly film form can now intersect with staging within theatre broadcasts, a goal that Branagh himself has articulated: 'I believe that, working with the talented director Bejamin Caron, we can bring the immediacy and excitement of the live stage production into cinemas. We will employ film techniques to make these broadcasts truly cinematic, without in any way compromising the theatrical experience' (qtd. in Shenton 2015). Live captured in black and white CinemaScope, this production persistently but subtly separates the broadcast spectators from the actual theatregoers at the Garrick, where reality is of necessity in full colour despite the production's monochrome set design and costuming. Moreover, as Michael Billington notes, the production's staging evokes film: 'You feel Fellini is due any moment to film it with a movie camera' (2016). Unlike the 1972 BTA theatre broadcast of *Much Ado about Nothing* (Osborne 2006: 58–9), the KBTCLive *Romeo and Juliet* effectively uses cinematic and theatrical coding reciprocally by integrating its cinematically informed production design with evocative black-and-white filming.

Collaboration between cinematic form and stage design is also evident in Simon Godwin's 2017 *Twelfth Night*, captured for NTLive by Robin Lough. Hinted at in the digital programme cover's video of a tuxedo-clad Malvolia climbing angled stairs and bursting a balloon under foot in an endless loop, the production's clever rotating stage and pincer staircases not only physically embody the play's 'whirligig of time' but also enable a number of visually impressive and exhilaratingly hazardous stage effects. Moreover, in addition to producing a sense of successive 'frames', the rotating stage and stairs correlate neatly with angled shots and more circular panning than I recall from earlier NTLive broadcasts. The stage movement also allied the theatre broadcast spectators with other in-theatre audience members who heard the laughter rolling through the theatre before Malvolia, entirely attired in burlesque yellow and reclining on the staircase, circled into view. The simultaneous effects of film and stage movement are enhanced by the aural presence of the theatre audience, particularly their laughter (see Aebischer, Chapter 7). As these broadcasts show in different ways, increasing collusion between filming and staging subtly reshapes liveness. Cinematic reinforcement of theatrical production design turns liveness into their shared effect.

Interval training

Theatre broadcasts also appropriate and revise the interval, a stage convention implicated in the dynamics of theatrical liveness. In the theatre, the interval offers the audience temporary release (or perhaps banishment) from the performance, freedom to move about and converse, and a communal waiting for the action to resume on stage. Arguably, by restoring those spectators temporarily to their own real experience, theatrical intervals not only enable complex set changes but also remind spectators that what they are watching may be live, but it is fictional rather than real. As spectators move between levels of liveness, migrating back and forth through different realities, intervals enhance the experience of live performance by temporarily withholding it.

Incorporating the interval into the theatre broadcast transplants theatrical experience into this new performance field (see Bennett, Chapter 2; Elam, Chapter 13; Martinez, Chapter 14), offering different source theatres their opportunity not only for branding and promotion, but also for an even more structured release from the 'live' experience. Essentially theatre broadcasts both introduce and eliminate the interval. They signal the gap in the 'live' performance but often fill at least part of that gap, sometimes with synchronous backstage interviews but often with obviously pre-recorded materials that are demonstrably less 'live' than the performance itself.

The interval for the KBTCLive *Romeo and Juliet* incorporated information about national and historical context of the production design in a text-based slide show apparently projected on the curtain in the theatre during the in-house interval:

What is the age of consent in Italy?
The age is 15

What is *passeggiata*?
The art of taking a walk in the evening to socialize

When did Italian women get the right to vote?
1945

How many Italian civilian and military personal died in WWII?
457,000
. . .
What was one of the most influential developments?
Television

What is *sprezzatura*?
Studied nonchalance

This question-and-response structure turned intermission into education. Just as important, the slideshow's rhythmically regular, predictable linking of language contrasted the film's less predictable and thus more 'lively' close-ups, medium shots and overhead shots. In fact, the clunky and apparently dated technology of an all-text slideshow underscored the greater sophistication of cinematic juxtapositions within the theatre broadcast overall.

More interesting, the transformation of the stage curtain into screen for projection interacted with the other deployments of the curtain – Branagh's greeting and comments about live theatre before the curtain, Juliet's taking poison behind a more translucent veil-like curtain in silhouette, and her pulling down that obstruction as she 'died'. The performances before, on and behind various curtains are production features in the KBTCLive *Romeo and Juliet* that link this stage production to film while complicating the curtain/screen relationship in receiving venues. This theatre broadcast, like many others, reconstructs the interval as performance and the performance itself within the interval.

Fast forward

The emergence and ongoing development of theatrical broadcasting suggest that liveness no longer calls for cinematic strategies that invoke presence in the theatre in the same way that earlier efforts did. Theatre broadcast directors now face audiences considerably more immersed in techno-proximal interactions and progressively more attuned to degrees of liveness because of cinematic and digital trends that are likely to continue influencing developments in theatre broadcast. Like Burton's 1960's 'Electronovision', which has re-emerged from the 1960s with a vengeance in theatre broadcasts, 3D cinema has also returned to movie theatres and could easily be the next immersive step in theatre-to-screen broadcasting. After all, motion capture has entered the RSC's Shakespeare on stage with Doran's 2016 *Tempest*. Theatre broadcasts in 3D could give the cinema spectators a virtual seat in the house or on the stage. As with any technology-inspired performance innovation, a move to 3D would entail retrofitting venues, likely favouring the already renovated cineplexes over multi-performance venues like Maine's Waterville Opera House, which could not screen event cinema until after their 2012 renovation.

Another emergent performance platform, gaming, promises even more immersive experience to encourage participants in their experience of liveness. Gaming-style VR could embed audiences as participants in site-specific productions and enliven currently 'canned' backstage tours. Linked to changing sophistication in audio and visual reproduction, such experimentation on both fronts is likely to continue the more pervasive online and virtual liveness effects become.

At the moment, theatre broadcasts garner their influence and profitability from both wide screen limited release as events and from blending cinematic and theatrical artfulness to create intimacy and dynamic engagement. 'Liveness' in this current mode is more than a marketing or venue gimmick, and its interactions with cinematic form are more complex than earlier filming of theatrical productions. The move to theatre broadcasts in cinemas along side television or computer screens – a shift I did not anticipate in 2006 – has precipitated a merging of performance and promotion practices that reflects on and elaborates an increasingly digitized common ground.

By engaging our evolving sense of 'liveness' within an endlessly reproduced world, theatre broadcasting has reshaped and will continue to test definitions of liveness by replacing an opposition between cinema and theatre with paratextual, contextual and spectatorial collaboration. Within the warp of digitization, we are weaving performance modes – and their paratexts – ever more closely together and shifting emphasis from the liveness inherent in the productions to liveness in their reception. I once concluded that digital recording of live theatre would 'recreate as well as reproduce Shakespearean performance' (2006: 64). I now believe that theatre broadcasting is reshaping cinematic practice in service of relocated and asynchronous collective experience – both putting stress on and stressing 'liveness' in the process.

References

Auslander, P. (1999), *Liveness: Performance in a Mediatized Culture*, London: Routledge.
Australian Council for the Arts (2008), '"Don't Panic": The impact of digital technology on the major performing arts industry'. Available online:

http://www.australiacouncil.gov.au/workspace/uploads/files/research/dont_panic_digital_discussion_-54325cbb827ba.pdf (accessed 1 June 2017).

Balme, C.B. (2006), 'Audio Theatre: The Mediatization of Theatrical Space', in F. Chapple and C. Kattenbelt (eds), *Intermediality in Theatre and Performance*, Amsterdam: Rodopi, 117–124.

Barker, M. (2013), *Live to Your Local Cinema: The Remarkable Rise of Livecasting*, New York: St. Martin's Press.

Cochrane, B. and F. Bonner (2014), 'Screening from the Met, the NT, or the House: What Changes with the Live Relay', *Adaptation* 7 (2): 121–33.

Fotheringham, R. (2016), 'Screening Live Performance: Australia's Major Theatre Companies in the Age of Digital Transmission', *Australasian Drama Studies* 68: 3–33.

Hornby, R. (2011), 'National Theatre Live', *Hudson Review* 64: 196–202.

Hunter, L.B. (2017), 'Digital Theatricality: Flickering Documents in Unsteady Archives', *Amodern 7: Ephemera and Ephemerality*. Available online: http://amodern.net/article/digital-theatricality/ (accessed 1 March 2018).

Kernan, L. (2004), *Coming Attractions: Reading American Movie Trailers*, Austin: University of Texas Press.

NTLive (2010), 'National Theatre *Hamlet*', YouTube, 13 October. Available online: https://youtu.be/-Dv_BSDXXbY?list=PL9C36281237500DC7 (accessed 23 May 2017).

NTLive (2011), 'The Best of British Theatre Broadcast to Cinemas', YouTube, 7 December. Available online: http://youtu.be/zCMou5vTP-k (accessed 22 May 2017).

National Theatre (2017a), '*Coriolanus* Digital Programme', *National Theatre Backstage*, Mobile App, Version 1.9.1. Available online: https://itunes.apple.com/gb/app/national-theatre-backstage/id1006110950?mt=8 (accessed 1 February 2017).

National Theatre (2017b). 'Taster Programme', NTLive App 1.10.0. Available online: https://www.nationaltheatre.org.uk/digital (accessed 15 July 2017).

Osborne, L.E. (2006), 'Speculations on Shakespearean Cinematic Liveness', *Shakespeare Bulletin* 24 (3): 49–65.

Paterson, E. and L. Stevens (2013), 'From Shakespeare to Super Bowl: Theatre and Global Liveness', *Australasian Drama Studies* 62: 148–62.

RSC (2017), *The Tempest: Digital Programme*. RSC app. 6.0. Developer: John T. Goode. Available online: https://itunes.apple.com/us/app/rsc-live/id1012890597?mt=8 (accessed 3 July 2017).

Shenton, M. (2015), 'Kenneth Branagh Productions to Be Broadcast Internationally in Live Screening', *Playbill*, 11 September. Available online: http://www.playbill.com/article/kenneth-branagh-productions-to-be-broadcast-internationally-in-live-screenings-com-361846 (accessed 14 July 2017).

Smith, D. (2010), '*All's Well That Ends Well*', *Shakespeare in Southern Africa* 22: 47–9.

Vollans, E. (2015), 'So just what is a Trailer, Anyway?', *Arts Marketing* 5 (2): 112–25.

Appendix

Digital Theatre Broadcasts of Shakespeare, 2003–17

Rachael Nicholas

This filmography contains stage productions of Shakespeare plays, or their adaptations, that were filmed digitally, in their entirety, in front of live theatre audience members for wider distribution (live or recorded) up to the end of October 2017. An asterisk in the 'Mode of distribution' column indicates that a DVD of the production is commercially available.

All of the productions that were filmed as part of the 'Globe to Globe' festival at Shakespeare's Globe in 2012 appear here as one entry. Thirty-four of the recordings are available online via Globe Player. For detailed information about individual productions see *A Year of Shakespeare: Re-Living the World Shakespeare Festival* (2013), edited by Paul Edmonson, Paul Prescott and Erin Sullivan.

Broadcast/ Release Date	Play	Theatre Space	Theatre Company	Director for Stage	Broadcast Company	Director for screen	Producer for screen	Mode of distribution
7 Sept 2003	Richard II	Globe Theatre	Shakespeare's Globe	Tim Carroll	BBC	Sue Judd	Alison Havell	Live television broadcast, BBC4.
4 Sept 2004	Measure for Measure	Globe Theatre	Shakespeare's Globe	John Dove	BBC	Janet Fraser Cook	Alison Havell, Alison Willett	Live television broadcast, BBC4.
27 Sept 2007	Othello	Globe Theatre	Shakespeare's Globe	Wilson Milam	Heritage Theatre	Derek Bailey	Robert Marshall	DVD only. Recorded live in 2007.*
1 Oct 2009	All's Well that Ends Well	Olivier	National Theatre	Marianne Elliott	NTLive	Robin Lough	David Sabel	Cinema. Live transmission.
14 Feb 2010	Romeo and Juliet	Globe Theatre	Shakespeare's Globe	Dominic Dromgoole	Globe on Screen	Kriss Russman	Hans Petri	Cinema. Recorded over two performances in 2009.*
26 March 2010	The Comedy of Errors	Clapham Community Project	RSC/Told by an Idiot	Paul Hunter	Digital Theatre	Robert Delamere	Tom Shaw	Online. Digital Theatre website. Recorded 11 December 2009.
12 April 2010	Love's Labour's Lost	Globe Theatre	Shakespeare's Globe	Dominic Dromgoole	Globe on Screen	Ian Russell	James Whitbourn	Cinema. Recorded over two performances in 2009.*
14 June 2010	As You Like It	Globe Theatre	Shakespeare's Globe	Thea Sharrock	Globe on Screen	Kriss Russman	James Whitbourn	Cinema. Recorded over two performances in 2009.*

Broadcast/ Release Date	Play	Theatre Space	Theatre Company	Director for Stage	Broadcast Company	Director for screen	Producer for screen	Mode of distribution
9 Dec 2010	Hamlet	Olivier	National Theatre	Nicholas Hytner	NTLive	Robin Lough	David Sabel	Cinema. Live transmission.
3 Feb 2011	King Lear	Donmar Warehouse	Donmar Warehouse	Michael Grandage	NTLive	Robin Lough	David Sabel	Cinema. Live transmission.
14 Feb 2011	As You Like It	Courtyard, Stratford-upon-Avon	RSC	Michael Boyd	Digital Theatre	Robert Delamere	Tom Shaw	Online. Digital Theatre website. Recorded over two performances, 1 and 2 September 2010.
27 June 2011	The Merry Wives of Windsor	Globe Theatre	Shakespeare's Globe	Christopher Luscombe	Globe on Screen	Robin Lough	Dominic Dromgoole	Cinema. Recorded over two performances in 2010.*
1 Aug 2011	Henry IV Part 1	Globe Theatre	Shakespeare's Globe	Dominic Dromgoole	Globe on Screen	Robin Lough	Dominic Dromgoole	Cinema. Recorded over two performances in 2010.*
18 Aug 2011	Henry IV Part 2	Globe Theatre	Shakespeare's Globe	Dominic Dromgoole	Globe on Screen	Robin Lough	Dominic Dromgoole	Cinema. Recorded over two performances in 2010.*
15 Sept 2011	Henry VIII	Globe Theatre	Shakespeare's Globe	Mark Rosenblatt	Globe on Screen	Robin Lough	Dominic Dromgoole	Cinema. Recorded over two performances in 2010.*

Broadcast/ Release Date	Play	Theatre Space	Theatre Company	Director for Stage	Broadcast Company	Director for screen	Producer for screen	Mode of distribution
24 Nov 2011	Macbeth	Liverpool Everyman and Playhouse	Liverpool Everyman	Gemma Bodinetz	Digital Theatre	Robert Delamere	Tom Shaw	Online. Digital Theatre website. Recorded over two performances, 8 and 9 June 2011.
13 Dec 2011	Much Ado About Nothing	Wyndham's Theatre, London	Sonia Friedman Productions	Josie Rourke	Digital Theatre	Robert Delamere	Tom Shaw	Online. Digital Theatre website. Recorded September 2011.
12 Feb 2012	King Lear	Almeida	Almeida Theatre	Michael Attenborough	Digital Theatre	Robert Delamere	Tom Shaw	Online. Digital Theatre website. Recorded over two performances, 4 and 5 October 2012.
1 March 2012	Comedy of Errors	Olivier	National Theatre	Dominic Cooke	NTLive	Tim van Someren	David Sabel	Cinema. Live transmission.
23 April–9 June 2012	Globe to Globe Festival (Complete Works)	Globe Theatre	Shakespeare's Globe	Tom Bird (Festival Director)	Globe on Screen/The Space	Ian Russell: 30 of the productions. Ross MacGibbon: Henry V	Dominic Dromgoole	32 of the productions were streamed live online on The Space website. Live transmissions.

Broadcast/ Release Date	Play	Theatre Space	Theatre Company	Director for Stage	Broadcast Company	Director for screen	Producer for screen	Mode of distribution
14 June 2012	The Tempest	Festival Theatre Stratford, Ontario	Stratford (Ontario) Festival	Des McAnuff	Stratford Festival/ Melbar Entertainment Group	Shelagh O'Brien	Barry Avrich	Cinema. Recorded live over two performances in 2010.*
13 Aug 2012	2008: Macbeth	Lowland Hall, Edinburgh	TR Warszawa	Grzegorz Jarzyna	Edinburgh International Festival and Adam Mickiewicz Institute	Not known	Not known	Online: *Guardian* website. Live transmission.
26 Sept 2012	All's Well that Ends Well	Globe Theatre	Shakespeare's Globe	John Dove	Globe on Screen	Robin Lough	Dominic Dromgoole	Cinema. Recorded over two performances in 2011.*
20 Oct 2012	Much Ado About Nothing	Globe Theatre	Shakespeare's Globe	John Dove	Globe on Screen	Robin Lough	Dominic Dromgoole	Cinema. Recorded over two performances in 2011.*
1 Nov 2012	Timon of Athens	Olivier	National Theatre	Nicholas Hytner	NTLive	Robin Lough	Emma Keith	Cinema. Live transmission.
9 June 2013	Henry V	Globe Theatre	Shakespeare's Globe	Dominic Dromgoole	Globe on Screen	Ross MacGibbon	Dominic Dromgoole	Cinema. Recorded over two performances in 2012.*

Broadcast/ Release Date	Play	Theatre Space	Theatre Company	Director for Stage	Broadcast Company	Director for screen	Producer for screen	Mode of distribution
1 July 2013	Twelfth Night	Globe Theatre	Shakespeare's Globe	Tim Carroll	Globe on Screen	Ian Russell	Dominic Dromgoole	Cinema. Recorded over two performances in 2012.*
20 July 2013	Macbeth	Hallé St Peters Church, Manchester	Manchester International Festival	Rob Ashford and Kenneth Branagh	NTLive	Tim van Someren	Emma Keith	Cinema. Live transmission.
29 July 2013	The Taming of the Shrew	Globe Theatre	Shakespeare's Globe	Toby Frow	Globe on Screen	Ross MacGibbon	Dominic Dromgoole	Cinema. Recorded over two performances in 2012.*
24 Aug 2013	Henry VI: Harry the Sixth, The Houses of York and Lancaster, The True Tragedy of the Duke of York (three-part trilogy)	Monken Hadley Common, Barnet	Shakespeare's Globe	Nick Bagnall	Globe on Screen	Ian Russell	Dominic Dromgoole	Online: The Space. Live transmission.
26 Sept 2013	Othello	Olivier	National Theatre	Nicholas Hytner	NTLive	Robin Lough	Emma Keith	Cinema. Live transmission.

Broadcast/ Release Date	Play	Theatre Space	Theatre Company	Director for Stage	Broadcast Company	Director for screen	Producer for screen	Mode of distribution
13 Nov 2013	Richard II	RST	RSC	Gregory Doran	RSCLive	Robin Lough	John Wyver	Cinema. Live transmission. Online: BBC Shakespeare Lives website (23 April 2016)*
30 Jan 2014	Coriolanus	Donmar Warehouse	Donmar Warehouse	Josie Rourke	NTLive	Tim van Someren	Emma Keith	Cinema. Live transmission.
13 Feb 2014	Romeo and Juliet	Richard Rodgers Theatre, New York	n/a	David Leveaux	Broadway HD	Don Roy King	Stewart F. Lane and Bonnie Comley	Cinema. Online. Recorded over two performances on 27 November 2013.*
1 May 2014	King Lear	Olivier	National Theatre	Sam Mendes	NTLive	Robin Lough	Emma Keith	Cinema. Live transmission.
14 May 2014	Henry IV Part 1	RST	RSC	Gregory Doran	RSCLive	Robin Lough	John Wyver	Cinema. Live transmission.*
28 May 2014	The Tempest	Globe Theatre	Shakespeare's Globe	Jeremy Herrin	Globe on Screen	Ian Russell	Dominic Dromgoole	Cinema. Recorded over two performances in 2013.*
18 June 2014	Henry IV Part 2	RST	RSC	Gregory Doran	RSCLive	Robin Lough	John Wyver	Cinema. Live transmission.*

Broadcast/ Release Date	Play	Theatre Space	Theatre Company	Director for Stage	Broadcast Company	Director for screen	Producer for screen	Mode of distribution
25 June 2014	Macbeth	Globe Theatre	Shakespeare's Globe	Eve Best	Globe on Screen	Sue Judd	Dominic Dromgoole	Cinema. Recorded over two performances in 2013.*
15 July 2014	A Midsummer Night's Dream	Globe Theatre	Shakespeare's Globe	Dominic Dromgoole	Globe on Screen	Robin Lough	Dominic Dromgoole	Cinema. Recorded over two performances in 2013.*
3 Sept 2014	Two Gentlemen of Verona	RST	RSC	Simon Godwin	RSCLive	Robin Lough	John Wyver	Cinema. Live transmission.*
11 Feb 2015	Love's Labour's Lost	RST	RSC	Christopher Luscombe	RSCLive	Robin Lough	John Wyver	Cinema. Live transmission.*
25 Feb 2015	King Lear	Festival Theatre Stratford, Ontario	Stratford (Ontario) Festival	Antoni Cimolino	Stratford Festival HD	Joan Tosoni	Barry Avrich	Cinema. US TV broadcast 6 Sept 2015. Recorded live 21 Oct 2014.*
4 March 2015	Love's Labour's Won, or Much Ado About Nothing	RST	RSC	Christopher Luscombe	RSCLive	Robin Lough	John Wyver	Cinema. Live transmission.*

Broadcast/ Release Date	Play	Theatre Space	Theatre Company	Director for Stage	Broadcast Company	Director for screen	Producer for screen	Mode of distribution
23 March 2015	Hamlet	Royal Exchange Manchester	Royal Exchange Theatre	Sarah Frankcom	Hamlet the Film Ltd	Margaret Williams	Anne Beresford and Debbie Gray	Cinema, Sky Arts TV (29 June 2015). Recorded over a number of performances in 2014.*
26 March 2015	Titus Andronicus	Globe Theatre	Shakespeare's Globe	Lucy Bailey	Globe on Screen	Ian Russell	Dominic Dromgoole	Cinema. Recorded over two performances in 2014.*
8 April 2015	King John	Tom Patterson Theatre, Ontario	Stratford (Ontario) Festival	Tim Carroll	Stratford Festival HD	Barry Avrich	Barry Avrich	Cinema. US TV broadcast 27 Sept 2015. Recorded live 26 Sept 2014.*
22 April 2015	Measure for Measure	Silk Street Theatre, Barbican	Cheek by Jowl	Declan Donnellan	Roundhouse Digital Productions	Thomas Bowles	Marta Sala Font	Online: embedded YouTube link on various sites. Live transmission.
30 April 2015	Julius Caesar	Globe Theatre	Shakespeare's Globe	Dominic Dromgoole	Globe on Screen	Ross MacGibbon	Dominic Dromgoole	Cinema. Recorded over two performances in 2014.*
21 May 2015	Antony and Cleopatra	Tom Patterson Theatre, Ontario	Stratford (Ontario) Festival	Gary Griffin	Stratford Festival HD	Barry Avrich	Barry Avrich	Cinema. US TV broadcast 20 Sep 2015. Recorded live 25 Sep 2014.*

Broadcast/ Release Date	Play	Theatre Space	Theatre Company	Director for Stage	Broadcast Company	Director for screen	Producer for screen	Mode of distribution
4 June 2015	Antony and Cleopatra	Globe Theatre	Shakespeare's Globe	Jonathan Munby	Globe on Screen	Ian Russell	Dominic Dromgoole	Cinema. Recorded over two performances in 2014.*
21 June 2015	A Midsummer Night's Dream	Samuel H. Scripps Mainstage, Polonsky Shakespeare Center, Brooklyn, New York	Theatre for a New Audience	Julie Taymor	Ealing Studios/ Londinium Films	Rodrigo Prieto	Lynn Hendee, Ben Latham	Cinema. Recorded over three performances in 2013.
25 June 2015	The Comedy of Errors	Globe Theatre	Shakespeare's Globe	Blanche MacIntyre	Globe on Screen	Ross MacGibbon	Dominic Dromgoole	Cinema. Recorded over two performances in 2014.*
25 June–4 July 2015[1]	Complete Works: Table Top Shakespeare	Berliner Festspiele, Berlin	Forced Entertainment	Tim Etchells	Forced Entertainment	N/A	N/A	Online: embedded YouTube link on various sites. Live transmission.
22 July 2015	The Merchant of Venice	RST	RSC	Polly Findlay	RSCLive	Robin Lough	John Wyver	Cinema. Live transmission.*
26 Aug 2015	Othello	RST	RSC	Iqbal Khan	RSCLive	Robin Lough	John Wyver	Cinema. Live transmission.*

Broadcast/ Release Date	Play	Theatre Space	Theatre Company	Director for Stage	Broadcast Company	Director for screen	Producer for screen	Mode of distribution
15 Oct 2015	Hamlet	Barbican Theatre	Sonia Friedman Productions	Lyndsey Turner	NTLive	Robin Lough	Emma Keith	Cinema. Live transmission.
21 Oct 2015	Henry V	RST	RSC	Gregory Doran	RSCLive	Robin Lough	John Wyver	Cinema. Live transmission.*
12 Nov 2015	King Lear	The Maria, Young Vic	Belarus Free Theatre	Vladimir Shcherban	CultureHub	Not known	Not known	Online: Belarus Free Theatre website. Live transmission.
26 Nov 2015	The Winter's Tale	Garrick Theatre	Kenneth Branagh Theatre Company	Rob Ashford and Kenneth Branagh	Kenneth Branagh Theatre Live	Benjamin Caron	Jez Breadin and Simon Fisher	Cinema. Live transmission.
25 Feb 2016	As You Like It	Olivier	National Theatre	Polly Findlay	NTLive	Tim van Someren	Emma Keith	Cinema. Live transmission.
12 March 2016	The Taming of the Shrew	Festival Theatre Stratford, Ontario	Stratford (Ontario) Festival	Chris Abraham	Stratford Festival HD	Barry Avrich	Barry Avrich	Cinema. CBC-TV broadcast 12 March 2016. Recorded live 29 Sept 2015.*
23 April 2016	The Adventures of Pericles	Tom Patterson Theatre, Ontario	Stratford (Ontario) Festival	Scott Wentworth	Stratford Festival HD	Barry Avrich	Barry Avrich	Cinema. CBC-TV broadcast 4 Sept 2016. Recorded live 15 Sept 2015.*

Broadcast/ Release Date	Play	Theatre Space	Theatre Company	Director for Stage	Broadcast Company	Director for screen	Producer for screen	Mode of distribution
25 April 2016	Macbeth	Tara Theatre, London (Tara Arts)	Black Theatre Live in association with Tara Arts and Queen's Hall Arts	Jatinder Verma	Pilot Theatre	Ben Pugh	Johnathan Kennedy	Online: Black Theatre Live website.
6 May 2016	Measure for Measure	Globe Theatre	Shakespeare's Globe	Dominic Dromgoole	Globe on Screen	Ross MacGibbon	Dominic Dromgoole	Cinema. Recorded over two performances in 2015.
7 May 2016	Hamlet	Festival Theatre Stratford, Ontario	Stratford (Ontario) Festival	Antoni Cimolino	Stratford Festival HD	Shelagh O'Brien	Barry Avrich	Cinema. CBC-TV Broadcast 7 May 2016. Recorded live 22 Sept 2015.*
8 June 2016	Hamlet	RST	RSC	Simon Godwin	RSCLive	Robin Lough	John Wyver	Cinema. Live transmission.*
10 June 2016	The Merchant of Venice	Globe Theatre	Shakespeare's Globe	Jonathan Munby	Globe on Screen	Robin Lough	Dominic Dromgoole	Cinema. Recorded over two performances in 2015.*
24 June 2016	Richard II	Globe Theatre	Shakespeare's Globe	Simon Godwin	Globe on Screen	Ian Russell	Dominic Dromgoole	Cinema. Recorded over two performances in 2015.*

Broadcast/ Release Date	Play	Theatre Space	Theatre Company	Director for Stage	Broadcast Company	Director for screen	Producer for screen	Mode of distribution
7 July 2016	Romeo and Juliet	Garrick Theatre	Kenneth Branagh Theatre Company	Rob Ashford and Kenneth Branagh	Kenneth Branagh Theatre Live	Benjamin Caron	Jez Breadin	Cinema. Live transmission.
11 July 2016	King Lear	Royal Exchange Manchester	Talawa Theatre Company	Michael Buffong	Lion Eyes TV/Saffron Cherry TV	Bridget Caldwell	Caroline Roberts-Cherry	Online: BBC iPlayer (UK), BBC.* Shakespeare Lives website (International). BBC broadcast 25 Dec 2016. Recorded over two performances.
21 July 2016	Richard III	Almeida Theatre	Almeida Theatre	Rupert Goold	Almeida Theatre Live	Robin Lough	John Wyver	Cinema. Live transmission.
11 Sept 2016	A Midsummer Night's Dream	Globe Theatre	Shakespeare's Globe	Emma Rice	BBC Arts	Ian Russell	Lotte Buchan and Jessica Lusk	Online: BBC iPlayer (UK), BBC Shakespeare Lives website (International). Live transmission.
28 Sept 2016	Cymbeline	RST	RSC	Melly Still	RSCLive	Matthew Woodward	John Wyver	Cinema. Live transmission.*
12 Oct 2016	King Lear	RST	RSC	Gregory Doran	RSCLive	Robin Lough	John Wyver	Cinema. Live transmission.*

Broadcast/ Release Date	Play	Theatre Space	Theatre Company	Director for Stage	Broadcast Company	Director for screen	Producer for screen	Mode of distribution
13 Oct 2016	Roméo et Juliette	Salle Richelieu, Paris	Comédie-Française	Éric Ruf	Comédie-Française / Pathé Live	Don Kent	Not known	Cinema. Live transmission.
14 Oct 2016	Lear/Cordelia (two-play adaptation of King Lear)	Attenborough Arts Centre, Leicester	1623 Theatre Company	Ben Spiller (Lear), Louie Ingram (Cordelia)	Pilot Theatre	Ben Pugh	Ben Pugh	Online: YouTube and 1623 website. Live transmission.
27 Oct 2016	Hamlet	Tara Theatre, London (Tara Arts)	Black Theatre Live in association with Watford Palace Theatre and Stratford Circus Arts Centre	Jeffery Kissoon	Pilot Theatre	Ben Pugh	Jonathan Kennedy	Online: Black Theatre Live website. Live transmission.
11 Jan 2017	The Tempest	RST	RSC	Gregory Doran	RSCLive	Dewi Humphreys	John Wyver	Cinema. Live transmission.*
14 Feb 2017	Macbeth	Caerphilly Castle	Theatr Genedlaethol Cymru	Arwel Gruffydd	Theatr Genedlaethol Cymru	Emyr Jenkins	Rhian A. Davies	Cinema. Live transmission.

Broadcast/ Release Date	Play	Theatre Space	Theatre Company	Director for Stage	Broadcast Company	Director for screen	Producer for screen	Mode of distribution
18 March 2017	Macbeth	Festival Theatre Stratford, Ontario	Stratford (Ontario) Festival	Antoni Cimolino	Stratford Festival HD	Shelagh O'Brien	Barry Avrich	Cinema, CBC-TV broadcast 20 Aug 2017. Recorded live in 2016.*
6 April 2017	Twelfth Night	Olivier	National Theatre	Simon Godwin	NTLive	Robin Lough	Emma Keith	Cinema. Live transmission.
19 April 2017	The Winter's Tale	Silk Street Theatre, Barbican	Cheek by Jowl	Declan Donnellan	Riverside Studios	Ross MacGibbon	Janie Valentine	Online: embedded YouTube link on various sites and Facebook Live. Live transmission.
26 April 2017	Julius Caesar	RST	RSC	Angus Jackson	RSCLive	Dewi Humphreys	John Wyver	Cinema. Live transmission.*
29 April 2017	Love's Labour's Lost	Festival Theatre Stratford, Ontario	Stratford (Ontario) Festival	John Caird	Stratford Festival HD	Barry Avrich	Barry Avrich	Cinema, CBC-TV broadcast 27 Aug 2017. Recorded live in 2015.*
24 May 2017	Antony and Cleopatra	RST	RSC	Iqbal Khan	RSCLive	Robin Lough	John Wyver	Cinema. Live transmission.*

Broadcast/ Release Date	Play	Theatre Space	Theatre Company	Director for Stage	Broadcast Company	Director for screen	Producer for screen	Mode of distribution
12 July 2017	Julius Caesar	Donmar King's Cross	Donmar Warehouse	Phyllida Lloyd	Illuminations	Rhodri Huw	John Wyver	Cinema. Recorded over two performances in 2017; UK premiere on 24 June 2017.
9 Aug 2017	Titus Andronicus	RST	RSC	Blanche McIntyre	RSCLive	Matthew Woodward	John Wyver	Cinema. Live transmission.*
11 Oct 2017	Coriolanus	RST	RSC	Angus Jackson	RSCLive	Robin Lough	John Wyver	Cinema. Live transmission.*

[1] This production was livestreamed online again from Theaterfestival Basel, Switzerland, September 2016.

INDEX OF THEATRE BROADCASTS OF SHAKESPEARE

All's Well that Ends Well
  NTLive (2009), dir. Elliott/Lough
  30, 120
Antony and Cleopatra
  RSCLive (2017), dir. Khan/Lough
  95–7, 98, 105, 150
As You Like It
  Globe (2010), dir. Sharrock/
  Russman 125
  NTLive (2016), dir. Findlay/van
  Someren 118–20
Comedy of Errors
  NTLive (2012), dir. Cooke/van
  Someren 46, 52, 150
Complete Works: Table Top
  Shakespeare
  Forced Entertainment (2015), dir.
  Etchells 5, 77–8, 84–9
Coriolanus
  NTLive (2014), dir. Rourke/van
  Someren 46, 77, 78, 79–84,
  85–6, 90, 150, 178, 179, 180–1
Cymbeline
  RSCLive (2016), dir. Still/Lough 95
Globe to Globe Festival
  Globe (2012), dir. various/Russell/
  McGibbon 9, 31, 186, 227
Hamlet
  NTLive (2010), dir. Hytner/Lough
  46, 52, 178, 193, 217–18,
  220–1
  Hamlet the Film Ltd (2015), dir.
  Frankcom/Williams 31–2, 154
  NTLive (2015), dir. Turner/Lough
  12, 32, 41, 46, 47, 139, 178,
  179, 180, 187, 193–8,
  199–204, 218
  Black Theatre Live (2016), dir.
  Kissoon/Pugh 153, 155–6
  RSCLive (2016), dir. Godwin/
  Lough 95, 150, 152, 154
  BBC/Illuminations Media (2018)
  dir. Icke/Huw 32
Henry IV, Part 1
  RSCLive (2014), dir. Doran/Lough
  35
Henry IV
  Illuminations (2018), dir. Lloyd/
  Huw 32
Henry V
  Globe (2012), dir. Dromgoole/
  MacGibbon 9
  RSCLive (2015), dir. Doran/Lough
  35, 103, 105
Julius Caesar
  RSCLive (2017), dir. Jackson/
  Humphreys 95–6, 97–9, 103,
  105, 106
  Illuminations Media (2017),
  dir. Lloyd/Huw 1–2, 3–5, 7,
  28, 32
  NTLive (2018), dir. Hytner/
  Grech-Smith 36, 46
King Lear
  NTLive (2011), dir. Grandage/
  Lough 31
  NTLive (2014), dir. Mendes/Lough
  178
  Stratford Festival (2015), dir.
  Cimolino/Tosoni 139
  Talawa (2016), dir. Buffong/Riley
  and Sen 32, 34, 152, 154–5,
  157
  RSCLive (2016), dir. Doran/Lough
  95, 187
Love's Labour's Lost
  RSCLive (2015), dir. Luscombe/
  Lough 103, 105, 108

Measure for Measure
  Globe (2004), dir. Dove/Cook
  Cheek by Jowl (2015), dir.
    Donnellan/Bowles 85, 163–72
Midsummer Night's Dream
  Globe (2016), dir. Rice/Russell 32,
    52, 63, 68–72, 127–8
Othello
  NTLive (2013), dir. Hytner/Lough
    34, 41, 46, 52, 150, 178
  RSCLive (2015), dir. Khan/Lough
    103, 105, 106, 108–9, 150
Pericles
  Stratford Festival (2016), dir.
    Wentworth/Avrich 140–2
Richard II
  Globe (2003), dir. Carroll/Judd 3,
    68, 103, 105–6, 108, 124–5, 149
  RSCLive (2013) dir. Doran/Lough
    41, 47, 187
Richard III
  Almeida (2016), dir. Goold/Lough
    32, 48–50, 51, 54, 196
Romeo and Juliet
  KBTCLive (2016), dir. Ashford and
    Branagh/Caron 47–8, 53, 63–8,
    69–71, 187, 196, 217, 222–4
  Comédie-Française (2016), dir. Ruf/
    Kent 208–12
The Tempest
  Stratford Festival (2012), dir.
    McAnuff/O'Brien
  RSCLive (2017), dir. Doran/
    Humphreys 187–8, 189,
    219–20
  Illuminations Media (2018), dir.
    Lloyd/Huw 32
Timon of Athens
  NTLive (2012), dir. Hytner/Lough
    46, 121–2
Twelfth Night
  NTLive (2017), dir. Godwin/Lough
    129–30, 150, 217, 223
Two Gentlemen of Verona
  RSCLive (2014), dir. Godwin/
    Lough 103, 105, 107–8
Winter's Tale
  KBTCLive (2015), dir. Ashford and
    Branagh/Caron 32, 41, 47–8, 64,
    181, 187
  Cheek by Jowl (2017), dir.
    Donnellan/MacGibbon 32, 41,
    72–3, 61

INDEX OF NAMES AND TERMS

50 Years on Stage (NTLive) 21, 33–4

Abbott, Daisy 82, 83, 90
Abramović, Marina 59–60, 62, 72, 73
access 1, 4, 6, 9, 12, 19, 21, 22, 25, 29, 30, 31, 35, 42, 44, 50, 52, 53, 80, 81, 83, 84, 88, 89, 90, 114, 115, 118, 121, 123, 124, 126, 127, 129, 134, 136, 152, 155, 156, 167, 177, 178, 182, 185, 200, 208, 209, 211, 216, 220, 222
Act For Change Project 150
Aebischer, Pascale 4, 5, 11, 12, 31, 32, 35, 36, 67, 68, 85, 108, 124, 154, 162, 169, 171, 189, 193, 196, 223
affect 60, 115–17, 122, 126, 163, 189, 190, 147
affective 8, 11, 62, 63, 115–17, 118, 120, 121, 122, 124, 125, 126, 128, 129, 189
Aldridge, Ira 147, 155, 156
Alexander, Sam 108
aliveness 7, 10, 60, 60–3, 65, 66, 67, 72–3, 115, 118, 122, 124
Almeida Theatre 3, 32, 36, 48
Almeida Theatre Live 8, 32, 48–54, 196
ambience *see* atmosphere
Anderson, Lindsay 21
Angadi, Darien 148
Arbuckle, Sean 141
architecture 11, 20, 26–8, 34–5, 48–9, 51, 104, 113, 123–30, 163, 164–7, 200–1, 204, 208–9, 211–12
archive 2, 5, 8, 11, 23, 26, 33, 34, 89, 96, 117, 135–6, 138, 140–2, 143, 149, 150, 155, 157, 167, 179, 194, 195, 216, 220
Arsentyev, Alexander 165, 166

Arts Council England (ACE) 8, 21, 23, 27, 31, 44, 45, 114, 148, 151, 154, 155, 156, 179
Ashford, Rob 63, 71, 187, 196, 217
atmosphere 25, 35, 97, 100, 115–16, 119–20, 122–6, 127–30, 139–40, 179, 185, 217–18
The Audience 187
audience performance: *see also* aliveness 78–90, 60–1, 104–6, 109, 126
audience *see* broadcast audience; cinema audience; online audience; theatre audience
audio *see* sound
audio commentary 77–84, 85–6, 220–1
Auslander, Philip 19, 60–1, 63, 135, 162, 186, 189, 197, 217
Aviva 49, 54, 121
Avrich, Barry 140, 141

Bahl, Ankur 128
Bailey, Nicholas 149
Bakhtin, Mikhail 61, 63
Barbican Theatre, London 45
  main auditorium 30, 32, 41, 46, 178, 195, 199, 202, 221
  Silk Street Theatre 161, 162, 165
Barker, Martin 61, 62, 77, 83, 84, 98–9, 122, 163, 166, 172, 178, 186, 189, 196, 216, 221
Barnes-Worrell, Elliot 108
Bassindale, Martin 107
Bath, Jon 47, 48, 54
Bay-Cheng, Sarah 7, 141, 143
BBC 8, 10, 19–21, 22–5, 28, 29, 30, 32–5, 47, 68, 69, 113, 114, 121, 124, 125, 126–7, 148, 155–7

BBC iPlayer 32, 155, 157
BBC Shakespeare series 8, 148, 150
Bazin, André 200
Beale, Simon Russell 33, 46, 122, 219
Beaton, Norman 148, 151
Belarus Free Theatre 85
Bennett, Edward 108
Bennett, Nigel 143
Bennett-Warner, Pippa 150
Birmingham Repertory Theatre 155
Black Theatre Live 150, 151–6
Bliss, Will 107
Blocking 96, 107, 167, 169, 171, 197
Bolshoi Ballet 42, 50, 193, 208
Bonner, Frances 6, 13, 135, 137, 141, 143, 197, 202, 203, 219
Bowie, David 45, 68
Bowles, Thomas 163, 170
Box of Broadcasts 157
Brahim, Suliane 210
Branagh, Kenneth 32, 41, 47–8, 63–6, 72, 79, 181, 187, 196, 217, 222, 224
brand 2, 11, 42, 45–8, 49, 51, 53, 64, 66, 104, 114, 130, 186, 191, 217, 223
Black Theatre Live 153, 154
Brewster, Yvonne 151
Bridge Theatre Company 36, 46
British Black and Asian Shakespeare Performance Database 148, 152, 158
British Council 8–9, 31, 32, 53, 68, 190, 191
British Home Entertainment 24–5
British national identity 8–9, 23–4, 49, 53–4, 114, 218
broadcast audience 5, 10, 62–5, 77, 106, 115–18, 122–9, 201–2, 208–12, 220–3
Broadway Theatre Archive 216
Brook, Peter 21, 23, 133–4, 142, 149, 152, 194
Brooke, Sian 202
Buckeridge, Flo 117, 118, 129
Buffong, Michael 151, 152, 153–5, 157
Buliung, Evan 141
Burge, Stuart 20, 24–6
Burnett, Mark 2, 23
Burton, Richard 25, 136, 216, 224
Buzzfeed 10, 87, 88

Caldwell, Bridget 34, 155
Carson, Christie 114, 124, 126, 128
camera 10, 95, 98, 201, 209, 222
    acting for camera 10, 95–101, 203, 218
    camera feed 5, 166
    camera footage 164
    camera position 1, 15, 31, 97, 98, 99, 100, 104, 107, 116, 127, 139, 165
    camera rehearsal 97, 119, 172
    crane camera 31, 97, 98, 119, 120, 122
    hand-held camera 211–12
    mobile camera 24, 97, 119, 120, 122, 140, 143, 197, 209
    multiple cameras 2, 4, 6, 23, 26, 29, 31, 85, 96, 97, 115, 118, 127, 165, 167, 209
    presence 104–6, 108, 119
    single camera 30, 50, 55, 85, 88, 139
    static or fixed camera 140, 142, 143, 167
    track camera 31, 106–7, 119, 122, 209, 210, 119
camera work 5, 28, 49, 82, 115, 116, 118, 119, 120, 121, 122, 124, 125, 127, 129, 130, 139, 143, 165 9, 179, 196–7, 201–4, 219
    close up 26, 28, 50, 106, 141, 143, 153, 167, 169, 170, 197, 202–3, 204, 210, 211, 218 19, 224
    establishing shot 122, 125, 166, 170, 221
    high angle 120, 122, 166, 222, 224
    low angle 26
    medium shot 26, 28, 168, 197, 211, 224
    pan 203, 209, 210, 223
    wide shot 30, 166, 197, 203, 204, 209, 210–11
    zoom 49, 119, 121, 141, 165
Caron, Ben 64, 217, 222
Carroll, Tim 124
CBC Presents the Stratford Festival 31, 138, 139
Cheek by Jowl 3, 10, 11, 31, 32, 72, 85, 162–72
Cheng, Chui-Yee 126
Chichester Festival Theatre 22, 24, 25

INDEX OF NAMES AND TERMS 247

Cimolino, Antoni 138-9, 143-4
cinema 1, 19-22, 23, 24-9, 30, 31-2,
    33-6, 61, 114, 116, 117, 138-9,
    154, 178, 185-6, 188-9, 193-8,
    199-200, 207-8, 225
  cinematic form 5, 6, 12-13, 20, 23,
    25-6, 28, 30-1, 34, 64, 67, 80,
    87-8, 96, 97-100, 119, 138-43,
    167-71, 195-8, 200-4, 211,
    216-19, 221-5
  event cinema 1, 6, 10, 41-3, 44-6,
    48-54, 69, 225
cinema audience 1-2, 7-6, 11-9, 72,
    77-85, 95, 97, 99-100, 103, 105,
    107, 109, 115-20, 122-30, 135-9,
    140-4, 162, 163, 166, 177-82,
    188-90, 195-8, 199-204, 208-12,
    217-18, 221-3
CinemaLive 129
Cineteca (Bologna) 194-6
Cochrane, Bernadette 3, 13, 135, 137,
    141, 143, 197, 202, 203, 219
co-creation 3
colonialism 8
Comédie-Française 8, 9, 12, 32, 43,
    207-12
community 2, 7, 10, 12, 13, 47, 51,
    61-2, 64-73, 78, 81, 100, 85-7,
    125-6, 128-30, 137, 161-2, 165,
    172, 189, 195-8, 200-1, 204, 223
  of reception (or community of
    perception) 199-204
*Complete Works: Tabletop
    Shakespeare* 5, 77, 78, 84-8
Complicité 156
co-presence *see* presence
Corden, James 116-17
corpsing 108, 116, 125. *See also* laughter
Corrigan, James 96
countdown timer 51, 161-2
Croll, Doña 151
Cultural Olympiad 31, 32
Cumberbatch, Benedict 11, 41, 46-7,
    139, 178, 179, 186, 196, 197,
    199, 201, 202, 203, 218, 219
*The Curious Incident of the Dog in the
    Night-Time* 181

De Certeau, Michel 78-9, 81, 115,
    116, 118, 123, 128

De Jersey, Peter 80
delayed screening 136-7, 188, 217
demography 44, 156, 180-2, 185,
    187-90
Dench, Judi 33, 47, 64
Dexter, John 20
digital programme 79-81, 91, 182,
    219-21, 223
digital theatre 30, 31, 34, 155
direct address 4, 30, 97, 122, 128, 129,
    171, 201, 209-10, 211-12
director's address 103, 105
disgust 122, 127. *See also* affect
Disiru, Sope 150
distance 11, 67, 72, 98, 99, 106, 124,
    165-7, 169, 189, 199-201
distribution 1, 4, 9, 11, 13, 29, 31, 42,
    48, 53, 88, 90-1, 114, 139-40,
    164, 217, 227
diversity 42, 71, 72, 90, 114, 149-50,
    191
Donmar Warehouse 1, 4, 6, 8, 31, 32, 41,
    45, 46, 77, 79-80, 82, 217, 220-1
Donnellan, Declan 162-3, 167, 168-70
Doran, Gregory 30, 31, 34, 52, 103,
    105, 108, 149, 187, 189, 225
Dromgoole, Dominic 9, 115, 125
durational performance 78, 87-9
DVD 4, 32, 68, 78, 80-3, 96, 114,
    124-5, 138-9, 144, 150, 154,
    157, 200, 220-1, 227
DVD commentary 77, 79-84, 220-1

Edinburgh International Film Festival
    4-5
editing 6, 116, 119, 120, 167, 197,
    201, 217. *See also* live mix
education 5, 22, 53, 81, 118, 138, 149,
    155, 157, 163, 167, 172, 190,
    212, 224. *See also* National
    Theatre. On Demand. In
    Schools; RSC Schools
    Broadcasts
Elba, Idris 150
electronovision 25, 216-17, 224
emotion *see* affect
encore screening 4, 41, 51, 54, 77,
    79-84, 55, 136, 138, 140, 187,
    188, 190, 193, 197, 199, 215,
    217, 218, 220

Equity (British Actors' Equity) 138, 148–9
Essiedu, Paapa 150, 152
Etchells, Tim 78, 86, 87–8
event/eventness 1–2, 6–7, 9, 10, 21, 23, 25, 33, 41–7, 49–54, 59–63, 65–9, 78, 80, 82–3, 105–6, 109, 115, 124, 128, 133–9, 142, 144, 154, 162–3, 172, 179, 187, 188–9, 193–8, 199–200, 208, 216, 219, 222, 225
exhibition 43, 50, 190, 193
Eyre, Richard 33, 149
Ezra, Daniel 51

Facebook 10, 51, 87, 90, 117, 118, 181
Facebook Live 90
fan communities 2, 7, 8, 11, 13, 68–9, 81–4, 90, 181–2
Fearon, Ray 150
features *see* paratexts
Feore, Colm 139, 143
Fiennes, Joseph 34
Fiennes, Ralph 41, 48, 50, 187
film *see* cinema
Findlay, Deborah 80
Findlay, Polly 118
Finlay, Frank 26, 34
Flickr 59
forced entertainment 5, 32, 77, 78, 84–9, 223
Fox, Phoebe 129
framing 3, 5, 8, 12, 13, 28, 30, 82, 116, 120, 124, 127, 129, 166–72, 210, 221
Frankcom, Sarah 154
Frankenstein 178–80, 219
Fraser, Hadley 80
Freud, Emma 51, 82–3, 121, 136

Garrick Theatre, London 32, 41, 47, 217, 221–2
Gatwa, Ncuti 128
genre 2, 6, 9, 10, 32, 45, 54, 193, 195–6, 201
Giannachi, Gabriella 6, 7
global community 2, 7–9, 182, 197–8, 215–6
global distribution 2, 8, 10, 13, 44–5, 47, 53–4, 185, 207

Globe *see* Shakespeare's Globe
Globe on Screen 114, 68, 124
Globe performativity 114, 123–8, 129–30
Globe Player 9
Globe to Globe 9, 31, 186, 227
Glynn, Johnny 107
Godwin, Simon 129, 217, 223
Gonon, Christian 209
Goold, Rupert 32, 50, 51, 149, 196
Greenhalgh, Susanne 3, 6, 10, 22, 29, 31, 32, 67, 88, 97, 114, 118, 130, 149, 166, 194
Greig, Tamsin 46, 51, 129
Guthrie, Tyrone 35

Hall, Peter 99, 21, 22, 23, 27, 33, 34
Hall, Stuart 6
Hall, Tony 32
Hamlet (1969) 20, 27–8
Hamlet at Elsinore 22
Hastie, Rob 80
Heath, Gordon 148
Heim, Caroline 78, 80, 81, 90
Henry, Lenny 46, 150
Herbert, Jocelyn 25
Heritage Theatre 30
Hiddleston, Tom 46, 79–84, 178, 180, 186, 220–1
Higlett, Simon 108
Holdbrook-Smith, Kobna 150
Holland, Peter 135, 136, 138, 143, 199–200, 204
Holm, Ian 149
Hopkins, Anthony 148
Hornby, Richard 20, 211
Hunter, Lindsay Brandon 220
Hutson, Martin 97–100
hybridity 2, 6, 10, 13, 20, 23, 24, 33, 35–6, 69, 78–9, 85, 126, 129–30, 185, 193, 195–6, 200, 204, 216, 219–20
Hytner, Nicholas 29–30, 33–4, 36, 46, 113, 115, 121–2, 134–7, 144, 201, 178, 193, 217, 218

Illuminations Media 1–2, 13, 30–1, 33
illusionism (performance style) 118–20, 123, 129
Imaginarium Studios 187

INDEX OF NAMES AND TERMS

immediacy 7, 25–6, 33, 60, 100, 108, 120, 160, 190, 216, 216, 222
immersion 2, 11, 12, 118, 120, 123, 129, 200, 217
Instagram 87
Intel 187
interaction 2, 3, 8, 10, 12, 21, 61–3, 70–2, 84, 86–7, 90, 119–20, 129, 135, 167, 203, 210, 216, 221–5
intermediality 7, 20, 34, 196
intermission *see* interval
interval 49–50, 65, 68, 70, 82–4, 104, 115, 116, 127, 154, 161, 188, 196, 201, 209, 218, 223–4
intimacy 4, 31, 97–9, 119–20, 162, 167, 216, 220–1, 225
Irvine, Adrian 149

Jacobi, Derek 46, 64, 222
James, Amber 96–7
James, Lily 48, 64, 65, 186
Jones, James Earl 148, 158
Judd, Sue 124

KBTCLive (Kenneth Branagh Theatre Company Live) 3, 8, 24, 32, 41, 47, 48, 53, 63–8, 185, 187, 191, 196, 217, 222–4
Keith, Emma 128
Kellner, William 25–6
Kennedy, Jonathan 151–2, 154–6
Kent, Don 5, 209, 212
Khalilulina, Anna 164, 169, 171
Kingsley, Ben 148
Kinnear, Rory 34, 46, 218
Kirwan, Peter 4, 5, 11, 31, 32, 51, 64, 82, 85, 108
Klein, Suzy 105, 107
Kurzel, Justin 187
Kuzichev, Andrei 167

Lacroix, Christian 209
Lang, Kirsty 51
Lapotaire, Jane 108
Laskey, Jack 125
laughter 8, 22, 116–17, 120–1, 125, 127–9, 137, 196, 209, 216, 223. *See also* affect; corpsing
Lawrance, Tamara 150

Lester, Adrian 33, 34, 46, 98–9, 100, 149, 150
Lion Eyes TV 155
live mix 4, 96, 106, 119, 163, 196
liveness 1–2, 7–8, 10–13, 20, 49–51, 59–73, 85–6, 100–1, 108–9, 113, 115–20, 122–30, 133–9, 133, 141–4, 161–4, 167, 171–2, 185–6, 196–9, 215–25
live-tweeting 69–72, 85–8, 89–91
Live-to-Digital Report (ACE) 7–8, 69
livestream 5, 7–8, 11, 31, 71, 84–90, 161–72, 186, 188
living 67, 124
Lloyd, Phyllida 1–4, 7, 28, 32
Lopez, Jérémy 210
Lough, Robin 30, 31, 41, 121–2, 115–16, 118, 121–2, 129, 178, 193, 217, 223
Louis-Calixte, Pierre 211
Luhrmann, Baz 42

Madden, Richard 48, 64–5
Manchester International Festival 41, 46
marketing 7, 10, 25, 45–51, 52, 54, 66, 100, 118, 136, 136–8, 144, 157, 178–9, 182, 208, 225. *See also* trailer
Maxwell Martin, Anna 33
McFarlane, Cassie 148
McGann, Jerome J. 5–6
McMullan, Tim 125
Meerkat 87
Meow Meow 68
Metropolitan Opera House 44, 222
The Met: Live in HD 29, 42, 45, 208, 218, 222
Mirren, Helen 186, 187
motion capture 225
Msamati, Lucian 150
multi-tasking 128
Museum of Modern Art, New York 59

National Theatre 33–4, 24, 29, 35, 41, 42, 44–6, 48–9, 52–3, 64, 79, 99, 113–26, 129
  Lyttelton 27, 115–16
  Olivier 27, 29–30, 33, 50, 99, 114, 115, 117–20, 122, 129, 193, 218

INDEX OF NAMES AND TERMS

National Theatre Archive 117, 130, 136, 138, 179
National Theatre Backstage app 79–84
National Theatre. On Demand. In Schools. 52, 128
NESTA 7, 43, 45–6, 48–9, 135–6, 156
Netlytic 63, 66, 70–1
network 7–8, 13, 79, 84, 86, 89–91, 100, 134–7, 162, 193, 197–8
Norfolk, Mark 152–3, 154
Norris, Rufus 119, 128
NTLive (National Theatre Live) 3, 7–9, 11–12, 13, 24, 25, 30, 31, 33–4, 36, 42–7, 48–4, 62, 77–85, 96, 114, 115–23, 126, 127, 128, 129, 130, 134–5, 138, 139–40, 141–2, 150, 154, 155–7, 177–82, 185, 187, 191, 193–4, 195, 197–9, 200, 202–4, 207, 215–23
Nunn, Trevor 29, 46, 149

Old Vic Theatre 20, 22, 24–6, 27, 29, 34
Olivier, Laurence 22, 24–6, 29, 34, 153
O'Neill, Stephen 6
One Man, Two Guvnors 115–20
on-demand 5, 52, 124, 128–9, 138, 144, 200. *See also* pay-to-view
online audience 9, 10–13, 59–63, 85, 88, 127–8, 161–3, 68–73, 77–9, 84–91
open stage 20, 25, 27–8, 31–2, 35, 114–15
Ormerod, Nick 73, 162–70
Osborne, John 21
Osborne, Laurie 8, 20, 49, 130, 196, 216, 219, 221, 222
Othello (1965) 20, 24–6
Ouimette, Stephen 139
outside broadcast 13, 20–3, 32, 34–5, 104
Owen, Katy 127
Oyelowo, David 150

paratext 2, 5, 7, 12, 35, 49, 78, 82–4, 100, 115, 118–25, 127, 130, 154, 195, 217, 219, 221, 225
participation 2, 7–8, 10–13, 51, 72, 77, 88–91, 115–30, 136–7, 141–3, 161–4, 216–17, 220

Pathé Live 8, 32, 207–9
pay-to-view 30. *See also* on-demand
Peake, Maxine 32, 154
Performance Plus 138
Periscope 87
Phèdre 30, 42, 136, 140
Phelan, Peggy 60–1, 179
phenomenology 2, 61–2, 115, 185–7, 189
Pilot Theatre 154
place 5, 22, 26, 41–2, 54, 59–62, 65, 72, 78, 115–30, 137, 150
platform 4, 6, 8, 9, 10, 13, 30, 31, 32, 52, 66, 67, 73, 87, 90, 114, 117–18, 127, 177–8, 182, 225
Plummer, Christopher 139
postproduction 2, 4–5, 72, 124, 156, 163–72
presence 2–4, 7–8, 12–13, 24, 27–8, 35–6, 59–63, 61–7, 69–72, 78–9, 114–18, 120–30, 133–7, 140–4, 161–2, 164–72, 185–7, 190, 211, 217, 220–3
presentation (performance style) 114–15, 123–30
presenter 34, 50–1, 82–3, 105, 109, 118, 121, 124, 127, 136
production companies 3, 8–9, 11–13, 19–23, 30–5, 47–48, 54, 72, 79, 85, 89, 90–1, 114–15, 117–18, 150–7, 162–4, 177, 207
production values 9, 51
programmes *see* digital programmes
promotion *see* marketing; trailer
Proscenium 10, 20, 25–7, 29–30, 32–6, 106, 108, 114, 115, 200, 204, 210–11
proximity 4, 7, 12–13, 62–3, 65, 72–3, 98, 134–7, 167, 199–202, 210–12
Pryce, Jonathan 186
Pugh, Ben 154
Purcell, Stephen 43, 68, 114, 124, 130

Quarshie, Hugh 148, 150
Quartley, Mark 187
Queen's Hall, Hexham 156
Quinn, Leigh 107

INDEX OF NAMES AND TERMS

race 33, 71, 147–59
radio 44, 61, 85
receiving venues 3, 8, 221–4
Redgrave, Vanessa 48
remediation 2, 3, 5, 12, 20, 34–5, 212
revenue 2, 41, 43–8, 54, 87
Rice, Emma 32, 63, 68–72, 126–9,
Richardson, Tony 20, 21, 27–8, 31
risk 26, 48, 50, 51, 53, 54, 69, 96–7, 114, 124, 139, 141, 151, 163, 171
Rix, Oliver 106
Roundhouse 20, 27–8, 31, 164
Rourke, Josie 80–3, 178, 187, 217, 220–1
Royal Exchange Theatre, Manchester 31, 32, 151–5
RSC (Royal Shakespeare Company) 29–33, 34–5, 47, 52–3, 95–101, 103–9, 139, 150, 152, 219–20
RSCLive (RSC Live from Stratford-upon-Avon) 9, 24, 25, 30, 34–5, 47, 79, 85, 95–101, 103–9, 139, 140, 150, 157, 161, 185, 187–8, 207, 219–20
RSC Schools' Broadcasts 52–3
RST (Royal Shakespeare Theatre) 30–1, 34–5, 95, 97–101, 103–9, 139
Ruf, Éric 208–9, 212
Ruparelia, Jay 148
Russell, Ian 68, 126–7
Russman, Kriss 125
Rylance, Mark 68–70, 115, 128

Sabel, David 1, 33, 203
Sack, Daniel 42, 52
Saffron Cherry TV 155
Salle Richelieu 208–12
Sangaré, Bakary 209–10
serialization 78, 87–8
set design 25–6, 27–8, 33, 34, 35, 114, 209, 222
sexuality 51, 70–1, 164
Shakespeare Live! (RSCLive) 21, 33, 34–5
'Shakespeare Lives' 32, 68, 127, 155, 157

Shakespeare quatercentenary 1964 20, 22–3, 25, 27
2016 20, 32, 34–5, 42, 118, 153, 190, 191, 193, 208
commemoration 20, 23–4, 29, 32–3, 34–5
'Shakespeare Unlocked' 31, 52
Shakespeare's Globe 3, 7, 8, 9, 11, 29, 30, 31, 47, 63, 68–72, 85, 113, 123–30, 149, 185, 207, 227
Sharp, Verity 51
Sharrock, Thea 125
Shaughnessy, Robert 20, 28
Simon, Josette 150
Simpson, Natalie 95–7, 100–1
simultaneity 7–8, 62–3, 126, 135–7, 139, 196–7
Sky Arts 50, 54, 154
Smith, Maggie 26
social media 5, 8, 13, 51, 59–72, 85–91, 100, 105–6, 108, 118, 126–8, 134, 154, 162–3, 177–82, 217
sound 21, 27, 34, 43, 68, 77, 79–82, 84–6, 96, 97, 106, 108–9, 116, 120, 124–9, 143, 153, 168, 181, 188, 196, 199, 208–9, 211, 218, 220, 221, 225
South Bank 24, 26, 27, 33, 36, 113, 116–30
Sowole, Raphael 152
The Space 9, 31, 155, 193
space 1–2, 11–12, 20, 23–8, 29–32, 35–6, 68, 78–81, 85, 97–8, 99–100, 103–5, 113–30, 135–7, 140–2, 150, 155, 163, 164–72, 189, 197–201, 204, 209–12, 217, 220–4
spatial dynamics 3, 10, 11, 20, 22, 23–8, 29–32, 34–6, 62, 85, 88, 106–8, 115–30, 140–1, 163–7, 171, 199–201, 209–12
spectatorship 2–3, 7–8, 10, 12–13, 26, 60–73, 78, 82–91, 105, 114–30, 134–7, 139–44, 199, 219–23, 225
sponsorship 49–50, 54, 121, 188
star 1, 10, 12, 31, 32, 46–8, 53, 63, 68, 79, 81–4, 86, 89, 139, 148, 149, 178–9, 185, 186, 187, 199, 218

INDEX OF NAMES AND TERMS

Starr, Nick 36
strategy 44, 48, 51, 53, 79, 81–4, 86–9, 123–4, 154, 156
Stratford Festival HD 11, 31, 47, 136, 137–44
Stratford Festival, Canada 136
subtitles 179–82, 190–1, 196
Sullivan, Erin 5, 10, 32, 33, 34, 78, 85–6, 115, 117, 120, 125, 126, 128, 142, 166, 202, 209–10, 227
Supple, Tim 149
Syal, Meera 64, 127–8

tactic 78–9, 82, 84–6, 89–90, 128, 181
Talawa Theatre Company 150–7, 11, 32, 34
Tang Shu Wing Theatre Studio 186, 189
Tara Arts 32, 85, 151, 154, 155
Tate, Catherine 34
television 3, 4, 6, 10, 19, 20, 21–2, 28, 31, 33–4, 46–7, 68–9, 82, 87–9, 95, 97–100, 119, 124–30, 134, 136, 138–9, 149, 154–7, 190, 200, 208, 216–18, 221, 224–5. *See also* BBC
temporality *see* time
Tennant, David 34, 47, 106, 149, 186
Terera, Giles 150
Terry, Michelle 129
Thackeray, Lucy 128
theatre audience 3–4, 6, 9, 10, 12, 78, 95, 98, 99–100, 103–9, 114–20, 122–9, 138–9, 141–2, 144, 153, 156, 162–5, 171–2, 196, 199–204, 208–10, 212, 223, 227
Théâtrephone 43–4
thrust stage 3, 31, 34, 97, 99, 106, 107, 114, 143, 200
ticket pricing 44
time 1–2, 5, 12, 22, 25, 33, 43, 50, 51, 52, 59–60, 61–8, 85, 86–9, 96, 104–5, 107–8, 115–17, 123–6, 133–7, 141–4, 155, 161–2, 172, 188, 189–90, 196–8, 199, 201, 204, 217, 223
Tosoni, Joan 139

touring 53, 151, 154–5, 162–3, 186, 207, 208
tourism 49, 54, 104
trace 4, 67, 133–4, 144
trailer 8, 25, 48–50, 54, 80, 215, 218–19
translation 106, 142, 180–2, 186, 191, 208, 210
Turner, Lyndsey 12, 32, 41, 139, 178, 180, 187, 193, 199, 218
Twitter 10, 51, 63–73, 78–9, 84–9, 100, 117–18, 180–2

Ubu Roi 163
Uncle Vanya 24

value(s) 21–2, 24, 25, 30, 34, 35, 42, 45, 49, 51, 82–3, 138, 144, 171–2, 189–90
van Hove, Ivo 139, 211
van Kampen, Claire 124
van Someren, Tim 6, 33, 80, 118, 119–20, 122, 178
Verma, Jatinder 151
Virgin Mobile 54

Waldmann, Alex 98–100
Walter, Harriet 1
Warner Brothers 25, 181
Warner, Deborah 14
Warner, Tamsen 216, 217, 222
Warrington, Don 152–5
Wars of the Roses 23–4
Waterville Opera House, Maine 216–17, 221–2
Wentworth, Scott 140–3
Whishaw, Ben 46
Williams, Margaret 154
Winter's Tale (RSC, 1999) 30
Woodall, Andrew 97–100
Wyver, John 1–2, 3, 6, 19, 21, 23, 24, 30–1, 32, 34, 35, 62, 95, 96, 106, 108, 115, 140, 141, 142, 143, 167, 204

YouTube 60, 87, 218

www.ingramcontent.com/pod-product-compliance
Lightning Source LLC
Chambersburg PA
CBHW062131300426
44115CB00012BA/1883